MUIRHEAD LIBRARY OF PHILOSOPHY

An admirable statement of the aims of the Library of Philosophy was provided by the first editor, the late Professor J. H. Muirhead, in his description of the original programme printed in Erdmann's *History of Philosophy* under the date 1890. This was slightly modified in subsequent volumes to take the form of the following statement:

'The Muirhead Library of Philosophy was designed as a contribution to the History of Modern Philosophy under the heads: first of Different Schools of Thought—Sensationalist, Realist, Idealist, Intuitivist; secondly of different Subjects—Psychology, Ethics, Political Philosophy, Theology. While much had been done in England in tracing the course of evolution in nature, history, economics, morals and religion, little had been done in tracing the development of thought on these subjects. Yet "the evolution of opinion is part of the whole evolution".

'By the co-operation of different writers in carrying out this plan it was hoped that a thoroughness and completeness of treatment, otherwise unattainable, might be secured. It was believed also that from writers mainly British and American fuller consideration of English Philosophy than it had hitherto received might be looked for. In the earlier series of books containing, among others, Bosanquet's *History of Aesthetic*, Pfleiderer's *Rational Theology since Kant*, Albee's *History of English Utilitarianism*, Bonar's *Philosphy and Political Economy*, Brett's *History of Psychology*, Ritchie's *Natural Rights*, these objects were to a large extent effected.

'In the meantime original work of a high order was being produced both in England and America by such writers as Bradley, Stout, Bertrand Russell, Baldwin, Urban, Montague, and others, and a new interest in foreign works, German, French and Italian, which had either become classical or were attracting public attention, had developed. The scope of the Library thus became extended into something more international, and it is entering on the fifth decade of its existence in the hope that it may contribute to that mutual understanding between countries which is so pressing a need of the present time.'

The need which Professor Muirhead stressed is no less pressing today, and few will deny that philosophy has much to do with enabling us to meet it, although no one, least of all Muirhead himself, would regard that as the sole, or even the main, object of philosophy. As

Professor Muirhead continues to lend the distinction of his name to the Library of Philosophy it seemed not inappropriate to allow him to recall us to these aims in his own words. The emphasis on the history of thought also seemed to me very timely; and the number of important works promised for the Library in the very near future augur well for the continued fulfilment, in this and other ways, of the expectations of the original editor.

H. D. LEWIS

MUIRHEAD LIBRARY OF PHILOSOPHY

General Editor: H. D. Lewis
Professor of History and Philosophy of Religion in the University of London

The Analysis of Mind BERTRAND RUSSELL 8th impression
Clarity is Not Enough by H. D. LEWIS
Coleridge as Philosopher by J. H. MUIRHEAD 3rd impression
The Commonplace Book of G. E. Moore edited by C. LEWY
Contemporary American Philosophy edited by G. P. ADAMS and W. P. MONTAGUE 2nd impression
Contemporary British Philosophy First and second series edited by J. H. MUIRHEAD 2nd impression
Contemporary British Philosophy third series edited by H. D. LEWIS 2nd impression
Contemporary Indian Philosophy edited by RADHAKRISHNAN and J. H. MUIRHEAD 2nd edition
Doctrine and Argument in Indian Philosophy by NINIAN SMART
Ethics by NICOLAI HARTMANN translated by STANTON COIT 3 vols
Freedom and History by H. D. LEWIS
The Good Will: A Study in the Coherence Theory of Goodness by H. J. PATON
Hegel: A Re-Examination by J. N. FINDLAY
Hegel's Science of Logic translated by W. H. JOHNSTON and L. G. STRUTHERS 2 vols 3rd impression
History of Æsthetic by B. BOSANQUET 2nd edition 5th impression
Histry of English Utilitarianism by E. ALBEE 2nd impression
History of Psychology by G. S. BRETT edited by R. S. PETERS abridged one-volume edition 2nd edition
Human Knowledge by BERTRAND RUSSELL 4th impression
A Hundred Years of British Philosophy by RODOLF METZ translated by J. H. HARVEY, T. E. JESSOP, HENRY STURT 2nd impression
Ideas: A General Introduction to Pure Phenomenology by EDMUND HUSSERL translated by W. R. BOYCE GIBSON 3rd impression
Imagination by E. J. FURLONG
Indian Philosophy by RADHAKRISHNAN 2 vols revised 2nd edition
Introduction to Mathematical Philosophy by BERTRAND RUSSELL 2nd edition 10th impression
Kant's First Critique by H. W. CASSIRER
Kant's Metaphysic of Experience by H. J. PATON 3rd impression

Know Thyself by BERNADINO VARISCO translated by GUGLIELMO SALVADORI
Language and Reality by WILBUR MARSHALL URBAN 3rd impression
Matter and Memory by HENRI BERGSON translated by N. M. PAUL and W. S. PALMER 7th impression
The Modern Predicament by H. J. PATON 3rd impression
Natural Rights by D. G. RITCHIE 3rd edition 5th impression
Nature, Mind and Modern Science by E. HARRIS
The Nature of Thought by BRAND BLANSHARD 3rd impression
On Selfhood and Godhood by C. A. CAMPBELL
Our Experience of God by H. D. LEWIS
The Phenomenology of Mind by G. W. F. HEGEL translated by SIR JAMES BAILLIE revised 2nd edition 5th impression
Philosophical Papers by G. E. MOORE 2nd impression
Philosophy and Religion by AXEL HÄGERSTRÖM
Philosophy of Whitehead by W. MAYS
The Principal Upanishads by RADHAKRISHNAN
The Problems of Perception by R. J. HIRST
Reason and Goodness by BRAND BLANSHARD
The Relevance of Whitehead by IVOR LECLERC
Some Main Problems of Philosophy by G. E. MOORE 3rd impression
The Theological Frontier of Ethics by W. G. MACLAGAN
Time and Free Will by HENRI BERGSON translated by F. G. POGSON 7th impression
The Ways of Knowing: or The Methods of Philosophy by W. P. MONTAGUE 6th impression
Values and Intentions by J. N. FINDLAY

Muirhead Library of Philosophy
EDITED BY H. D. LEWIS

MEMORY

MEMORY

By
BRIAN SMITH

LONDON: GEORGE ALLEN & UNWIN LTD
NEW YORK: HUMANITIES PRESS INC.

FIRST PUBLISHED IN 1966

This book is copyright under the Berne Convention. Apart from any fair dealing for the purposes of private study, research, criticism or review, as permitted under the Copyright Act, 1956, no portion may be reproduced by any process without written permission. Inquiries should be made to the publishers

© *George Allen & Unwin Ltd, 1966*

'*Library of Congress Catalog Card No: 65-27341*'

DEDICATION
To Bob Brown

PRINTED IN GREAT BRITAIN

CONTENTS

I. *Doubting the Authority of our Memories* page 13

II. *What do we mean by 'Remembering'?* 32

III. *Kinds of Memory* 57

IV. *Memories and Memory Claims* 79

V. *Remembering how to* 105

VI. IMAGES—*The Subjects of Imagery* 136

VII. IMAGES—*The Function of Imagery* 157

VIII. *Conclusions* 186

Index 213

The author would like to thank the Humanities Research Council of Australia for their help in making the publication of this book possible.

CHAPTER I

DOUBTING THE AUTHORITY OF OUR MEMORIES

THE 'INITIAL AUTHORITY' OF MEMORY

Nearly every work on 'remembering' introduces us to the 'sceptic' whose task it is to show us not only that memory plays us false, but that our memories, however essential they are to the everyday conduct of our affairs, should never be trusted since nothing can ever conclusively prove that any given memory is not false. We could reply to this sceptic that the same kind of arguments as he uses could equally well be employed to show that we cannot prove conclusively that a given memory is not true, that by seeking logical criteria for what is essentially an empirical question he is setting himself a logically impossible task. The introduction of this sceptic is a useful device for raising questions, but we must take care not to allow it to suggest to us that a sceptical or tentative attitude to all of our memories may be a reasonable position to hold. Clearly it is not. We all of us answer questions about our past experiences without any hesitation or doubt, we sit on chairs with the utmost confidence that they will support us, we walk along familiar roads with complete certainty that they will lead us to where we wish to go.

It may be objected that the sceptic does not in fact doubt the authority of all his memories, he only insists that memory is always *logically* open to doubt, that though in fact many memories are reliable, and are known to be reliable, it is always logically possible that we are mistaken. But if this is all he claims he is a poor sort of sceptic, for few if any people would wish to disagree with him. Being sceptical involves rejecting, or holding strong reservations about, some view seriously put forward by its adherents. A man may be sceptical about the virtues of socialism or the truth of the Christian doctrines. In these cases some idea is put forward for his consideration, which has not, or need not have been, previously entertained at all.

But when we first come to consider the credentials of memory we have already tacitly accepted them, have taken memory for granted, trusted it implicitly, and experienced surprise and alarm when it has proved unworthy of that trust. It is not the ordinary function of memory, but its capacity for giving us unpleasant surprises, that first leads us to enquire into its workings and the question we then ask ourselves is not 'How is it that memory can be informative?'—but—'How is it that memory is sometimes misinformative?'. My own memory is one thing, surely, that I can, and must, trust. Yet experience teaches me to treat it with caution.

It is certain, however, that we do not always, or even often, doubt our own memories. They have an initial authority which usually cannot be gainsaid. Even when evidence to the contrary is very strong we are inclined to stand by the authority of our own memories. A book is not where I remember leaving it. I ask who has moved it. Every one assures me that he has not. Yet I am quite confident that somebody *must have* done so. I find the reply, 'You must have made a mistake' a quite unconvincing answer to my insistence that I remember putting it there.

Perhaps I *have* made a mistake. Perhaps I came back and moved it myself 'unthinkingly'. Perhaps I left it there yesterday, not today. Certainly, assuming that nobody is lying, somebody is mis-remembering. The saving fact is that if such a question is pursued long enough, the mis-rememberer nearly always finds himself out. For other people this 'finding out' will simply amount to the recall of something which had been temporarily forgotten. For the agent it may be a matter of revising or repudiating what he had regarded as his memory of the event.

What I have called the initial authority of memory—the belief about the past which is quite independent of any outside evidence—does not guarantee the truth of any claim about the past. But it is inseparable from whatever we accept as remembering; we would not regard ourselves as remembering otherwise. It is present in varying degrees, so that sometimes it is possible for us to 'back down', to admit that we are probably wrong, not because of any revision or variation of our memories, but simply because we have the experience of misremembering, and in the light of this the degree of confidence we feel in our memories is insufficient to withstand the pressure of external counter-evidence. But at other times we feel absolutely sure, on the authority of the memory experience alone, that we are not mistaken.

Of course, being absolutely sure is at best a particular state of mind. Frequently two people claim to be absolutely sure of incompatible things. And which of them has the better right to be sure cannot be decided wholly according to which of them happens in fact to be right. If, for instance, one savage believes the earth to be flat because he has observed that unsupported bodies always fall, whilst another believes it to be globular simply because this seems to him a more satisfactory shape, then the second happens to be right *in* his belief, but the first seems to have the better right to hold his belief. In the case of direct remembering, however, there seems to be at least a *prima-facie* case for allowing the one who is in fact right the right to be sure.

It is well to bear in mind that for every 'memory' which clashes with the memory reports of other people, there are countless others that fit easily and naturally into the general scheme of known fact. Our strongly authoritative memories are rarely challenged, either by the memories of other people or by the facts as presented to us. Our less strongly authoritative memories can usually be made to dovetail with the testimony of other people and with the facts as we find them by minor, and quite 'painless', modifications. Most of our memories have both 'strong' and 'weak' parts. If I 'remember' coming to work at 9.30 a.m. yesterday, and I am told by my neighbour that he saw me at home at 9.45, I would normally be quite happy to reconsider my 'memory'. Had he claimed that he saw me at home all day my reaction would have been quite different. I remember very definitely that I went to work, but much less definitely that it was at 9.30 a.m.

Nevertheless the whole of the original 'memory' had *some* degree of initial authority, the weakness of which became apparent only when my claim was challenged. In fact it is generally only when any memory is challenged by present facts, or by the testimony of other people, or by subsequent memories of one's own, that the question of the degree of its initial authority arises at all. And because it is so easy to say, *after* a successful challenge—'No, I wasn't remembering that at all' or 'Of course, that was the day before' or 'It certainly happened; it doesn't much matter where', we are apt to overlook the fact that all our memories come to us in the first place with the same kind, if not the same degree, of initial authority. We are apt to overlook it, that is, until the need to abandon a really firm memory-belief in the light of counter evidence forces us to wonder just what sort of authority a memory can ever really have.

THE CAUSES OF DOUBT

The question, 'Wherein does the authority of memory lie?' is not just a 'philosopher's puzzle', it is a problem which must present itself sooner or later to any thinking person. The man who seems to remember something quite clearly but discovers that he *must* be mistaken is bound to ask himself—'What is peculiar about this case? How is it that my memory, usually so reliable, has let me down this time?' And when the only peculiar thing he can find is that this memory gave him the wrong answer, he must inevitably wonder how many of his memories which happen *not* to have been challenged have been equally false, and how he can *ever* know that he is not being deluded.

Moreover, the errors of memory are by no means all of the same kind. There does not seem to be any situation, or group of situations, in which we can say 'Here I must be on my guard against delusion', or 'Here I am completely safe'. Why then are we so confident and unhesitant about our memories? Is it simply a matter of a beneficial tendency to be overcredulous as some pragmatically inclined philosophers have suggested? Or is there a secure and indubitable basis of memory that justifies our belief that whatever errors of remembering we may make, further remembering can eventually set matters right for us; that doubt, though it can exist, cannot go on forever?

It does not seem enough to say that our memories are more often found to be right than wrong, that we are comparatively rarely surprised; this is a necessary, but not a sufficient, condition for our confidence. Very few people are ever struck by lightning, but in general people are apprehensive of lightning in a quite different way from that in which they are apprehensive of being misled by their own memories. Our memories seem to be 'in our own control' in a way that lightning is not. We seem to have some ground for assurance more fundamental than the mere averaging of instances. The guarantee that I get with my watch does not ensure that it will not go wrong, only that if it does the makers will replace it with another—and if necessary another again—until I have one which is reliable. They are in a position to give such a guarantee because, in addition to their observation that their watches do not in fact generally go wrong, they have a knowledge of their design and structure which satisfies them that the watches *ought* not to go wrong. Therefore if one of them does so it must be as the result of some accidental departure from that design and structure. We feel that if we had some analogous insight into the structure of memory itself, we should be able to understand why, and not only how, particular memories are false. We should be able to guarantee our memories in the way that the watchmaker guarantees his watches. But it is this insight into the structure of memory which is so hard to achieve. First, I want to consider in detail the particular ways in which memory can play us false, and then go on to look at the general problems which the various kinds of error raise about the authority of memory.

Whatever can be remembered can also, *ipso facto*, be forgotten. Forgetting, i.e. failing to remember what we are in a position to remember, may be regarded as total or partial. We might call the complete failure to recollect some past experience, total forgetting. But, of course, since the fact that I am not now recollecting a certain experience does not entail that I never again shall do so, the only occasions when I can be said to be totally forgetting are those when the temporary total forgetfulness is made apparent; when I am asked what I did on a certain day and am quite unable to answer, or I am asked how I enjoyed the film I saw on the previous evening and I look blank and ask 'What film?' The question of forgetting can only arise when the assumption is made that something is, or should be, remembered.

We might also speak of total forgetting in cases of failure to recognize or inability to perform once mastered tasks. A house in which I know that I once lived looks quite unfamiliar to me; a man who appears to be a total stranger shows by his behaviour that I ought to know him; I am surprised to hear that a new coat I have bought is 'exactly like' one I had some years ago. I mount a bicycle after many years of driving a car and fall off because I simply cannot balance; or when I am asked to work out the square root of a number by simple arithmetic I find that I have forgotten where to start. In all these cases, as in the first, the failure of memory is apparent only as the result of other knowledge, not itself direct memory.

B

It is, however, the cases we would tend to regard simply as partial 'lapses of memory' which most commonly concern us, because they are continually brought home to us without the aid of any independent authority. I do recognize a man's face but cannot remember his name; I remember, however, that I have heard it. I distinctly remember a certain cricket match but cannot remember who was wicket-keeper, though I remember remarking how good he was. Such omissions of memory we find particularly irritating. For memory tells us enough, as it were, to make us feel that it should tell us more; it supplies the blanks but refuses to fill them.

Now, in all these cases we are not so much doing something as *not doing* something. And it may be felt, therefore, that whilst they are omissions, they are not strictly errors. We do not say that the boy who has not even attempted the examination question has got it wrong, but this boy gets no more marks, and may even get less, than the boy who *has* attempted it and *got it wrong*. And consider the case where we are confident that only three people were present at a meeting we attended, not because we did not notice the fourth at the time—we may have spoken to him—but simply because, quite unaccountably, we do not remember him. A three-man conference is clearly a different thing from a four-man conference. Omissions, *though not themselves errors of memory*, are certainly a source of such errors.

The positive case, the memory error proper, is less frequent perhaps, but by no means infrequent. I 'remember' locking the door, but when I come home it is not locked. I am asked what colour my friend's car is and I immediately reply 'blue'. I 'see it quite plainly'—but when he arrives it is brown, and it has not been re-painted. The distressing thing is that, although I must accept the evidence in such cases, and sometimes am able to say, 'Of course—it is Bill's car that is blue', or 'It was yesterday that I locked the door', there are times when the original 'memory' seems to persist as strongly authoritative as ever, and I must simply allow myself to remain mystified for fear of becoming a bore on the question.

One particular kind of memory error is often associated with George IV because he is alleged to have 'remembered' leading a charge at Waterloo. Though this type of error might be regarded simply as an extreme case of error of commission, we may well feel that the difference from the cases cited above is not only one of degree. For in those cases there seems to be the misplacement rather than the sheer invention of a memory. I *have* locked doors and *have* seen blue cars, but George IV never led a charge anywhere. The difference seems parallel in many ways to that between illusion and hallucination; the one has a basis in fact which the other has not. It is true, of course, that there was in fact a Battle of Waterloo which *did not* include George IV, just as there are elephants which *are not* pink; even an hallucination must be relatable to actual fact in order to carry the conviction which it does. Nevertheless the distinction between being relatable to fact in this way and being based on fact in the manner of a misplaced memory or misinterpreted visual experience should be quite clear.[1] I shall therefore call such extreme cases 'mnemic hallucinations'. These are not to be confused with memories of hallucinations, memories which may themselves be perfectly veridical and in no way deceptive. But the somewhat grandiose term 'hallucination' must not mislead us into thinking that something like a charge at Waterloo must be involved. A man is doing the same kind of thing as George IV, though less spectacularly, if, having seen his colleagues at school with boils on their necks, and having vividly imagined how unpleasant such a boil would feel, he subsequently 'remembers' having a boil on his own neck as a boy.

The reverse position is also possible; what is in fact memory is sometimes taken to be imagination. A man awakes in the morning after a wild night out. Quite dispassionately he contemplates the picture of his friends and himself climbing lamp posts, breaking windows, being apprehended by the police—and suddenly he realises that it all really happened. We might say here that his drunken state had given a dream-like quality to his experiences so that the recall of them felt at first more like imagining than remembering. But there is no reason why this same error should not occur under perfectly normal conditions, and ample evidence that it sometimes does. A composer may be dismayed to hear played on the radio the very melody which he himself had just

[1] At this stage I am simply setting out the apparent 'kinds of error'. In Chapter VI I shall argue against any rigid distinction here.

'composed', and realise that he *must have been* remembering, not imagining, as he wrote. It is very hard to be certain of the complete originality of one's own work. I have, for instance, a shrewd suspicion that my example of the boil on the neck in the preceding paragraph is something I read once, though I cannot say where or when. Nor is this error confined to what we might call 'creative activity'. A friend of mine recently showed surprise at finding a full packet of cigarettes in his pocket. I asked him if he did not remember buying them and he replied that he 'supposed he did'. He had been aware, he said, in some way, of having gone into the shop for them, but he had not thought it had really happened. Had I pressed him further he would probably have said that though he was contemplating, or perhaps having images of, the shop visit there was no feeling of familiarity about it, no 'this happened' endorsement. But 'feelings of familiarity' can be very tricky. Most of us have at some time experienced the rather uncanny feeling, often called the *deja vu* experience, that some incident, some view, some group of words or sounds, was familiar to us, so that, although this strange familiarity is felt after the event (or is noted by us after the event) it seems as if from the first instant we *could have* predicted exactly what would follow, much as we could if we were watching a film for the second time. We do not generally think of these experiences as remembering. Rather we should be inclined to describe them as 'as if we were remembering', and to suspect that the odd experience is caused by some unplaced or 'unconscious' memory of a very similar incident. The worrying thing is that if we ask why it feels as if we are remembering, the only answer possible seems to be that we have a sense of familiarity. But, since this also seems to be all we can say when we are asked what it is like to recognize something, and since some epistemologists have regarded this same sense of familiarity as the feature which distinguishes memory from imagination, when something feels familiar we like to know *why* it feels familiar. If, in the *deja vu* case, we can have a sense of familiarity for no reason that we or anybody else can discover, what right have we to regard this same sense of familiarity as the hallmark of recognition and recollection?

Perhaps the greatest confidence shaker of all is the conflict which arises between our own memories. I am describing some event I have experienced—'Last Saturday afternoon—no, morning—I'm sorry, Sunday morning, a fellow got out of a black car—no, it was a green utility—and walked straight into a puddle without looking—wait, I remember now, he did see it but . . .' and so on. A fairly normal reconstruction, we may say, by the time-honoured method of trial and error. But why the error; why the need for trial? Why did the wrong answers come up in the first place? And if one correction is necessary how do we know another is not—and another? For these changes are not always simply modifications or elaborations, they are often downright contradictions.

The extent of the problem is seen more clearly when the contradictions are spaced out, as it were, in time, when we remember both the event and our earlier 'remembering' of it, and find that they do not tally. We are frequently obliged to correct one memory-claim in the light of another later memory of the same event. There is the further difficulty that even when one memory-version has given place to another, this does not mean that it is vanquished for all time. When we are climbing hills, it often happens that just before we reach what we have been taking to be the peak another 'peak' comes into view. This can happen many times in the same climb, but when we do reach the real peak there can be no further doubt about it. Conflicting memories do not seem to be like this; there is no simple set of fixed criteria for distinguishing the true from the false.

Each specific failure of memory brings its own contribution to our suspicion about the validity of memory as a whole—not just an empty suspicion that 'it could always be otherwise', but a real suspicion that 'it always may be otherwise'. And the consideration of memory in more general terms only seems to confirm this suspicion.

It seems wholly natural to think of memory, rightly or wrongly, as being closely akin to perception. Yet on examination the analogy soon runs into difficulties. We see things by looking with our eyes, hear things by listening with our ears, and the things we see and hear are there for anybody to see and hear. But memories seem almost to come and go of their own accord; all we can say is that we are aware of them, or aware of something *because* of them. A man can lose his memory just as he can lose his eyesight, but whereas in the latter case we can tell by physically examining him that he is incapable of seeing, in the former case all we can know is that he does not in fact remember anything prior to a certain time. Or, with a different kind of loss or failure of memory, we know that he is very poor at remembering things. Memory does not seem to be quite *like* anything else. We may well feel driven to allow that our ability to remember things is a quite unaccountable 'brute fact' which defies any attempt at 'structural analysis'.

We might say that even if memory is totally unlike perception from a physiological or organic standpoint, at least it is like it from a functional standpoint; memory provides us with knowledge of the past just as perception provides us with the knowledge of the present. But this will not do. Whilst it might well help to convey to a child how the word 'remember' is used, it can cast no light upon what remembering is, nor is it strictly true. Perception is usually the acquiring of knowledge by a combination of present sensory stimulus and memory dispositions. Thus both sense perception and memory are needed for our knowledge of both the past and the present. That we could not know the past without memory is true only because we could not *know anything* without memory, in the ordinary sense of 'know'. That I know about some past event is no proof that I remember the event in question; I could be reading about it in a book. And, because this is so, the fact that I am able to relate some incident that I *did in fact witness* is no *proof* that I am actually remembering it at the time. My inability to relate an incident may prove that I am not now remembering it (allowing that I have no language difficulty), but my ability to relate it is no more than a fair indication that I am remembering. It is sometimes very hard indeed to sort out our actual memories from knowledge acquired by other means. This is amply illustrated by what Von Leyden has called 'the childhood test case'.[1]

This is, in effect, the general problem arising out of errors of commission as such, and 'mnemic hallucinations' in particular. Most of us have some favourite memories of our own childhood;

[1] W. von Leyden, *Remembering*, London, Duckworth, 1960, p. 38 ff.

our first visit to the seaside; or the time we climbed on to the back of the pony and were thrown off. Not uncommonly such memories are accompanied by quite vivid visual imagery. It is alarming therefore, when we discover, on revisiting the seaside place, that it is simply nothing like our 'memory' of it, or we learn from a visiting uncle that it was not ourselves at all but our brothers who were thrown from the pony. On reflection we realise that we were, in any case, far too young to remember so clearly. We guess, rightly no doubt, that our images were built up in our imaginations by stories we heard our parents and their friends tell, and that these images became so familiar to us that they felt like memories— and still do feel like memories. In a sense, perhaps they are; they are the memories of our earlier imaginings. But this is not what we took them to be.

We may then begin to wonder how many more of our childhood memories are memories only in this derivative sense. The real problem is not those that are plainly false but those that are substantially true. After all, if our uncle had confirmed instead of denied that we were thrown by the pony, we should still think we remembered the incident itself though our 'memory' would not be one whit different. And why only childhood memories? If there is nothing save counter evidence to show us the difference between our remembered experiences and our remembered imaginings, and if we are capable—as clearly we are—of imagining situations involving ourselves as they are reported to us, then how can we ever know what we are really remembering and what we only seem to be remembering?

Closely allied to this is another difficulty arising out of the free play of our imaginations. When we remember a state of affairs we remember it as it appeared to us. This is quite natural, right and proper, so long as we always remain capable of distinguishing the state of affairs from our own attitudes towards it. But do we always? I remember very little about a certain Latin master except that he was a great villain with a cruel smile and a rasping voice. If I were to meet him again it is not improbable that I should find him a charming gentleman. I remember the annual fair on Gretham village green as a much more grand affair than any such local fairs are nowadays, yet it seems unlikely that it really was so. Everyone can supply examples of this kind of distortion from his own experience. Some time ago the name of a lad I was at school with came up in conversation and I immediately had a clear visual image of him. But on reflection I realised that the image was of a man my own age, not of a boy at all, almost as if the memory had grown up with me. Because I had always thought of him as my contemporary I remembered him as my contemporary.

Suppose I make an ordinary perceptual error; I think that it is Black and not White that has won the race I am watching. A little later I discover my error and learn that the winner was White. Notwithstanding this there is no small chance that I will subsequently 'remember' seeing Black win. I have quite genuinely thought this, seen *what I took* to be this, why should I not *remember* this? Samuel Alexander may perhaps have overstated the case when he wrote: 'Though we do not often attend to our past mental states, we never remember a past object without some consciousness however faint of the past state',[1] but there can be little doubt that our feelings and attitudes and interpretations frequently do intrude into our recollections of past events we have witnessed, and that, within the memory, the event and the attitude (the subjective colouration of it) are very hard to separate.

Of course, since I *did* discover that the winner was really White, it could be claimed that I might remember this, that I *have a capacity* for remembering it. But having a capacity is not much good here and now if it is not being actualized; and no memory 'capacity' can guarantee its own permanence. When I ask my friend 'Do you remember the night the bomb fell?' I may be told 'Yes—and I'm not likely to forget it', or even 'Yes, I shall never forget it'. But this last is a somewhat reckless claim; 'permanent memories', like permanent waves, are not always permanent. There is no intrinsic difference between those memories which last a lifetime and those which soon disappear for ever. Even the fact that I remember having 'remembered' something every day for the past year, cannot guarantee that I shall ever remember it again. Nor can it guarantee that, if I do remember it again, I shall not misremember it in some way. We may say with some justification that the fact that I have remembered it correctly many times in the past makes it inductively probable that I shall remember it

[1] Samuel Alexander, *Space, Time and Deity*, Vol. 1, London, Macmillan, N.D. p. 125.

correctly again, but this is to assume that my remembering of my previous memory is accurate. And it always *is* a matter of assuming; the only checking available to us is to think again.

It may be protested that remembering again is not the only way we have of confirming memories. If what I remember is that I have bought milk each day this month the account from the milk man surely confirms this. And my memory that I have promised to take my wife to the theatre is surely confirmed by the fact that she has just entered dressed in her best clothes. Certainly these occurrences do not specifically establish that the events I claim to remember did occur, but when the initial authority of my memories has already provided the hypotheses all that is required is that these be strengthened.

All this is true. Indeed it would be a bad look-out for us if it were not. But there are a number of reasons why it may relieve, but cannot solve, the problem we are faced with.

At best cause/effect evidence tells in favour of this or that memory. If it *always* told in favour no problem would present itself since we would have no inductive grounds for doubting the authority of memory. But, as we have seen, all too often the evidence points to our having misremembered. The successful confirmation of one memory, therefore, does not necessarily increase the probability of the truth of another. I grant that we may discover from experience that we tend to remember more reliably in dealing with one type of question than in dealing with another type. But the value of such a discovery rests upon our ability to 'classify' questions, and can never be more than a useful rule of thumb. Each individual memory may stand or fall quite independently of any others without detriment to such a 'rule'. The point is that it is not always obvious *how* we can confirm a memory in the way that it *is* obvious how we must verify a perception. If it were obvious the cross-questioning of witnesses would be a waste of time. For instance, I may remember very clearly that I saw a man pedal down the road on a bicycle at 5 a.m., but how could I possibly prove it, even to myself? Certainly there is a man somewhere who *could* confirm my claim, but even if I found the man in question he may well deny it.

And supposing independent supporting evidence were always available, it would still be quite impossible in practice to confirm *every* memory by it; there simply would not be time. Only when we have already cause to doubt do we seek confirmation to allay that doubt. We seek it in further memories, in the testimony of other people, and in present conditions as we perceive them. What evidence we are able to find is an empirical question, dependent upon the circumstances of the case. And whether or not it does in fact allay our doubts is ultimately a psychological question. The expression 'reasonable doubt' may be used in law. But what constitutes reasonable doubt cannot be laid down by the law or by any other source of decisions.

Even when independent evidence does support a particular memory, such evidence can never be conclusive. For, no matter what form it takes, it always presupposes the accuracy of some other memory or memories. If I remember that the vicar called, and then support this memory by remembering that my wife remarked how shabby his coat was and that my daughter spilled tea over his trousers, I may well be satisfied that my original memory is correct. But it is hanging, so to speak, by a sky-hook; the supporting memories are not themselves independently supported. If I rely on the testimony of other people—the neighbours agree that the vicar did call that day—then I am only adding their memories to my own to give it extra weight. If I find his hat left in the hall I must remember that it *is* his hat, and even if it has his calling card inside it marked with the date of his visit, I can take this as conclusive evidence of his visit only on the assumption that such objects do not materialize in such places of their own accord. And this assumption, arising as it does out of our ability to associate observed instances with similar previously observed instances, presupposes the validity of memory. Furthermore, even when the assumption has become an accepted maxim it can be retained, as a maxim, only by memory. Even an established inductive rule *can* be forgotten. Under strong emotional stress men have been known to try to walk through walls, and children are notoriously capable of forgetting that eggs break when dropped on the floor.

We may feel that the only satisfactory guarantee would be a direct comparison of the past event with the memory of it; and simply because the past *is past* it cannot be held up for present comparison. It is as if some object lay on the other side of a high wall and we could see it only with the aid of a mirror held aloft.

We may complain that the mirror reverses what we see, and overcome this difficulty by using two mirrors periscope fashion. We may suspect that part of what we see is a fault in the mirror itself and demand a better mirror, or a whole battery of mirrors to enable us to compare the reflections. But if we ask how we can know that the mirrors do in fact show us what is on the other side of the wall, no amount of improved mirrors will help us.

Now, suppose all the mirrors were slightly distorted and each showed a slightly different picture; and suppose also that they were flexible and liable therefore to change the nature of their distortions when directed to a new object, thus making it impossible to check them by comparing the reflections they showed with any visible object. We might well feel then that we *could never know exactly* how the thing on the other side of the wall looked. The only really satisfactory course would be to climb the wall and see for ourselves the thing as it actually is. But the 'wall' we are concerned with is *time*, and this by its nature can be 'climbed' only from one side.

There is a further difficulty which is not always fully realized. Not only is it impossible to compare our memories with the events of which they are the memories; but because the present is, as it were, always slipping away from us into the past we cannot even compare our memories with what purport to be the effects of the original events (or, more properly, with our inferences from those 'effects'). For what I am comparing must always be, not the memory itself, but my memory of that memory.

Suppose that today I remember building, a short while ago, a castle in the sand. Tomorrow I go to the beach and there it is. I say, 'Yes, just as I remembered it yesterday'. But how do I then *know* it is just as I remembered it yesterday? The sight of the sand castle itself may well influence my memory of my previous remembering. Again, suppose I 'hear' for my children a poem they are committing to memory and notice that they make a number of errors and omissions. When they are finished I say nothing; I just hand the book back to them and they read it again for themselves. They may well be quite satisfied that they got it exactly right. Of course, if they had written the poem down instead of just saying it their errors would have been there to be seen, and in any case they generally believe me when I assure them that they *did* say this or that wrong. But in most cases when we wish to confirm a memory we have neither record of, nor independent witness to, our actual 'act of remembering'.

It seems that at every stage a further question can be asked, a further doubt raised. We feel that, in some way, every memory must carry within itself its own credentials. Yet we seem quite unable to isolate them.

What if a true memory *always felt different* from a false one? But then there would just not *be* any false ones. Nothing could then count as a 'false memory' since, being false, it would be seen not to be a memory. (We can, of course, distinguish remembering from imagining—however hard it may be to describe the difference in terms of experience itself—but do we want to call imagining false remembering?) And what would have to count as one memory? How could we separate the true part from the false part if, say, I remembered a pair of black brogue shoes instead of a pair of brown brogue shoes.

The only sort of 'feeling different' we seem able to conceive is in our own degree of confidence—the initial authority of the memory itself. And this, as we have seen, far from preventing errors of memory, is the very thing which promotes them.

BEING UNABLE TO DOUBT A MEMORY

Nevertheless, we say, there *must* be some memories which we simply cannot doubt; the complete sceptic, after all, is just a device, not a real man. Our task now is to discover what, in view of all that we have said, this *inability* to doubt can amount to. Initially there are two quite distinct possibilities: 'I cannot doubt' could refer simply to an empirical or psychological fact, or it could mean that it would be logically self-contradictory to doubt.

It is simply a matter of fact that I cannot seriously doubt (which means that I cannot doubt), that my name is Smith, that I had bacon and eggs and tomatoes for lunch today, that I have a wife and two children. I could be misremembering—I could be imagining—I could be dreaming—but I happen to know that I am not. These are plain facts, and, however hard they may be to reconcile with some philosophical theories, to deny them is to be guilty either of frivolity or of blatant falsehood. Nor do I need to justify, in any ordinary sense of that word, these and other similarly certain beliefs.

But our concern is not to justify particular memories but to examine memory itself in the hope of discovering *why* certain memories *are* self-justifying. And if we reject the 'beneficial overcredulity' thesis, we seem bound to allow that the psychological certainty we feel must have at least some logical basis—else what can 'rational grounds for believing' mean?

We may say that it is logically demonstrable that *some* memories are true—for otherwise the question of the truth or falsity of any given memory could not arise at all. Our only grounds for doubting one memory are, or at least include, our assumption of the reliability of others. It may be protested that the incompatibility of two 'memories' proves only that at least one is false—not that the other is true. But the very notion of incompatibility can derive only from the assumption that memory is reliable. If our experience were other than it is we should not hold the same pairs of instances incompatible, but to even suggest that our experience might be different is to presuppose that we do remember it (in general) correctly.[1]

But it is not enough to establish that there are true memories; we must also be able to identify them, to distinguish them from false ones as they arise. And, as we have seen, every attempt to achieve this distinction by logical demonstration must fail since the demonstration always assumes part of what it seeks to prove.

There is, however, another possibility. To say it is logically improper to raise doubts about a particular class of memories *may mean* only that this particular class of memories is of the wrong logical type for doubt to apply to.

I cannot climb Everest; I am neither trained nor fit enough. I cannot at once both climb and descend (except perhaps by walking up the 'down' escalator); this is logically contradictory. And I cannot climb the floor; this is simply inapplicable—floors are not things to be climbed. Now, propositions, judgments and

[1] H. H. Price makes this point at length in his contribution to the Symposium: Memory-Knowledge—*Aristotelian Society Supplementary* Volume XV—'What can Philosophy Determine'—1936, pp 16 ff. I am only claiming, however, that the *truth* of some memories is presupposed by our questioning the authority of memory. I make no claim that the *infallibility* of any memory is presupposed.

inferences are the sort of things it makes sense to doubt. Events, entities, qualities, are not the sort of things it makes sense to doubt; we can only doubt something *about* them. The categorial difference between those things we can doubt, in the normal sense of that word, and those things we simply cannot, may be made plainer by the following distinction.

When we say a proposition is false we are saying something about the proposition itself. But, when we apply the term 'false', as in common speech we often do, to such things as teeth and hair and the bottoms of suitcases, we are really saying that these things are designed (or simply happen) to make us think that they are something other than they are and so lead us to formulate false propositions, to make false inferences; we are saying that they are, in some way, misleading, or potentially misleading. But nothing is *intrinsically* misleading. Whether and to what extent anything is misleading is a contingent empirical question—whether and to what extent it does in fact mislead *somebody* into expectancies which will not be fulfilled. It is important also to realize that a statement is not necessarily misleading simply because it is false. The message on the old man's placard—'The end of the world is at hand', is almost certainly false; but it is misleading only if somebody takes it seriously and starts repenting.

The placard itself may well be misleading and intentionally so, if the natural inference that the old man bearing it is a religious crank is in fact not true: he may be a spy or a detective. The placard is then a sign for most of us of something which is not the case—it is a misleading sign. And, conversely, a true statement at the literal level can be grossly misleading, as Macbeth discovered to his cost.[1] If I say 'I didn't give the chocolate to the baby' when in fact I had put it on the table and watched him take it, then I am being both truthful and misleading at the same time. This is why inflections play so large a part in everyday speech.

The importance of this distinction is that, whereas what is false is simply false and that is all there is to it, that anything is misleading is contingent upon someone's being misled by it. A *sign* is always *of* something *for* somebody. It is always possible therefore

---

[1] 'And be these juggling fiends no more believed,
    That palter with us in a double sense;
    That keep the word of promise to our ear,
    And break it to our hope.' Act V, Sc. VIII

that some other person will be 'rightly led' by the same sign, or that the one originally misled will correct his error although the object which operated as a sign remains unaltered. If it can be shown that a great deal of what we call 'remembering' lies at the subinferential level, we may find therein the warrant we are looking for to justify the psychological certainty we do in fact achieve about most of our memories. Our task, therefore, is to discover what kinds or parts of memory, if any, can properly be said to be true or false, and what kinds or parts, if any, can properly be said, at worst, to be misleading.

CHAPTER II

WHAT DO WE MEAN BY 'REMEMBERING'?

CAN MEMORY BE DEFINED?

Before going any further we must try to decide just what is to count as memory, bearing in mind, however, that we are discovering, not legislating about what memory is. We must, therefore, give an equal hearing to every claimant that even seems to be an instance of remembering.

William James defines 'memory' thus: '*It is the knowledge of an event or fact, of which meantime we have not been thinking, with the additional consciousness that we have thought or experienced it before.*'[1] He is very definite in his view that the mere occurrence of an image in the mind *without this additional consciousness* does not constitute a memory, even though the image may be a faithful representation of some previous experience. 'Such a revival is obviously not a *memory*, whatever else it may be; it is simply a duplicate, a second event, having absolutely no connection with the first event except that it happens to resemble it.' The same view—that to be remembering we must know we are remembering—seems to be implicit in Bertrand Russell's claim:[2] 'If we are to know—as it is supposed we do—that images are "copies", accurate or inaccurate, of past events, something more than the mere occurrences of images must go to constitute this knowledge. For the mere occurrence, by itself, would not suggest any connection with anything that had happened before'. The idea that to remember is always to refer back consciously to the past commends itself to common sense and seems generally to accord with common usage. But it raises certain difficulties.

I feel that we must distinguish the *memories* which we have from the *remembering* which we do. When I speak of a memory

---

[1] William James, *Principles of Psychology*, Vol.1, London, Constable, 1950, p. 648 (His italics).
[2] Bertrand Russell, *The Analysis of Mind*, London: Allen & Unwin, 1921, p. 160.

I am having I clearly *must* be consciously aware of some happening as belonging to the past. Yet it does make sense, I believe, to say of some other man that he is remembering certain past events even though that man is not then conscious of these events as past. It is enough that he is able to relate, recognize, perform or verify *because* he has in fact had a certain experience in the past, whether or not he is aware at the time of the connection between that past experience and his present activity. We can speak, quite properly and normally, after the event, of having remembered, even though the particular memories in question were not recognized as such. I may, for instance, make an assertion of fact and, when I am asked how I know, reply, after some consideration, that I remember it. Under these circumstances it would seem very odd to say that I started to remember it only when replying to the question—especially as my reply shows that, since my knowledge is based upon my own past experience, I must have been remembering it already.

Prima facie, remembering is one way of knowing things. It has been strenuously denied by some writers[1] that remembering is ever a way of *getting to know* things, but it would seem simply perverse to deny that it is one way of actually knowing something here and now.

Now, if I could not know that a bird is sitting on that chimney pot without also knowing that I know that a bird is sitting there, then I could not know this without knowing that I know it—and so on *ad infinitum*. It follows that I need not be (though I may be) aware that I know something in order to know it.

And if the 'knowing' in question is remembering, whereas I *might* know that I am remembering a certain event, I could remember it perfectly well without any 'additional consciousness' at all. Russell is quite right when he says that something more than the mere occurrence of an image is necessary; it is also necessary that we recognize it, that is, see it *as* something. But it is a further, and usually quite unnecessary, step to see ourselves as seeing it as something.

In Chapter I, I claimed that there could be occasions when we take our remembering to be imagining. If we were to accept

[1] E.g. G. Ryle, Cf. *The Concept of Mind*, London, Hutchinson, 1949, p. 247 ff.

James's definition we would have to say of such cases that the remembering commences only when we realize that we are remembering, notwithstanding that nothing else is changed thereby. And if, as is certainly possible, we never do realize this, we should never have remembered the event at all. We should have *imagined* it, even though every detail is in fact a representation to us of our own past experience.

Whether we are deliberately trying to remember something or simply allowing our memories to 'wander', the arrival at a particular piece of remembered information may be the culmination of quite a long process, involving, as we saw in the previous chapter,[1] the consideration and rejection of various propositions and images. Suppose, for example, that an old wartime colleague telephones to say that he is in town and asks me to meet him. As I try to remember his appearance a number of images arise in my mind. Each one is quickly replaced by another—I know that they are not of the man in question—until at last I have an image which I know immediately *is* the one I want.

But who are these other gentlemen in Naval uniform whose images appeared to me? They are not the man I was 'looking for', so I did not stop to enquire—yet it seems highly likely that each was a real person, not just a figment of my imagination and, if so, can we say anything but that I must have been remembering them? The same thing applies when we remember the face but not the name; the names which suggest themselves to us are usually real names, names we have actually encountered, though not the name we want. And if, instead of simply discarding the 'unsuccessful applicants', we take the trouble to try to identify them, we are often successful. It is when we are interested only in who they *are not*, rather than in who they are, that they must remain anonymous. I may perhaps pause in my pursuit to say 'No, that's old Jim. He joined us later'—but my doing so does not seem to make any difference to the fact that it *is* old Jim, and that I *am* remembering him. I do not need to maintain that we can *always* identify or 'place' these 'intermediate stages of memory'. If we can sometimes do so this shows that those 'identified' are in fact memory-images; and surely we do not want to say that they are *made* memory-images, only by our stopping to consider them.

[1] See pp. 20 and 21.

James's definition seems to demand a third group of experiences, neither memory nor imagination yet in some way of the same 'kind' as these, a sort of 'potential memory', and I can see no justification for the postulation of such an additional class. If we wanted to call anything 'potential memory' surely it would be those experiences we have had and *might* remember.

It is tempting to define 'memory' as simply 'Our knowledge of the past', or, less incautiously, 'Our knowledge of our own past experience', because this seems to be straightforward and clear-cut and to embrace everything we might want to call memory. Unfortunately, however, it also embraces a great deal we might *not* want to call memory.

As we saw in Chapter I,[1] knowing the past is not necessarily the same thing as remembering the past, even when the past in question is our own. It may be suggested, therefore, that in order to make the attempted definition function as a definition we rephrase it as—*direct* knowledge of our own past experiences. But what does the word 'direct' mean here? Perhaps—causally dependent upon our own past experience—but the causal dependence is something we infer, it is no part of the individual experiences. These must be knowledge of the past in a particular though quite ordinary way. But the only description we can give of this particular and ordinary way is—remembering.

Perhaps we can give a negative definition: Remembering is being certain about past facts without the aid of testimony and inference. This is, in effect, the position adopted by Sir Roy Harrod. 'A memory', he says, 'is an imaginative structure to which the truth symbol adheres without there being any apparent grounds for the adherence. Memories, in fine, are members of the class of wholly irrational beliefs recognized as such (definition)'.[2] He argues that the irrationality of the beliefs does not render it irrational to hold them. But even if we accept this argument the definition is hardly satisfactory. It is difficult to see how it can exclude articles of faith and mere prejudices. We might extend the definition to exclude these specifically but then I cannot but feel that we would be defining memory by what it is not—making

---

[1] P. 23.
[2] Roy Harrod, *Foundations of Inductive Logic*, London, Macmillan, 1956, p. 187.

it a mere residue after the more specific kinds of belief have been extracted.

This definition is also open to the same objection as that put forward by James. Whilst it accepts as memory whatever commends itself to us as memory, it makes no provision for memory which is not recognized as such, memory to which the 'truth symbol' does not adhere. Unless, that is, we take the 'truth symbol' to be nothing more than our failure to judge 'this is false'.

I have shown that 'Knowledge of our past experience' is too wide to function as a definition. In another way it may well prove also too narrow. By adhering to the factual critreion it abandons the psychological criterion altogether. If it isn't true it isn't remembered. Now, whilst this seems to be a quite reasonable stand it is not without problems. There is obviously a strong case for insisting that 'remember', like 'know', should apply only to what is in fact the case (or *was* the case). And it may seem that we are tacitly following this rule whenever we say 'I seem to remember'. For it may be argued that there would be no point in saying 'seem' unless we felt that something over and above the present experience itself were needed to qualify the event as a memory. Thus 'seem to remember' may stand to 'remember' much as 'believe' stands to 'know'.

But at what point, then, would we be justified in dropping the 'seem to'? Only when 'independent evidence' is produced? 'I seem to remember' usually denotes a low degree of 'initial authority'—'Don't put too much weight upon this recollection, it may be wrong'. Certainly there is not the same *prima-facie* absurdity in saying 'I seem to remember it clearly, yet it could not have happened' as there is in saying 'I believe it, but it is not so'.[1] The two cases are not really parallel. For when I say 'I know' I am saying 'I believe and I have adequate grounds for believing', but when I say 'I remember' am I saying 'I seem to remember and . . . ' and what? It hardly seems to make sense to talk of adequate grounds for seeming to remember.

'Knowledge of our past' provides us with neither an exclusive

---

[1] We might, of course say 'I can't help thinking it is so although I know that it is not' but this reports successive states of mind. It is not a claim to (now) both think and not think it is so.

definition of memory nor an effective criterion by which we can identify instances of memory when they occur. Seeming memories are not labelled 'fact' or 'fiction'—to the extent that they seem to be memories they seem to be an awareness of facts about the past. So that our only means of establishing that some seemingly remembered event did in fact occur is by more remembering of the same kind. To say that a seeming memory is really a memory only if it is true, tells us something quite important about how we normally use the word 'memory', but it provides no means of identifying our memories as such. We are obliged to face the general problem that if we define 'remembering' as 'knowing the past' we must then define 'the past'. The *Concise Oxford Dictionary* gives 'gone by in time'. But our concept of temporal sequence seems, *prima facie* at least, to rest heavily upon our ability to distinguish the perception of events from the memory of events by the natures of the experiences involved. In order to make the 'pastness' of the event contemplated the criterion of our remembering that event, we must first show how our concept of the past is derived without reference to any 'memory-experience'.[1]

A fairly recent attempt to cut away the aura of mystery from memory is the claim that 'remembered' means simply 'learnt and not forgotten'.[2] The advantage of this move is that it seems to give clear rules for deciding what is remembered and what is not:—Did I learn this by instruction, perception, practice? Have I retained what I learnt, i.e. am I now capable of relating, recalling, performing, properly?—Then I remember. And if it be objected that I may not be remembering *that* I ever learnt the thing, the advocates of this view are generally prepared to say that this is of no importance, that it is sufficient that it is the kind of thing which *would have to be* learnt. The only valid test for memory is the ability to perform appropriately when called upon to do so.

The difficulty here is that if we are to know that we are remembering—and surely we often do know this—then we must know that our performances are 'appropriate'. But, I may consider that I am performing appropriately, i.e. according to what I have learnt, whilst someone else considers that I am not. How

---
[1] There have, of course, been several attempts to free the concept of the past from memory, some of which will be considered in Chapter VIII.
[2] Principally associated with G. Ryle. Cf. *The Concept of Mind*, p. 272 ff.

could the issue be decided except by reference to the learning process remembered in some other way? I feel that there is an attempt here to define a 'genus', memory, in terms of one of its sub-species, 'learning'. This is apparent when we consider the assertion 'I remember his face'. I certainly never 'learnt his face'. And though I may perhaps have learnt *to describe* his face, a moment's reflection will show that 'I remember his face' not only is not equivalent to 'I can describe his face', it does not even entail that I have ever attempted (let alone learnt) to do so. Nor does it mean simply that I have learnt to identify his face, a claim we may feel obliged to allow if, in fact, I do recognize him when I meet him again. I can remember someone's face, and know that I remember it, though I see him only once in my life.

We know well enough what we are doing when we are learning something—a part in a play, or how to swim, or the order of colours in the rainbow, or our twelve-times table—we are committing something to memory, or, if you prefer, acquiring a skill. But when we ask what it is for that something to *have been learnt*, what can we say but that, as a result of past efforts, we can do, or do know, the something in question? Learning is *one kind* of remembering: remembering directed to the acquisition of some particular talent. For, when we consider *how* we learn anything, what the 'efforts' in question amount to, we find that, in so far as they affect the issue at all, these efforts are themselves simply 'little rememberings'. The observation of anyone learning a part in a play, or going through the early stages of learning to drive, will show this very clearly. What *could* learning be except piecemeal remembering?[1] I can see a rainbow a thousand times but unless I remember which colour joins which I shall never learn the order of the colours. Learning entails remembering—having learnt entails having remembered, and going on remembering. Now, what of not forgetting?

It is notorious that things we cannot remember today may come back to us as clear as ever tomorrow. Sometimes events from long ago come back to us with surprising clarity, and some

[1] Or the 'drilling' of the physical faculties in some set way. This is discussed more fully in Chapter V.

psychologists believe that nothing we have experienced is ever totally lost to us, a belief which is supported in some measure by the 'unearthing' of lost memories under hypnosis. At what stage, then, can we say we have forgotten something? I often enough do say this, but all that I mean is that at this moment I am unable to recall it. If the matter is important I may be urged to try harder to remember, and I may be successful. Or I may adopt the technique of thinking about something else in the hope that the recollection will 'come to me of its own accord'.

Clearly the only meaning of 'forgotten' which permits verification is 'not recalled or recognized *now*'. Asking which memories are 'quite forgotten' is like asking which of the young men at the university will live to be octogenarians. The only possible answer is 'Wait and see', notwithstanding that some of them are plainly healthier than others. Wittgenstein asks the question[1]—If I knew something yesterday but do not know it today, at what time did I stop knowing it?—There just does not seem to be any way of answering. We want to say I ceased to know it at the moment I lost the ability to relate the something in question. But the loss can be noticed only when the relating is attempted.

Thus if I say 'I have not forgotten what I once learnt' it is not entirely clear what I am claiming. If I simply mean 'I am now doing something which I once learnt how to do' then this is certainly good evidence that I remember something—something which, as we have seen, is itself a complex of earlier rememberings. But this only instantiates the concept of remembering, it cannot serve to define it. In the same way 'I observe that the meadow is very green' shows that I have colour vision but it does not provide a definition of the concept of colour.

Of course, when we consider how we *would* attempt to define colour, it is hard to see what we could do *except* say 'It's the kind of experience you have when you see a green field—' and so on. And perhaps when we attempt to define memory the position is much the same. Friedrich Waismann attributed much of the misunderstanding in philosophy to— 'something of great significance, the fact, namely, that language is never complete for

[1] L. Wittgenstein, *Philosophical Investigations*, 2nd ed., Oxford, Blackwell, 1958, pt. 1, para. 182 ff. p. 73 eff.

the expression of all ideas, on the contrary, that it has an essential openness'.[1] And he introduces the term 'open texture concept' in his article 'Verifiability' for those of our empirical concepts which are elastic in their coverage. 'Open texture is a very fundamental characteristic of most, though not of all, empirical concepts, and it is this texture which prevents us from verifying conclusively most of our empirical statements'.[2] The distinction between 'closed' and 'open texture' is fairly straightforward. Whereas there are exact rules for determining whether or not a given poem is a sonnet, there are no such exact rules for determining on every occasion whether a given animal is a cat. If the poem has one line too many or one rhyme out of place it is not a sonnet. But the cat may have no tail, or have three legs, or bark like a dog; the point at which we stop calling it a cat is a matter for decision. A term may be introduced into the language to refer to a closed concept —closed in the sense that *all* possibilities are already catered for; but when a term is evolved to refer to a group of similar instances found in the world, no exact rules are laid down for its use and we have an open-texture concept. In the first case we have a set of absolute rules, in the second a set of descriptions which must be met with to a substantial degree.

We can safely assert that memory is a 'natural' rather than a 'formal' concept. We have applied the name to a certain kind of experience, recognized in ourselves and assumed in other people, we have not created it as a technical term to assist us in discussing such experiences. The concept evolves from specific instances, not *vice versa*, so that it would be classed as an open-texture concept. It does not follow, however, that it is also a *vague* concept. To use Waismann's examples, 'heap' and 'pink' are vague terms whereas 'gold' is a quite precise term, notwithstanding that if some novel material were to be found which met almost, though not quite, all the tests for gold, we should be obliged to *decide* whether to call it gold or to invent some new name for it. It is just a fortunate fact that such novel experiences occur comparatively rarely. Normally in the case of 'natural kinds' ostensive and formal definitions do in fact coincide in practice.[3] It is because of

[1] Analytic and Synthetic'. Pt. vi. *Analysis*. March 1953, p. 82.
[2] Reprinted in *Logic and Language*, ed. A. G. N. Flew, Oxford, Blackwell, 1951, p. 120.
[3] Indeed, I would suggest that this coincidence is the basis of what constitutes for us a 'natural kind'.

this that when 'novel experiences' do occur we are in a position to deal with them.

Now, if it were the case that some definition could be formed to embrace every instance that we in fact accept as memory, and exclude every instance that we do not, then the inadequacy of such a definition to deal with a totally novel experience which *might* occur need cause us no more distress than does the inadequacy of the definition of 'horse' to meet such an eventuality. 'Memory' would be an open-texture, but not a vague, concept. But each of our various attempts at exact definition has either excluded instances that many people do want to call memory, or included instances that most people do not want to call memory. Our problem, then, is not simply that our definition may have to be revised at some future date, but that no single definition can meet our *present* needs, can provide us with an effective criterion for all occasions. We seem forced to rely upon a series of distinct criteria which must be applied severally since they cannot, by their nature, be applied jointly.

Perhaps the ideal memory, the perfect exemplar, to use H. H. Price's term,[1] is that which both feels like a memory to ourselves and 'behaves' like a memory to other people. I remember that Aston Villa won the football match: I have a visual image of the winning goal being scored and I remember being delighted by the victory. I am able to tell everyone quite confidently who won the how they won, and to check my pools coupon. The people I speak to saw me go into the stadium and come away from it after the game was over. They also saw others coming away with Villa rosettes and happy smiles. Here is a memory which nobody but a professional sceptic would ever query.

Three distinct characteristics are involved:

(*a*) The experience has the initial authority of memory—the feeling of belief about a past event.

(*b*) There is strong independent evidence that: (i) what is claimed did in fact happen and (ii) I was in a position to perceive its happening and subsequently remember it.

(*c*) I am able to proceed with certain activities dependent for their execution upon a knowledge of the past event.

Where any two of these conditions hold we would normally

[1] Cf. H. H. Price, *Thinking and Experience*, London, Hutchinson, 1953, p.20.

speak of remembering. The first, however, unlike the second and third, seems to demand no additional support, only an absence of contradiction. Here we tend to say straight off 'I do remember' rather than 'I must be remembering'. For most of us the 'initial authority' constitutes the remembering. Since this is often referred to as a feeling of familiarity it may be well, at this juncture, to consider briefly what might be meant by this expression.

Hume held memories to be subjectively distinguishable from mere imaginings because they are more vivid. But Hume himself was forced to admit that on occasions mere imaginings may be more vivid, in any ordinary sense of that term, than memory-images. To preserve the notion of an intrinsic memory-indicator—the truth-symbol as Harrod calls it—empiricists have cast about for some other description which is not open to this objection. William James was perhaps the first to speak of a feeling of familiarity which accompanies, or arises out of, the memory, and *obliges* us to accept it as an account of our own past experience. Unfortunately however, although 'familiarity' has become, largely through the writings of Bertrand Russell, very widely accepted as the 'memory-mark', it is, like 'vividness', something of a makeshift. As R. F. Holland has pointed out,[1] a thing normally becomes familiar through long usage, and there is therefore no reason why our imaginings, since they may be repeatedly entertained by us, should not become more familiar than actual experiences we have had only once.

I hope that as we proceed we shall discover what it is that *makes* a memory 'feel familiar'. But for the present all that I mean by 'initial authority', whatever the explanation of it may be, is the feeling of belief manifested in our readiness to base our expectations, reasonings and testimony on the memory in question.

Any attempt to provide a definition which is also a means of identifying cases must force us to decide between a psychological, and private, criterion and a factual, and public, one.[2] Our alternatives are to treat remembering as we treat *knowing*, making our criterion *what was the case*, and basing it upon the way we generally

[1] 'The Empiricist Theory of Memory'. *Mind*, Vol. LXIII, 1954, p. 466 ff.
[2] Cf. *Remembering* Chapter IV—Von Leyden distinguishes what he calls the 'present approach' and the 'past approach' to memory.

use the word 'remember' in discourse, or to treat it as we treat *believing*, making our criterion a particular state of mind, and basing it upon the experience we *refer to* when we speak of remembering. If we were to take past fact as our sole criterion, then we would have to include many instances where there is no 'memory-feeling' at all; we could not distinguish between memory-knowledge and knowledge about the past from other sources. If we were to take the present belief about the past as our sole criterion, then we would have to include beliefs which are in fact unjustified; we would be obliged to maintain that *no* independent evidence about the past, however well established, could overthrow a memory-claim provided the belief were strongly held. We would be obliged to admit 'mnemic hallucinations' as memories.

Of course, what we want to say is that remembering is holding a true belief about the past as a result of having experienced the past in question. But we must recognize that whilst this may well be an adequate description of memory it in no way explains its authority. For we know it to be 'as a result of past experience' only by virtue of the present memory-experience, and in most cases we do in fact know the belief to be true by virtue of that 'memory-experience' alone without reference to any kind of causal story. It seems that we must allow that the terms 'memory' and 'remember' are applied, and quite properly applied, to a great many differing situations, and concentrate our attention on discovering the relationship between these. First, however, we must consider in detail what these different memory-situations are.

WAYS OF CLASSIFYING AND DISTINGUISHING MEMORIES

The first distinction which springs to my mind within the field of memory is the one I have made some use of already—between the memories we have and the remembering we do. We may well feel that a totally different classificatory system must apply to *what* we remember from that which applies to *how* we remember. It may seem comparable with the way in which different classificatory systems would apply if we were asked 'What did you run? The hundred yards, the egg and spoon race, or the all-Australia championship?' and if we were asked 'How did you run? Fast, bowlegged, or with increasing pace?' Certainly there are differences in the grammar which are applicable to memory and to remembering. I can remember quickly, or efficiently, or effortlessly, but I cannot have quick or efficient or effortless memories. On the other hand I can remember clearly, and this *is* having a clear memory of some event.

We must allow then, that there are some things we can say about remembering that we cannot say about memories, but are they, from our point of view, the important things? To preserve the analogy with running the subjects of memory would have to be such things as 'that farm', 'the man next door', 'yesterday's breakfast'; or perhaps, farms, people, breakfasts. But these are not the 'kinds' we are interested in. Rather we are interested in distinguishing between memories of: things, skills, states of mind, appearances, propositions. The more pertinent analogy would therefore be with running a race or running a lottery or running for Parliament—where *what* we do and *how* we do it are closely interwoven. Thus:

Remembering the look or the sound or the smell of something seems simply to *be* imaging. Perhaps it is not; perhaps I can remember exactly how something looked or felt without any image at all and perhaps I can have images without remembering at all. I shall dispute these possibilities in a later chapter[1] but for the present we must allow them. Nevertheless, to say that my memory takes the form of images seems to say as much about what I am remembering as about how I am remembering. It is very hard to imagine, for instance, how I could have an image of a proposition.

Remembering a skill, i.e. how to do something, may simply *be* doing it. Whether this 'really is' remembering or not need not concern us here.[2] All that is relevant is that, in so far as we do treat it as remembering, our reason for saying that what is remembered is a skill is that our manner of remembering is a skilled performance.

Again we must be careful not to prejudge the issue. It may prove that the remembering is quite distinct from the performing, but it is evident that there is a strong connection.

It could perhaps be held that the remembering of a factual relationship *could only be* the stating of a proposition. This is at least arguable. And it seems to be analytic to say that when the

[1] Chapter VII.   [2] This question is taken up in Chapter V.

mode of remembering *is* the stating of a proposition (assuming that there be such a mode of remembering), the subject of the memory must be a certain relationship which held, or is claimed to have held, between certain events, or proceedings, or situations.

We cannot remember without remembering something. I am suggesting further that we cannot remember in this or that way without remembering something of this or that kind. If this is a mere tautology then it is one which has frequently been overlooked. Too often people have sought to treat what we remember and how we remember as two distinct categories. On the other hand it would be equally wrong to ignore completely, as some philosophers have done, the differences between what can appropriately be said of remembering (as an activity) and what can appropriately be said only of memories (as the 'products' of that activity). In the next chapter I shall try to avoid both dangers by approaching the classifications of memory in the frameworks of what we remember and how we remember alternately. But first I want to make an initial distinction, a distinction we might say, between distinctions.

We have, on the one hand, the different sorts of things we can say about remembering because it is one kind of activity, and on the other hand, the different kinds of things that count as memories. An analogy may help to make this distinction clear. Discussing a colour we can say that it is bright or dull, clear or opaque, cheerful or gloomy, and we can argue as to whether it 'belongs' to the surface of an object or is 'dependent' upon a mind. Or quite differently, we can classify it as green or red or blue or orangey-red or bluey-green. Whilst the first list is of real enough distinctions, and these clearly are applicable to colours, they are also equally applicable to other things as well. The weather can be bright or dull, the fireside can be cheerful or gloomy, and the arguments about ontological status can be carried on about sounds or flavours. But the second list of alternatives lies *within* colour itself; it is the possible classes into which colours, and only colours, can fall. For convenience I shall call these primary and secondary distinctions respectively, and the two important points to note are:

The 'primary distinctions' are applicable irrespective of the 'kind' (the 'secondary' classification) in question.

'Secondary distinctions' apply only within the class under consideration. Primary distinctions apply to members of that *and other* classes.

An example of a primary distinction is that given in this chapter, between memories which are specifically believed and memories which are merely accepted in passing. This distinction, though applicable to memory, is by no means peculiar to memory; it applies equally to perception and prediction as well. In the case of memory one primary distinction is of the utmost importance, that between dispositional memory and memory occurrence. We shall need to be conscious of this distinction at every stage of our enquiry.

Whilst we can talk of remembering something either in the dispositional sense of being able to remember, or in the occurrent sense of actually remembering now, our being entitled to talk of remembering a given event in either sense entails that, on some occasions, we must be entitled to talk of remembering that event in the other sense. The fact that an event occurred yesterday and I recall it today is all the proof needed that I have retained that event in my memory. Furthermore it is the only proof possible that I have done so. It may well be that at some future date physiologists will be able to isolate 'memory traces' and thereby ascertain the existence of a memory-disposition. This is at least possible in principle, but *only because* memory dispositions *are* periodically actualized. For us to notice, and predict from, a correlation there must be two factors which correlate. Memory dispositions can be known to exist only because memory occurrences actualize them.[1]

Thus, whilst 'Do you remember . . . ?' is a different kind of question from 'Are you remembering . . . ?', it does not necessarily need a different kind of experience to enable us to answer it. Asking a man on his Golden Wedding day 'Do you remember your wedding day?' is quite different in intention from asking him 'Are you remembering your wedding day?' But though he may answer 'Yes' to the first question and 'No' to the second, there is an obvious sense in which he must, to be entitled to answer 'Yes' to the first question, be fulfilling at least some of the conditions required for answering 'Yes' to the second question

---

[1] This does not mean that they can be known not to exist if no memory occurrence is actualizing them. Cf. p. 39 above.

also. A memory disposition or capacity can be claimed only on the evidence of some memory occurrence, and *justly* claimed only on the evidence of a memory-occurrence directly related to the event claimed as remembered. This is the fact which people overlook when they claim to remember some event they have in fact long since forgotten. What they remember is simply the fact that they *did once* remember it, as when an old man starts to relate some incident from his youth and finds, to his astonishment, that he is unable to do so. Memory dispositions or capacities are not evident personal characteristics like the colour of our hair. Nor do we carry them about with us like the watch which must still be in my pocket because I put it there and have not taken it out.

'Does he remember this?', then, means 'Did he experience this and can he be expected to remember it', and our evidence for asserting that he does remember would normally be that he has remembered in the past. And 'Do you remember this?' generally means 'Can you remember this?' and is often used to ask us to try to remember. Or, if the object be particularly complicated—like a proof in geometry for instance—the question may mean 'Can you remember ever remembering this and if so could you do so again if you tried?'.

There is, however, a problem here. It is very hard to deny that quite often we seem to know things without thinking about them at all. We take the right action, give the right answer, select the right book, without experiencing anything that feels like an occurrent memory. Often these performances are quite complex; they are the kind of things we should say *need* to be remembered. Now, it may be possible to explain such spontaneous right actions wholly in terms of physiological conditioning. There seems no doubt that a great deal of spontaneous action must be so explained. But it would be precipitous, I think, to assume that this always *must* be the explanation. There may be situations in which there is occurrent memory but not a *new memory* occurrence.

What we discover by perception is retained by memory. Ten seconds after an event there seems no doubt that we are remembering not perceiving. The question of how and when this change occurs, if indeed there be any actual change, will be considered in my final chapter. But, even allowing that such a change *has* occurred, the memory we now have is not, properly speaking, a recollection. Though the memory takes the form of an awareness as distinct from merely an activity, the object of awareness has not been recalled into consciousness, for it has never left consciousness. Suppose I see a quite perfect rose and this makes such a strong impression upon me that when I turn away it remains in my mind—in the popular phrase 'it is still clearly before me'. I may have a continuous image of that rose for five minutes following my actually seeing it, during which time I may appear to be giving my full attention to all kinds of other matters. Nor does there seem any reason why such a capacity to 'hold' a thought should be confined to imagery. So there does not seem to be any logical reason why we could not continually remember something (without ever recollecting it in the ordinary sense of that word) for an indefinite period.

Thus, whilst the disposition/occurrence distinction is possible only where there are in fact periodical occurrences, there could be cases of remembering where the distinction simply does not apply. There may be some memories which are constantly, as people say, at the back of our minds. And in such cases we could equally well regard the memory as occurrent or as dispositional. It would be a mistake, I think, to draw too rigid a distinction between what is and what is not being specifically remembered at any given moment.

When we turn our attention to the secondary distinctions, immediately a host of questions spring to mind. Must events be remembered either in words or in images? What is the connection between a remembered event, a remembered fact, and the proposition in which the memories are expressed? Can we simply remember a proposition? How is this different from remembering a sentence? How is remembering a person or place connected with remembering the qualities of that person or place? Can remembering how to do something be in imagery? What is the relation between habit and memory? Is recognition a kind of recall? Or is recall a kind of recognition?

These are the kinds of question we now have to consider. From them emerge various candidates for consideration as 'kinds of remembering' or 'classes of memories'. Images, remembering states of mind, remembering in words and propositions, remembered events, remembered qualities, remembering how to, remembered facts, recognition—all these have their places, their

WHAT DO WE MEAN BY 'REMEMBERING'?

particular functions, in the general scheme of what we call memory. Our task is to decide what these particular functions are.

Something else emerges from our list of questions, the fact that the 'kinds' are not simple alternatives. I can contrast remembering *how to* swim with remembering *that* I had eggs for breakfast or remembering *what* my home looks like; but in each case the remembering may take the form of, or include, uttering words, framing propositions, or having images. I can contrast remembering a man's behaviour with remembering his appearance; but the remembering in either case may take the form of either recall or recognition. A memory-image seems to be a totally different sort of thing from a remembered proposition, though both may be means of remembering the same event. And recognizing something seems quite different from recalling something from another time and place. Yet it seems to make sense to talk of recognizing an image.

The upshot of all this is that before we can start to answer the question 'What kind of memory is this?' we have to ask 'What kind of question is this?'. Just as when I am asked 'What kind of soldier is he?' the question could mean 'Is he a Corporal or a Colonel?', or 'Is he an infantryman or a cavalryman?', or simply 'Is he a good soldier or a bad one?'. (The last is a primary distinction but the first two are secondary). Of course, in practice, I should avoid this difficulty by replying 'He's an infantry Corporal and a very good one'. It does no harm to throw in a little gratuitous information. But with memory this manoeuvre is not so easy. We know well enough that 'cavalryman' excludes 'infantryman', and 'Corporal' excludes 'Colonel'. But what 'kind of memory' excludes which other kind seems to vary with the point of view of the question, and it is vital therefore to know what the questioner is 'getting at'. For instance I might ask a man who is describing his friend to me, 'Do you have a visual image of him, or do you simply remember a number of facts about what he looks like?'. The question seems reasonable enough but it could be that to him the 'alternatives' may seem to amount to exactly the same thing, for he may be thinking only in terms of what he can state, and not, like myself, in terms of the mode of remembering which enables him to state it. And I cannot point out an image to him as I could point out a Corporal.

Nevertheless, most of us would allow that there are intelligible questions to be asked—and answered. 'Do you actually remember *how* he looked or just *that* he looked like Napoleon?'—'When you say you remember how to drive are you saying that you remember what you did on some previous occasion, or that you can now think through the rules of driving, or simply that given a car you could drive it?'—'Is the actual group of words the subject of your memory, or simply the way of expressing it?'. These questions make sense once we are in tune, as it were, with our questioner. It is only because this is so that we are able to talk intelligibly of kinds of memories at all. *There are* genuine alternatives within certain contexts of enquiry, and I hope that in the course of the next chapter it will become clearer what these contexts are, and what are the alternatives appropriate to them.

CHAPTER III

KINDS OF MEMORY

To claim 'I remember my grandfather' may be to claim more or less than to claim 'I remember my grandfather visiting us in Birmingham'. I could remember the man without remembering the visit. And I could remember the visit, in the sense of remembering things about it, without actually remembering the man at all. I could, for instance, recall certain outings at which someone, presumably my grandfather, was present. I might perhaps say 'I remember my grandfather' and mean nothing more than 'I could recognize a portrait of my grandfather if I saw one', but this would be a rather questionable use of 'remember'; it is natural to feel that to remember someone must at least be to be able to recall something about him, and to recall it from personal experience. My ability to recognize his portrait could hardly constitute remembering him since I could still have this ability even if he had died before I was born. My claim to remember my grandfather would be very hollow indeed if I were unable to relate from direct memory, a single incident which involved him or to give any description of him. In this case all that I would be entitled to say is that I remember certain events that occurred at a time when (so I am told) my grandfather was visiting.

Such considerations may lead us to reduce the memory of individuals to one way of talking about the memory of events. C. D. Broad, for example, writes 'All perceptual situations refer beyond themselves to physical things: if we confine ourselves to saying that we perceive a certain physical event we simply leave the further reference more vague than when we say that we perceive a certain physical thing. Now the same is true of perceptual memory. I say that I remember the Master of Trinity, and I say that I remember dining with him. But, on the one hand, I remember him only in so far as I remember the events in which he was concerned. And, on the other hand, when I remember any physical event I, *ipso facto*, remember to some extent the thing in which I believe this to have occurred.'[1]

[1] C. D. Broad, *The Mind and Its Place in Nature*, London, Routledge, 1925, p. 224.

But is it true that I can remember an individual *only* in remembering some event in which he was concerned? I have agreed that it would be hollow for me to claim to remember my grandfather if I were unable to relate *anything* about him; but surely I could describe him from memory without remembering *any event* in which he was concerned. Perhaps Broad includes in 'events' such things as 'having white whiskers'; it is noticeable that he says 'the thing *in which* I believe this to have occurred', not '*to* which'. But once we allow the traditional distinction between internal and external properties—and the question of remembering individuals could hardly arise at all if we do not allow it—then 'having white whiskers' does not refer to an event in the way that 'coming to dinner on Christmas Day 1936' refers to an event. There seems no reason why I could not remember him by means of memories of the former kind without any assistance from memories of the latter kind. My memory of him may simply be in the form of an image. Of course, I could remember *that* he had blue eyes and white whiskers and a Scottish accent without any image of him at all. But I can remember this kind of detail about people who I certainly do not remember—Oliver Cromwell for instance—and if this were all that constituted my memory of my grandfather, then, when I was asked 'Do you remember your grandfather?' I would be inclined to reply 'No, not really'. For I would have neither a mental picture of him (unless it were a purely imaginative one built up from verbal descriptions) nor any direct memory of his actions. The ability to describe and classify a person does not, of itself, constitute a memory of that person, though clearly, it does constitute a memory of something.

The claim 'I remember grandfather' is justified then if:

(*a*) I remember events in which grandfather was personally involved in such a way that the memories of those events would have been quite different had he not been present; or

(*b*) I have certain images (usually visual though not necessarily so) of him which I know to originate from my actual past perception of him; or

(*c*) I remember certain facts about his personal appearance or his doings which are directly traceable to judgments made in his presence, i.e. I can remember the occasions of making the judgments in question.

I feel that (*c*) would be merely a case of remembering propositions about him (as in the Oliver Cromwell case) unless I in fact remembered some event in which he was involved. The memory *that* he had white whiskers, even coupled with the belief that I learnt this fact from observing him when he visited us, would hardly constitute a memory *of him*. Thus we can, I think, regard (*a*) and (*b*) as the only real alternatives. As a rule both these conditions hold, but either will suffice. I can have clear memories of people's participation in certain events, their doings and their sayings, and the way I felt about them at the time, without any imagery of those people. Thus even my failure to recognize a man does not entail that I do not remember him. Failing to recognize people we do in fact remember, in the other sense of the term, is quite a common experience. And, on the other hand, I can have a clear image which I know to be the image of a particular individual, and know to originate from my perception of that individual without being aware that I am remembering any particular event. Nevertheless, *the fact that I can be sure* that the imagery derives from my own past perception shows that *I am in fact* remembering a particular event (or number of events) whether I am conscious of this or not. To this extent we must allow that Broad is right. The distinction between events and individuals is only within what *I regard myself* as remembering.

It may be suggested that, when we remember an individual as distinct from remembering an event, what we are actually remembering is the group of sensible characteristics which for us make up the appearance of the individual in question. And in a sense this is quite correct; we could say that we are attributing a continuity and an identity to a remembered group of sensible characteristics. In the same way as we see a group of such characteristics *as* an individual we remember a group of them *as* an individual. Of course this does not mean that what we 'really see' is not a man at all but just a pattern of colours; as the English language is used what we see, *and what we remember*, is a particular individual. I can see no objection, however, to saying that I see a man *because* a pattern of colours is presented to my sight. And, at a particular time when our attention is focussed on the colours themselves, as a painter's might be, it is quite possible simply to see the pattern of colours and shapes *as such*. I could, for instance, observe the white patch which is an old man's moustache without otherwise noticing the old man at all. And, if I can notice an instance of a sensible quality without noticing the individual whose quality it is, then I *can* also remember it with the same detachment.

To remember an individual by way of imagery, then, *is* to remember a particular complex of sensible qualities; but it is to do more than this, it is to remember that complex of sensible qualities *as* that individual. This does not mean that the image must be indentified as of a particular individual *on a specified past occasion*. Indeed it is often maintained that the image need not necessarily be derived from any single perceptual occasion; it may have been developed throughout a series of different perceptual experiences with a consequent vagueness of detail. This claim is supported by the fact that if you think of someone you know well and then, after you are satisfied that you have a clear visual memory-image of his appearance, you ask yourself whether he is wearing a waistcoat or not, the chances are that you will be quite unable to say. Our images of particular people often seem more akin to impressionist paintings than to photographic representations. If the man or his photograph were before you instead of just 'before your memory' such vagueness would hardly be possible.[1]

I have argued that we might remember the sensible qualities—the sensed appearance—which normally signifies a particular individual without remembering that individual as such. I want now to suggest that in the same way we might remember the elements, so to speak, of a past event without remembering that event as such. In the strict sense we can remember only those events which occurred within our own experience—this seems to be unquestionable. But it is often assumed that experiencing an event means perceiving it to be an event of a particular description, the description we finally decide to give of it, and I doubt whether this assumption is justified. Suppose, for example, that I ask my son 'Do you remember the coalman delivering today?' and he replies 'No', but later adds 'I do remember hearing a big truck and a lot of crashing downstairs, and shortly after that I saw a very dusty man go past the window, though I did not, at the time, connect the two things.' Are we to say that he does, or does not, remember

[1] The question of 'vague' or 'generic' images is taken up at greater length later. See p. 181 ff.

the event describable as the coal's being delivered? He cannot remember thinking 'That is the coal being delivered' because he never thought it, but are we concerned with his past thoughts or with a past physical event? From his memories alone it is possible for him to reclassify the event, to think 'That *was* the coalman' where he earlier failed to think 'That *is* the coalman'. And since he *could have* made this reconstruction even if his attention had not been specifically drawn to the question, there is obviously a sense in which we must allow that he is remembering the event itself.

Now, a similar reconstruction is possible at a quite different level: not from events into other events, but from 'remembered appearances' into events and things. I have claimed that we see events and things *because* we 'see' instances of certain sensible qualities in certain relationships. Sometimes, however, we fail at the time to notice certain of the relationships, though these may subsequently prove to be very important ones. And sometimes we do notice the relationships without noticing what sensible qualities are related by them. For example, in a strange town I may look at the Town Hall clock, observe the time correctly, and yet be quite unable to say whether the hands of the clock were thick or thin, black or white. All I looked for, and all I saw, was the *relative positions* of the hands. And at other times I have been so foolish as to look up to see the time, return to my work and then realize that I have not noticed the time. I *have* seen the *clock*, including the hands and numbers upon it, but I have seen them only as a certain pattern of coloured shapes, and have failed to take note of those particular relationships between these coloured shapes which indicate the time to me. Yet when the circumstances are such that I cannot look again—perhaps I have just driven past the clock in a car—then sometimes I can read the time from my memory of the clock just as I should have read it from the clock itself. Notice how often an absent-minded clock-looker, when he is asked 'Well, what is it?', will pause a moment as if gathering his thoughts and then give the time quite correctly without looking again. What is happening is that he is remembering a group of sensible qualities which he recalls as related in a certain way— once it occurs to him to pay attention to that relationship.

Now, in most of our perceptions we observe both the 'clock' and the 'time', more or less exactly, and accordingly our memories of an event include both imagery and understanding of that event. But the memories of those events where only the 'time' is observed will normally be imageless (unless images are supplied subsequently by imagination). For we could not have a visual image of the clock-face and yet not know what it looked like. And the memories of those events where only the 'clock' is observed must remain a kind of uninterpreted imagery until such time as an interpretation is made of the imagery itself.

These, however, would be extreme cases. Such performances as 'telling the time from memory-image' are by no means frequent. It is in 'filling out' the memory of an event, supplying and correcting details, that memories of appearances play their main part. Suppose, for instance, that I have been involved in a road accident. I remember the event—how could I forget it?—but I was too agitated at the time to take in much of what was going on. So that later, when I am questioned, in addition to my propositional memories—*that* this happened and *that* I saw so-and-so—I must rely on my memories of the appearances presented to me by the event. I find that things which did not mean anything to me at the time begin to make sense. I realize that the visual image I have is 'of' the tray of a lorry projecting through the front window column of my car, and that the auditory image I have is 'of' the squeal of skidding tyres. Thus I am able to conclude that I must have braked hard and run into the tail of a lorry.[1]

We might well say that whether we are remembering individuals, qualities or events, the 'stuff' of our memories is the same; it is simply organized differently. And one important factor in the organization is the 'temporal locatability' we attribute to what is being remembered. This is an ugly expression but I do mean locatability, not location.

Although we speak of the 'same thing' occurring on successive occasions, any event is necessarily located at some specific time; anything occurring at a different time is a different event. Nevertheless I can remember an event very clearly and *wonder* when

---

[1] I do not wish to give the impression that I think of images as 'inspectables' which we produce to look at or listen to, like photographs and gramophone records. In Chapter VII I hope to show why the function of memory-images I have described here does not entail the existence of any such 'inspectables'.

it happened. Remembering when an event occurred seems to be a quite separate achievement from remembering that event. But the important point here is that it always *does make sense to wonder when it occurred*.

But, when what we regard ourselves as remembering is an individual and not an event, no specific temporal location seems applicable. And frequently individuals are remembered as participants in, not one event, but a series of events, the whole series giving rise to the memory of the one individual. The event, or events, in which the individual participated each occurred at some specific time, and *may be* remembered as doing so. But normally the essential feature of any memory of an individual is the assumption that there is a single continuous identity. Even in remembering *an* axeman I saw from a passing car, I make the implicit assumption that he may have gone on to chop other trees after I passed by.

It is possible, I grant, for an individual to be bounded, as it were, by one single event. The particularly striking pattern once made for me by a kaleidoscope is, as a particular pattern of coloured chips, an individual entity to which a proper name *could be* attached, just as military operations and tornadoes are frequently known by proper names nowadays, but it has neither a past nor a future. In this case the individual has no being outside of one single event, and to remember that individual is, therefore, always to remember a particular event which occurred at a particular time. But even here, to think of it *as* an individual rather than *as* an event is to hold temporal location to be irrelevant.

I have allowed that the memory of an individual *may be* simply the occurrence of a particular memory-image. Even where the image is too vague or schematic to pinpoint a particular past occasion we might still say 'This is as he appeared between the wars, as distinct from the way he has appeared since the last war'. But in such cases our right to say this may well depend upon the comparison of this image with another image of the same individual on a known occasion, or upon remembered propositions about him which have specific time-reference. It is difficult to see how else we could make such judgments.[1]

When an image derives from one particular occurrence in an individual's life, the subject of that image is, *ipso facto*, locatable in time. The question 'When was this?' would always be appro-

[1] This question is taken up at length in Chapter VIII. See p. 210 ff.

priate. It might be argued that a series of visual presentations which were very closely similar could give rise to an image which, so far as its intrinsic properties were concerned, could equally well be of any one of those visual presentations or all of them. I might, for instance, always park my car in the same place and have an image of it so parked. But whether I can ascribe a particular date to the subject imaged must then depend upon such minor details as whether the windows are up or down or whether there is a bicycle propped alongside. If such details form an essential part of the image, then what is being remembered is a particular event which occurred at a particular time; if they do not then what is being remembered is simply the continuous existent, my car.

A few pages back I claimed[1] that we can remember instances of qualities as distinct from remembering the things they are the qualities of. It may be felt that, since to remember a quality as such is always in a sense to abstract, the subject of the memory in such cases must be a universal. But this would be quite wrong. I could remember the particular blue shade of a certain evening sky simply as a shade of blue, and yet, in fact, my image would have arisen from the particular occasion when I noticed that particular evening sky. If we agree with Hume (and here I cannot disagree with him) that every image must have its origin in an impression or a number of impressions, then it seems possible, in principle at least, to locate in time the particular impression or impressions from which each image derives. If we avoid the term 'quality', a term suggestive of abstractions and universals, and talk instead of appearance, then it is plainly not only possible but necessary that the subject of the memory should be locatable in time. We can remember an appearance simply as an appearance, and this is, in effect, to remember a group of related sensible qualities. The possibility of our *becoming* aware, when we remember, of the relationship between these qualities, i.e. seeing them for the first time *as some thing*, rests upon their being the particular group that they are with the particular relationship that they have. There is an obvious sense, then, in which the appearance in question *is* an event, the occurrence of a particular group of coloured shapes and/or particular sounds, smells, and so on, in a particular relationship to each other from a given stand-

[1] See p. 53.

point, and as such it may be regarded as locatable in time like any other event.[1]

We have considered the senses in which we can be said to remember things and events. Now, in what sense can we be said to remember facts and propositions? Such claims as 'The world is the totality of facts' suggest to us that a fact is in some way substantial, the same sort of thing as an event. We do all use expressions like 'physical fact' but surely what we really mean is a fact about physical entities. *We cannot point to facts*, we can only assert them.[2] The fact itself is neither physical nor mental. Neither can it be true or false; though the assertion of it is *ipso facto* true. A fact is simply whatever is asserted by a true proposition. If yesterday it rained and tomorrow it will be fine, then it is now a fact that yesterday, December 6th, it rained and tomorrow, December 8th, it will be fine. And six months hence I shall still be correct in saying 'It *is* a fact that on December 6th, it rained and on December 8th, it was fine. Particular facts are timeless, notwithstanding that a specific temporal location may be built into the relationship which constitutes the fact. 'It is a fact that the sun is shining now' means 'It is a fact that the sun is shining at 11 a.m. on December 7, 1961', and this must remain a fact for all time.

Since a fact as such is timeless it cannot be past, and cannot, therefore, be remembered. We do not need to go into the difficult question of whether all facts are necessarily particular or whether there are universal facts. For if, for example, 'lying is immoral' is a fact and not simply a directive for the use of English words, then no variation of the occasion of uttering 'Lying is immoral' can affect the truth of the assertion. I feel, therefore, that it would be better not to speak of remembering facts. We may remember the events which gave rise to our knowing these facts, and we may also remember that we knew certain facts at some past time, but here again we are remembering events, not facts. My previous

[1] The 'remembered appearance' is in effect what Russell calls a 'perspective'. See Bertrand Russell, *Our Knowledge of the External World*, London, Allen & Unwin, 1926, p. 95 ff.

[2] I can assert that a man is running and draw attention to this fact by pointing at the man. But I am not thereby pointing at the fact that he is running any more than I am now sitting on a fact because it is a fact that there is a chair under me.

knowledge of the facts was itself an event, though it was a separate mental event, not the physical event which gave rise to my knowledge of the fact in question. And, lest it be objected here that we may not recall any occasion of such awareness, I hasten to point out that, as I have argued above,[1] the actual temporal location of an event is not an essential part of remembering that event.

But though facts are not the kind of things we can remember, we can and do know them *because* we remember; and usually what we remember are propositions. By remembering propositions we can remember a great deal about events without actually recalling the events themselves. If I were asked 'Do you recall your first day at school?' I might reply 'No, but I remember that it was raining'. It is here beside the point how I came to know that it was raining. We shall assume that it *is* a fact that it *was* raining. The point we are concerned with here is that my present knowledge of the fact may simply be my present memory of the proposition 'On my first day at school it rained'. In this case I could have known the fact by other means, I could have remembered the event itself, but our knowledge of facts concerning events we did not experience *must* depend upon remembered propositions. When I remember that Brutus stabbed Caesar I am not remembering Brutus or Caesar or the event; I am remembering the proposition 'Brutus stabbed Caesar', and possibly, though not necessarily, the occasion on which I learned this fact.

Frequently, when we assert facts, or alleged facts, i.e. when we frame propositions to ourselves or to other people, we are making inferences from what we perceive. I assert 'The Professor is leaving' because I see *what I take to be* the event, the Professor driving away, though all that I actually see is his car disappearing. And many such inferences can be made from the same perceptual experience, some at the time of the experience itself, some occurring later from the memory of that experience.

We may feel that to perceive at all is always, to some extent, to go beyond 'presented appearances'. I visually sense a patch of reddish colour, but I *see* a chimney pot, with three dimensions, a hard surface, and a definite function. So that when I remember

[1] See p. 56 of this chapter.

this experience I can remember both the appearance presented to me and the perceptual judgments I made when that appearance was presented to me, and also the further inferences I made as a result of my perceptions—such as that there was a fire burning in the house. And, of course, it would be very hard to draw any sharp line between what I am here calling 'perceptions' and what I am calling 'further inferences'. Since the presented appearances and the various 'judgments' based upon them are all memorable, the memory of a particular event is frequently a mixture of images and propositions, though, as pointed out earlier (the 'clock' and the 'time'), it *need not* be so.

As a result of what we might call the 'loose range' of perception and inference we not uncommonly change our minds about what we are seeing, even though the 'presented appearance' remains the same. What we took to be a menacing figure we later realise is merely a bush at the road side. And to change our minds in this way it is not always necessary to have another look at the object. The change may be made 'from memory'. We change our minds about what we saw, although (because, in fact) the *remembered* presented appearance remains the same. Suppose, for example, that I remember a police patrolman waiting at the side of the road to pounce on speeding motorists. But, even in my memory of him, there is something stiff about this policeman. And when, a little further on, I see another exactly similar police patrolman and, looking closer, I see that it is only a plywood dummy put out by the authorities to frighten motorists into obeying the law, I realize that my earlier perceptual judgment was wrong— the first 'policeman' also was only a dummy. And since I was able to make this correction on the strength of the memory I had of my earlier perceptual experience, I *might* have made it even if I had never encountered the second dummy. The point I am making is that the remembered propositions are separable from the remembered event. I can still *remember* the proposition 'There is a policeman' but I no longer *believe* it. I now realize that it was a conclusion to which I jumped, and, as it turned out, a wrong conclusion. But it is possible for me to realize this only because something else, the appearance actually presented to me, is separately and correctly remembered. The fact that the second 'policeman' was a dummy does not, of itself, show that the first was a dummy also.

If my memory of an event were wholly dependent upon the memories of propositions I formed at the time of witnessing that event, then nothing in my own memory of that event *could* prompt me to correct or modify those propositions. Therefore we must be careful to distinguish between propositions which are themselves remembered and propositions made subsequently *about* what is remembered, bearing in mind that the latter may themselves be remembered as propositions on subsequent occasions. If yesterday afternoon I saw Jones shake his fist menacingly at Jenkins, then the event I remember is simply Jones shaking his fist at Jenkins—whether I saw it *as* a threat or *as* a piece of play-acting. I may remember the proposition (and report the event accordingly) either that Jones threatened Jenkins or that Jones joked with Jenkins. At least one of these propositions would be false, but, as we have just seen, remembering a false proposition which reports, or claims to report, an event is not necessarily mis-remembering that event. The 'lesser claim'—'Jones shook his fist at Jenkins'—is still, as it were, included in the remembered proposition, and is still correct.

But here we strike a major problem. If I say, as I may seem to be implying, that remembering an event just is having an image—remembering (or 're-having') an uninterpreted sensory intake—and all other, propositional, memory is in some way incidental, not memory *of the event itself*, then I must explain how anything *wholly uninterpreted* could constitute the memory of an event *for me*. Indeed the notion of a cognitive experience which does not involve any recognition *that* A is B does not seem to be intelligible at all. The only alternative is to allow that *some* proposition, some classification, is an essential part of the memory of the event. And then the problem is: where can we draw the line? For it might well be objected at this point: why stop at whether or not the fist-shaking was a threat? That what Jones shook was his fist is itself an assumption I made from my observation of certain coloured shapes in a certain relationship. I have already allowed that there is no obvious line of demarcation between 'perceptions' and 'further inferences'. Does it not follow that no error, however gross, in the reporting of an event can ever prove that the event itself is not correctly remembered? Once we separate the remembering of propositions from the remembering of the events which they purport to be about, we can *always* attribute the error to the proposition.

Logically no amount of error in reporting a past event can prove that the actual memory of that event is inaccurate.[1]

In practice, however, there are perfectly adequate ways of deciding in any given case the point at which we must stand firm. For, though I may have the clearest possible memory of Jones shaking his fist at Jenkins, unless this is augmented by some additional knowledge of, say, a long standing dispute between them, it is still reasonable for me to say 'Perhaps he was not really angry, only pretending'. Whereas, only if my memory were very vague indeed—perhaps a memory of something witnessed in the half-light—would it be reasonable to say 'Perhaps it was not his fist at all, it only looked like it'.

If it is allowed, as surely it must be, that a physical event always involves physical things, not qualities or appearances, then those who insist on regarding the naming and classifying of all appearances as inferences are driven to also allow that no event can be witnessed in the full sense of that word until *some* inference has been made. I do not wish to suggest that there are two different kinds of inference, nor yet two rigid 'levels of inference'; clearly there are not. We could come to recognize anger behaviour before being able to recognize fists. What I do suggest is that we are all aware of a difference, *on any given occasion*, between the things and events we 'see straight off', even though we realize that logically we *could be* mistaken in these, and the things and events we infer from those we 'see straight off'. Both may be framed in propositions which, when later remembered, may be regarded by us as belonging to our memory of the event. But, whilst we are at liberty to abandon certain inferences without also abandoning our claims to remember the event, we cannot so easily abandon the initial assumptions from which those inferences were made. For instance, in one case I could say 'Yes, I do remember him shaking his fist, but I realize now that it was only in fun'. But in the other case I would have to say 'I thought I remembered him shaking his fist, but apparently he did not do so, and so I must have imagined it'.

It is important, at this point, to make it clear that remembering a proposition is not the same thing as remembering a sentence. A sentence which could be used to express a proposition might

[1] Compare the 'sceptic's argument' in the first paragraph of Chapter I.

in fact be used to express nothing at all. Children often learn and remember poems without having the remotest idea what they are about; my daughter would recite poems in French (which she certainly did not understand) when she was five years old. And it may well be that even in later life, in the case of much of the remembering that is manifested only in the ability to make appropriate verbal responses, what is being remembered is neither the event itself, nor a proposition made about it, but simply a sentence, a group of words.

When what is remembered is in fact a proposition it may be expressed in a variety of sentences. 'My father's brother gave me the price of a bicycle on my tenth birthday' and 'My Uncle Jim gave me five pounds the day I turned ten years old' may well express exactly the same proposition, that is, they may well refer to the same remembered event and report that event quite correctly—though, clearly, they *could* refer to two quite separate events. We shall consider later[1] in this chapter the question whether propositions are necessarily *in* language, but whether they are or not, they are certainly not necessarily in any particular phrasing of language. Those European-born Australians who have forgotten how to use their native tongues have not thereby forgotten the propositions they formulated in those tongues—but now they remember them in English.

It is not always easy to decide, however, on every occasion, what it is we are actually remembering: the events themselves, propositions about those events, or sentences previously used to express those propositions. I now remember, together with appropriate images, an event I once witnessed, a lion-taming act. Suppose I utter the proposition 'One lion jumped over the trainer's back whilst the other remained on the stool'. How is it possible for me to know whether this is a proposition I have just formed based upon my memory-image, or a memory I am having now of a proposition I formed at the time of the event? We might be tempted to say that if the details described are actually being imaged the former is the case, and if they are not the latter is the case. But this will not do. There is no reason why I should not remember correctly both the propositions I formed and the appearance presented to me. Furthermore, if my imagination is fertile and I am a 'good visualizer', then the memory of the pro-

[1] See p. 68 ff.

position may well prompt me to form an image of a lion jumping over a trainer even though I do not have an actual *memory*-image of the event.

And when we recite to ourselves 'Thirty days hath September . . .' are we remembering a sentence or a proposition or both? It is such problems as these which make introspection so suspect as a means of investigating memory. Yet, if we are not satisfied with a purely behaviourist account, it is the only means we have, or ever can have. And though introspection may not show us on every occasion whether what we are remembering is an event or a proposition or a sentence, or all of these, it can and does show us that these are all things we can remember, and that the remembering of each of them is in principle distinguishable.

MODES OF REMEMBERING

We have considered what it is that we remember; we must now consider how it is that we remember it. If I say that I am remembering the prizegiving and I am asked what form my memory of it takes, I may reply that I am having images of it, or that I am 'telling myself about it', or simply that I am thinking about it. These seem to be the three possible ways of remembering an event: in imagery, in words, or in concepts. But this is altogether too tidy. Apart from the fact that remembering an event might well involve a combination of all three, the term 'words', as we have seen, can refer either to propositions or to sentences; and it may be felt that the term 'concepts' refers to either words or images, rather than that it is an *alternative* 'mode' to them. We must, therefore, examine the relationships between these ways of remembering more closely.

When we remember in words we may be remembering propositions or we may simply be remembering particular expressions. If what we remember *is* the proposition—as when I remember the proposition that my grandfather had white whiskers—it seems that we are remembering a certain factual relationship perceived in the past, but now free, as it were, of the particular perceptual experience in which our knowledge of it originated. The memory *that* my grandfather had white whiskers, though quite correct, does not of itself enable me to draw a picture of those whiskers.

What I am remembering is simply an observation I once made; and I am remembering it in words, though not necessarily the same words as I originally employed to make the observation.

But if we are not remembering propositions as such, but forming propositions *about what we remember*, then although the remembering may be *conducted in words*, there must be some kind of occurrent memory for those words to refer to (or be stimulated by); and since this occurrent memory is not *of* propositions, the only remaining candidates seem to be images or imageless, wordless concepts. Anyone who argues that the words simply refer to, or are stimulated by, the remembered physical event itself, must explain how it is that sometimes what I saw *as* A I subsequently remember *as* B; how it is possible, as we have seen it is, for me to revise or modify assertions made from memory without the intervention of any 'additional evidence'.[1]

When what we remember is simply the words themselves, at least one of two things must be happening. Either we are simply having images of words, or we are making appropriate physical responses to a given stimulus. The second possibility I shall consider shortly.[2] Here I shall try only to substantiate the claim that remembering a sentence as such, if it is anything more than a verbal motor-response to a stimulus, must be in imagery.

Any symbol must have some sensible characteristics of its own. To function as a symbol it has to be something visible or audible or otherwise experiencable through the senses. Thus to remember symbols, as distinct from remembering their significance, is to remember sights, sounds, bodily feelings and so forth. So to remember words is either to have visual or auditory or kinaesthetic images, or else to remember propositions about the words themselves. This last is possible. We could, for instance, remember *that* the word 'place' begins with the same sounds as the word 'please' and ends with the same sound as the word 'race'. There is little doubt that linguists often do remember words in this way, but such memories can be of use to them only if they do have *some* memory-images of words, the words they are using for comparison. Unless, of course, they always spoke these words out loud to themselves. It seems certain that at some stage we do remember words, simply as words, straight off. It is true that often,

---

[1] See p. 61. This question is taken up at length in Chapter IV.
[2] See p. 71 ff.

having once uttered words, we are immediately afterwards aware of their usual meanings, as when a child 'parrots' a poem or the answer to a question asked him, and *then* realizes what the words he has used actually mean. But in this case the words, as such, have already been remembered. He understands them in the same way as he would have done if they had been uttered by somebody else. Provided there actually was an audible utterance, we could claim that this was simply motor-responsive physical activity. But if, as often happens, the remembering of the poem or of the verbal answer involves no utterance at all, no physical activity of any kind, then we seem obliged to allow that the words are themselves imaged.

There is a danger that such words as 'concept', 'thought' and 'idea' come to mean whatever we want them to mean. Hume used the word 'idea' as though it were synonymous with 'image', but he allowed it to 'spread' so as to take in relational properties which are clearly not imageable in the ordinary sense. In this way he was able to sidestep the problem of 'something in the mind which was not previously in the senses'. Abstract ideas have been a constant source of embarrassment to philosophers who, whilst paying lip-service to Berkeley's dictum that any idea must be the idea of something specific, have been uncomfortably aware that we *just do know what* 'above' and 'after' and 'greater than' mean in a way that is something more than just being able to put words in the right places in sentences, whether or not there are examples of these relationships before us, and without the necessity of specifically remembering any such examples.

If we allow, as surely we must, that it is possible to have a concept without also having an occurrent image, we might ask the question: Are images just one kind of concept; or is remembering and imagining in images an alternative to remembering and imagining in concepts?

To avoid question-begging, let us take the ability to recognize instances as coming under a particular concept, not as a definition, but simply as a test, of the possession of that concept. Then, since by virtue of having an image of a wombat I can recognize a wombat when I visit the zoo, the possession of an image does seem to meet the test for the possession of a concept. But the image itself is not the concept—for I can recognize a wombat by virtue of the image I have only if I can also frame the proposition about it 'This is an image of a wombat'. We might say then that to have an image *and identify it* as the image *of something* displays the possession of a concept of that thing.

But it would not follow that the possession of a concept *must* always involve the identification of an image. For we also have concepts of relationships—above, below, greater and so on—but we cannot have images which could be identified as *of* these, only images which *exemplify* them, provided we already have the concepts. I can have an image of a red patch above a blue patch, but not an image of aboveness. Aboveness is not even an ingredient of the image in the way that the red and blue patches may be said to be.

Further, to possess a concept is *at least* to be able to recognize instances of it. Even if we speak of the concept of a particular individual we can do so only because we treat the individual as a continuous existent and assert that various manifestations at different times are instances of a single concept. Thus a concept must always extend beyond any particular instance, involving thereby at least one relationship, similarity or continuity, which is itself not even exemplified by the image. That is why the judgment 'This is an image of a wombat' is required to provide a concept (or establish the existence of the concept) where there is already an image. Thus, whereas an image may exemplify a concept and the existence of an image may be a pre-requisite for a certain kind of concept,[1] an image, as such is neither an alternative to, nor a kind of, concept. Simply having an image is not a cognitive act.

Of course the mere ability to remember without images does not, in itself, establish the occurrence of what we might call 'bare concepts' or abstract ideas. It could be held that the possession of a concept is nothing but the dispositional ability to use the concept word properly. We must now consider the possibility of remembering without either imagery *or language*, a possibility which has often been denied by both Behaviourists and traditional Empiricists alike. I suggest that we might in fact be doing this in any of three cases: when we are remembering 'by doing', as when my remembering the way home is manifested simply in my going

[1] E.g. particular shades of colour. This question is taken up in Chapter VII.

home; when we recognize a presented instance without naming it to ourselves, as when I return a greeting though I am deep in conversation; and when we classify instances *in memory*, i.e. remember similarities, without the help of either names or images. To my mind the three cases are so strongly connected that to accept one of them is to be committed to accepting them all. Behaviourists must accept the first, and most Empiricists would, I think, accept the second. This being so, I shall try to show that they have no justification for rejecting the third.

When I simply 'go straight home' this is *prima-facie* evidence that I remember the way, but it is most unlikely that I have any images of the route, re-presenting to me previous journeys home, or that I formulate propositions to myself about what I am doing. Nevertheless going straight home is not a wholly automatic performance; I could not do it blindfolded without the aid of images and/or remembered propositions. It is essential at least that I recognize the route I am following. 'Remembering by doing' thus seems to reduce to recognizing, that is, to one special case of our second possibility, recognizing presented instances.

It is immaterial to our present argument whether the recognition in question is of kinds or of individuals. Recognition always is, or involves, or gives rise to, the noting of a similarity. When the similarity is sufficiently great *and we are also prepared to assume* spatiotemporal continuity then we speak of 'identity'; but this spatiotemporal continuity can only be assumed, not observed, or there could be no question of recognition. The streets I walk through on my way home are the same streets, but they are the same streets at different times, and the appearances they present are unlikely to be exactly the same on each occasion. Thus the recognition of individuals is simply the recognition of kinds with the additional assumption of continuity, and it is in no essential way different from that employed by a craftsman, a book-binder say, in plying his craft. He also remembers what to do without the aid of words or images, though the materials he works with are certainly not numerically the same on different occasions, nor are they always qualitatively the same. Unless we are prepared to say that his skill is *only* the exercise of a physiologically conditioned reflex, we seem obliged to say either that he *must be* having images or forming propositions or else that he does recognize kinds, register the similarities of past and present instances, without the aid of words or images.[1]

Now, if it is possible to recognize instances of a concept without the aid of language, and without images for comparison, then, in so far as any classification presupposes the comparison of present and absent instances, we must *have* the concept in order to recognize the instance. Or, to put it differently, if we have the capacity to recognize, we have, *ipso facto*, the concept of what is recognized. The onus is upon those who deny the existence of unnamed concepts to show how classification is possible without comparison. I find it difficult to take seriously the current view that thinking *just is* using language. The sponsors of this view have never really faced up to the question—how could we ever come to relate concept words to experienced instances unless we already had the concepts which these words signify? Talk about words and concepts evolving 'hand in hand' is more poetic than informative. Nor yet have they explained how it is that dumb animals (and deaf and dumb people) appear to think and remember in the normal sense of those terms.

If it is possible to have concepts without names for them, then there is no reason why we should not remember having such nameless concepts, and also remember in nameless concepts. The refusal to admit, and take account of, wordless thinking and remembering is, I believe, one of the greatest sources of confusion in the consideration of memory. All of us are sometimes unable to express ourselves; we fumble for words when we 'know very well what it is we want to say'. *How could* we know this unless we were already in possession of the concept we seek to name? Even the most fluent language users occasionally find that their thoughts have got ahead of their command of language. We would not need the aid of a vocabulary to feel surprise at the sight of a man walking on the ceiling—but we would need a concept of human behaviour.

I have already referred to 'remembering by doing'—what we

[1] This is not to discount the possibility that his action, or at least the greater part of it, might be purely automatic. See also Chapter V, p. 128 ff. and Chapter VIII, p. 188 ff.

might call public remembering. There are occasions when I have memories which I can, if I wish, 'keep to myself', and there seem also to be occasions when other people could point out to me that I am remembering something though I might not myself have realized this fact. In the first case I may avow 'I remember—' because I feel myself competent to relate some event, describe some past situation or thing, or perform some task; in the second case I may be told that I am remembering because I am in fact relating some event, describing some past situation or thing, or performing some task, in a way that indicates that *I must be remembering*.

But to say that I must be remembering is to suggest that my overt performance is really evidence of something else, some kind of mental act, and that it is the occurrence of this mental act which entitles me to say 'I remember'. But I do not always say, or even think, 'I remember'. Why then should an onlooker say 'You must be remembering because you are performing learned tasks or relating past experiences'? If it is assumed that what is going on is an exercise of memory, then, since all that is going on is there for him to see, is he not entitled to say 'This (your present performance or speech) *is* your remembering'? Now it should be clear from my earlier arguments that I do not hold the extreme view that *all* remembering either is public or could be public, in the sense that its privacy is the result only of our talking to ourselves instead of out loud. But though remembering *can* be private, it does not follow that all remembering must be private. If my *only* reason for saying 'I remember Jones' were the fact that I found myself describing him, or my *only* reason for saying that I remember how to navigate were the fact that I found myself using a sextant efficiently,[1] then there would be at least a *prima-facie* case for holding that remembering need not be private, that the onlooker is sometimes entitled to attest to my memory at the same time, and by the same authority, as I am myself.

There is a tendency to write off a great deal of what I have called 'public remembering' as mere habit, or habit-memory. With sufficient practice we come to give certain overt performances seemingly quite automatically. Yet, in general, though we do not want to say that we remember how to walk, we do want to say

[1] In Chapter V, I give reasons for denying that these are the *only* reasons.

that we remember how to cycle, although the child who 'lives on a bicycle' is probably no more conscious of his actions when he is cycling than when he is walking. The rationale for the distinction seems to rest only in the fact that to the question 'Can you cycle?', but not to the question 'Can you walk?', it seems reasonable to reply 'I used to be able to once—but now I may not remember how to'. But a man who has been laid up in hospital for a year could make this reply to the question about walking. It may be dangerous, therefore, to attribute any performance which *might* be called 'skilled' to 'pure habit'.

At the same time, what we are here calling habit may well be a factor in nearly all our performances. Even in a more complicated case like navigation, gripping the sextant correctly and opening the Nautical Almanac at exactly the right page are 'habitual' actions. And the vocal cords, no less than the hands, are susceptible to 'habit'. The child reciting a nursery rhyme may be going through the same kind of performance in this sense as the habitual cyclist. In the case of these vocal performances the distinction I have made between remembering propositions and remembering sentences is plainly important. But we cannot simply equate the former with memory-knowledge and the latter with habit. As we have seen, remembering sentences is, in many cases, simply having images. Whereas when we remember propositions it could be held that we are remembering past mental events, the fact that our reporting of an event is always *in* propositions does not prove that there is any additional mental process going on. The ability to use words meaningfully *may* be itself 'habitual'. Yet I cannot but feel that to say this would be to stretch the meaning of 'habitual' rather violently.

My fundamental objection to the whole notion of 'habit-memory' is the extreme vagueness, we might even say slipperiness, of the term 'habit'. There is a constant temptation to equate 'habit' with 'automatic response' whilst still using such phrases as 'he was in the habit of choosing his clothes very carefully' which suggest that habit is simply characteristic behaviour, the often repeated.

If I were to part my hair on opposite sides on alternate days, then in the course of a year I should have parted it one hundred and eighty-two times on the left side. But that I am in the habit of parting my hair on the left side is exactly what we would *not* say under these circumstances. We would say that I am in the habit of alternating my parting, and it might sometimes require careful remembering on my part to preserve the habit. The assertion that an act is habitual is nevertheless more often taken to report the *way* it is performed than the number of times it is performed. Yet we must be careful not to allow 'habitual' to become identified with 'automatic' or 'easy'. There is something very unsatisfactory about the way that Broad, for instance, simply identifies habit-memory with ease of remembering. He says: 'Repetition is not essential, though it is helpful, for the establishment of a habit-memory-power. A man, like Lord Macaulay, with a very quick and retentive verbal memory, may be able to repeat sentences or sets of nonsense syllables which he has met with only once'.[1] Surely if this man's memory of these sentences is not, in the first place, dependent upon repetition, then there is no reason why it should be classed as a 'habit-memory-power' however often it may be repeated.

The same problems apply to performances which are not overt, imaging for example. The fact that I now have an image of my father as I saw him eighteen months ago does not entail that I have had a similar image at any time during the intervening period; nor need we suppose that the image in question would be any different if I had. Yet if I had the same image regularly we might well say that I am in the habit of having it. Now, when I have a certain image habitually, to what extents is the latest occurrence of it causally dependent upon the original perceptual experience, upon the previous occurrence of it, and upon the whole series of occurrences of it to date? I do not see what grounds we could possibly have for answering this question one way or another. I am an habitual smoker in that I smoke cigarettes at very short intervals, and the observation of the fact that I have done so for many years makes it reasonable for anyone to expect me to continue to do so. Similarly I may assume that my having a series of images of a particular appearance of my father may make it more likely that I shall have that image again. But surely this only means that I have reason to believe that whatever it is that prompts me to have that image is a persistent factor, just as whatever it is that prompts me to smoke is presumably a persistent factor. To the question 'Why do you smoke?' the answer 'Just because it is a

[1] *The Mind and Its Place in Nature*, p. 225.

habit' is simply one way of saying 'I don't know'; an habitual smoker is simply one who smokes often and regularly. 'I smoke because it is a habit' reduces to 'I smoke because I smoke'.

This does not mean that to say that something is done from habit is always wholly uninformative. We may be saying in effect 'There is no special or peculiar reason in this case—it is just what I always do'. But any attempt to give a causal explanation in terms of habit is bound to be circular, I could say that it is my habit to have a certain image on receiving a stimulus of a certain kind. But the cause of the image is the stimulus, not the habit. What I have said of imaging seems to be equally true of remembering in general. I may remember the same event any number of times, so that I can fairly be said to be in the habit of remembering that event. But this seems to have no effect upon *the way I remember it*.

We are particularly prone to think of many of our overt skilled performances as 'habit-memories' simply because we assume them to be the kind of automatic responses which *could only arise* out of long repetition. But surely, if we are seeking some special kind of *explanation*, this must be in terms, not of habits, but of motor-responses to physiological stimuli. It is much safer, I feel, to avoid the term 'habit-memory' altogether, and concentrate on the question whether, and to what extent, overt skilled performances are mere motor-responses, physiological rather than intelligent performances. We are then faced with such questions as whether, when we 'remember how to swim' by actually swimming, as opposed, say, to rehearsing the movements on land, we are in fact *remembering* at all. We may be simply allowing our bodies to react to a physical stimulus. But this question we must defer to a later chapter.[1]

Finally, I want now to consider the distinction between recognition and recall, a distinction which H. H. Price has treated as fundamental to the whole analysis of memory.[2] When I recall an individual or an event, that individual or event was experienced by me at some earlier time, and its only representative, as it were, in the present experience is my memory of it. When I recognize something, that something is actually present to me; so that I cannot truly be said to be remembering *it*, for I am actually experiencing

---

[1] Chapter V.
[2] See *Thinking and Experience* Chapters II and III.

it. Therefore what I *remember* must be *something about it*. To recognize is always to classify.

When I recognize a No. 18 bus I am classifying what is before me as one of those buses which take such and such a route, and when I recognize my dog I am classifying what is before me as an episode, if I may so put it, in the life of one particular creature. But I do not generally seem to be remembering specifically any other members of the class of No. 18 buses or other episodes in my dog's life. At most I seem to be remembering *that there were* such other buses and episodes.

I might think to myself 'Here is the No. 18 bus', but on the other hand I might simply board the bus 'without thinking at all'. In the same way I reach out to take a book from the shelf I do not always seem to be consciously selecting the one I want; sometimes my hand just 'goes out to it'. Yet, in some sense, I *must have* associated the bus with other similarly routed buses, the book with other uses of it—otherwise why do I not constantly board wrong buses and select wrong books? 'The right bus', we might say, simply means 'the one that goes the same way as that one went', 'the right book' simply means 'the one that I used last time'. I grant that I do not go through life saying to myself such things as 'There is my wife; these are my feet; those are the stairs; here is the bannister', each utterance being accompanied by a set of memories of former experiences. All I do is grasp the bannister and run downstairs to where my wife is waiting. Yet I can do this only because I do, in some way, recognize all these things for what they are—and know thereby what to expect of them. So that although my behaviour may be the only indication, even to myself, that I am recognizing things, there would be something misleading about saying that the recognition is identical with the behaviour. There is still a difference between doing things intentionally and simply doing them by chance.

There are, of course, different ways of recognizing, but it is important to remember that the differences are only of what I have called the 'primary' kind.[1] The main distinction is that between 'consciously knowing' and merely 'accepting in passing': Recognition *is* recognition always by virtue of the same feature,

[1] See p. 45.

the acceptance of a presented instance as a member of some particular class (which may be the class of appearances of a particular individual). We cannot, therefore make 'secondary distinctions' in *how* we recognize, only in *what* we recognize on different occasions.

To recognize a particular person, place or thing is to accept what is presented as a manifestation of, or phase in, a particular continuous identity; to *identify* what is now presented with what has been presented before. For me to recognize my desk is for me to accept it as the same desk I have used on a number of previous occasions, and *as the result of* having used it on previous occasions, though these previous occasions need not be separately specified in my recognition. I say 'as the result of' because it does make sense to say of someone that he only *seems* to recognize something when he does in fact *accept* it.

It might be claimed that we can recognize individuals we have never seen before. For example, I might say 'I recognized you immediately from your father's description' or 'I recognized the boat from the picture in the brochure'. But what may actually be *recognized* in such cases is a particular shape or a particular 'look' which *has been* seen, or imagined, before. Where I simply accept something as the thing which has been described to me, this is not recognition of that thing in any ordinary sense.

Sometimes what we recognize is simply a particular quality in a thing. When I look at a passing car and see that it is blue I am recognizing the colour of that car. Probably I do not recognize the car itself; I may have never seen it before. But that I can later describe the car is proof that I did recognize certain of its qualities. We do not generally speak of recognizing qualities, only of noticing them. Yet in order to *notice them*—we must to some extent notice what they are, i.e. classify them (and generally, though not necessarily, name them); and this *is* recognition.

In ordinary speech we are inclined to say such things as 'I noticed that the car was blue—and recognized the shade as arctic blue'. This, I suggest, is only because being arctic blue seems to be the sort of thing we *need to* recognize (recognition having somehow a suggestion of deliberation about it), whilst being blue does not; it is too familiar to us. But clearly there is no fixed 'line of distinction' between qualities we recognize and qualities we simply notice. The principle difference in our use of the two terms is that 'notice' does not necessarily imply that the object has been seen before. Nevertheless, as soon as we *name* the object noticed, there is an implied assumption that at least some of its characteristics are being recognized.

Recognition need not be of particular objects or qualities. Just as I can recognize the approaching creature as *my* dog so I can recognize it as simply *a* dog. In both cases I am noting similarities; in the one case between what I am regarding as episodes in the history of a single individual, in the other case between what I am regarding as a series of different individuals. It might be felt that recognizing my dog is always a more specific recognition—that it must already be recognised as *a* dog before it can be specified as *my* dog. But this is not so. An infant can often recognize his own dog before he even knows of the existence of other dogs.

Whether we are concerned with individuals or kinds or qualities, in all the cases I have considered so far something actually before us is being classified or identified. I want now to consider whether we should still speak of recognition when what is being classified or identified is not actually before us. Now, I have allowed that, although the thing we recognize is present to us, the recognition must refer always beyond the present experience. As I put it in reference to the recognition of qualities, we must notice *what* it is. To recognize is to note a similarity, or perhaps I should say that to recognize is to *isolate* an area of similarity since it may well be that the capacity to recognize is logical*y* prior to the awareness of universals. So that, although what I recognize is the thing now before me, my recognizing it involves my noting of its similarity to other things not now before me. We might well ask, therefore, 'How does seeing an object and judging "That is my dog" differ in any important way from remembering an object and judging "That was my dog"?'. Do I recognize what is 'before my mind' in the same way as I recognize what is before my eyes?

We can, if we wish, simply decide that the term 'recognition' shall stand for only one type of classification: the classification of present events, things, qualities and relations, and that any other use of the term is metaphorical. Such a decision is in any case wise in that it avoids possible misunderstandings. But this does not answer the question, it simply avoids it. The real point at issue is whether it makes sense at all to talk of recognizing objects 'before the mind'.

Certainly my present *state of mind* is something I am now experiencing and can, therefore, recognize in the ordinary sense —assuming that it is classifiable and that I have experienced similar states of mind before. I can, for instance, usually recognize misery when I experience it. And it might be argued that my state of mind when I am remembering an event *includes* the event remembered. But the belief which I hold about some thing does not include that thing in any ordinary sense. Clem Attlee is not included in my belief that he is a great statesman in the way that he was included in the British War Cabinet, nor yet in the way that he is included in the denotation of 'British Prime Ministers'. And if I remember Clem Attlee my memory does not *include* him. It is of him or about him, and this is quite different.

The sense in which, and the extent to which, we may be recognizing events and individuals when we are remembering them seem to depend upon two questions: whether the event actually remembered is the physical event which occurred or the mental event which was our perception of it, a question we shall take up in the next chapter, and whether memory-images are in some sense 'before us' in a way that permits us to scutinize, and recognize or fail to recognize, them. This question we shall deal with in Chapter VII.

CHAPTER IV

MEMORIES AND MEMORY-CLAIMS

REMEMBERING AND REPORTING THE PAST

We have seen that it is quite possible to have and to express knowledge of a past event which is not dependent upon any actual memory of the event in question. I now want to make the point that, even when the knowledge is dependent upon an actual memory of the event, the claim to that knowledge, the proposition purporting to relate that event, is distinguished from the memory by virtue of which I make that claim. My memory-claim 'I had fish for lunch' may be made because of certain images I now have of my lunch and/or my remembering certain propositions such as 'This is good fish', and clearly it would be quite possible for us to have those images and to remember those propositions without, so to speak, advancing from them to this particular memory-claim, 'I had fish for lunch'. Nevertheless, as Wittgenstein has pointed out,[1] a word in a public language must have a public meaning, and since the established usage of words arises out of interpersonal communication, the public use of the words 'memory' and 'remembering' must rest upon the memory-claims we make rather than upon what we might call our private remembering. By 'private' here I mean essentially private in the sense of being below the level of communication, not simply in fact not communicated; my assertion about a past occurrence is as much a memory-claim if it is made to myself in the course of explaining or planning my own conduct, as if it is made out loud to an audience. Suppose, for instance, that I enter a bar and, recognizing a man I dislike, I avoid meeting him. My action may be no more considered than my avoiding walking into the gatepost as I leave my house. But if I say to myself 'That chap cornered me last week and bored me stiff', then I am making a definite memory-claim. It could have been made to anybody and would have conveyed the same information.

---

[1] *Investigations*, Pt. 1, para. 242 ff., p. 88e. See also para. 257 ff., p. 92e. But note that I am not committed to, nor do I in fact support, Wittgenstein's general view that all language is necessarily public.

Now, what is it that such a memory-claim refers to: a present mental state, a past mental state, a past public event, or a combination of all of these—my present mental state as related to past events? Before we answer 'all of these' it is well to consider that, unless I am deliberately introspecting for the purpose of examining my own 'remembering procedure', there seems to be no reason whatever why I should make a claim about anything but the past physical event itself. This is all that need interest myself or my listener if there be one. Neither he nor I need be concerned about my mental states in order to understand the claim.

Certainly if I were to say to a friend 'There was a riot here last week' he might be interested to know whether I in fact remembered this event or had simply been told about it. To this extent 'I remember the riot here last week' gives *him* more information than does 'There was a riot here last week'. But it is information not directly connected with the actual event—the first statement does not usually give *me* (the speaker) any information that the second does not. It may be protested here that neither assertion can give me any information since I am the one who is making it. But in making the claim I may be, so to speak, drawing together a group of otherwise disconnected recollections, not necessarily in order to draw a conclusion—I most probably drew a conclusion when I witnessed the event—but to provide premises from which to draw further, or different, conclusions. And for this purpose the addition of 'I remember' is quite superfluous. We can fairly conclude, then, that memory-claims *refer*, in normal cases, to the event remembered, not to the particular mental state which is the remembering of it. And since it is our memory-claims that are of public interest, the reliability of our memories must be judged by the accuracy with which our memory-claims report past events.

I have maintained that a memory-claim is a report about a past event, dependent upon a present mental event, or mental state. But what is this relationship of dependence? It clearly cannot be logical dependence since there is no reason why a true claim about the past, even about my own past, should not occur without any 'act of remembering' at all. It must, therefore, be causal dependence. We can say only that the memory is a causally necessary condition of the memory-claims; it is not both necessary and sufficient since the memory-claim may not be made at all, or it may be made wrongly. Nevertheless, when a true memory-claim is made there are causal (though not logical) grounds for supposing that there exists a memory or a group of memories which is itself in some sense 'correct'. We must, therefore, consider what sense of 'correct' is applicable to the actual memories.

It would be a gross mistake to assume that, because my memory-claim refers directly to a past event, my present mental state is not relevant to it. It is according to historical facts that a memory-claim is finally accepted or rejected, but it is by virtue of a present mental state that it is made at all. My present memory-claim that the film I saw was about Don Quixote refers to that film, not to the images and propositions now forming in my mind. Yet I am able to make that claim only because those images and propositions *are* now in my mind. A remembered proposition is something quite distinct from any particular form of words which might express it. And an image cannot be *expressed in* words at all, only at best *described by* them. Thus a memory-claim must always be, in a sense, an interpretation of a memory.

It may therefore be misleading, if not improper, to speak of the memories themselves as true or false. It can only be when something is asserted that truth or falsity applies. Of the memories themselves all we can say is that they do or do not 'recapture' or 'represent to us' the past event in a way that should lead to our making true memory-claims. Thus the accuracy of a memory-claim is in part causally dependent upon the extent to which the claim is in fact justified by the actual memory, the extent to which this particular memory or group of memories is *adequate grounds* for the making of this particular memory-claim.

I say 'adequate grounds' but clearly no memory (nor anything else) can be adequate *in itself*. It must be adequate *for* some purpose. It may be felt, nonetheless, that a memory can be *complete* in itself; we may feel that no detail can possibly be missing. My memory image of some man may seem to me to be every bit as detailed as an actual view of that man; and the memory of some brief experience may seem to recapture every moment and every aspect of that experience. It is beside the point that the memory-image may be without background and the experience as remembered may be totally out of context; within very small limits a memory may seem to be complete in this sense. Yet its *seeming* to be complete is a matter of our *not being conscious* of any deficiencies. Whether any memory, however small its scope, is in fact complete is very difficult, if not impossible, to decide. Furlong draws an analogy with the exact focussing of a telescope and says[1] 'But do we ever reach a term in the series [of increasingly detailed memories] that will correspond to the clearly focussed object . . .? I do not think we do. Will anyone claim that he has ever had a memory which he could not conceive of being more vivid and realistic?' We may feel that there must be *some level of particularity* at which memories are 'complete'—it is hard, for instance, to think what it would be like to have an incomplete memory of the colour of my car (it happens to be black), yet even here, we may claim that there are different 'shades of black' in different lights, and, be this as it may, to be 'complete' is not necessarily to be *adequate*. For to claim that I have a complete memory of my dog would surely amount to my claiming the ability to give a complete or full description of my dog by virtue of that memory—and what could possibly count as a full description?

We do better to avoid altogether the difficulties inherent in the idea of a 'complete memory' by assessing our memories solely in terms of their adequacy for some *specific* purposes. To decide whether a particular dog was a bull terrier or a fox terrier the sketchiest memory of it may serve my purpose, whereas if I am trying to decide whether it is my dog or my neighbour's that the postman is complaining about a most detailed memory of my dog may prove inadequate. The adequacy of memory is a contingent matter, something quite distinct from its degree of detail.

This does not mean, however, that it is *indifferent* to the degree of detail. The memory, however vague it may be as compared with some other memory of the same event, must at least be *detailed and precise enough* to support the memory-claim made.

We must be careful here not to confuse what I am calling a vague memory with what might be called a faint memory. A memory, like a picture or a description, is more or less precise, less or more vague, according to the extent that it includes or lacks detail. An outline sketch of a building is more vague than a detailed sketch or a photograph of the same building—though it may serve as well, or even better, to identify the building. An outline sketch

[1] E. J. Furlong, *A Study in Memory*, London, Nelson, 1951, p. 25.

of the Tower of Pisa, for instance, may direct our attention immediately to those features by which we have come to recognize it, whilst the detail included in a photograph may draw our attention away from them. In the same way a wealth of detail in the memory of an event may distract our attention from the very feature of the event with which we are most concerned. In his book *Defeat Into Victory* Field-Marshal Sir William Slim relates how, by having in his mind the sketchiest possible map of the area under his command, he was able to conduct his campaign in Burma unfettered by trifling detail and to keep his appraisal of the situation constantly in perspective.

It is important to note that vagueness (which is in any case a matter of degree) is not essentially correlated with faintness. The figure in a brightly lit room is more vague seen through frosted glass than seen through clear glass, but it is not necessarily more faint. In the case of clear and faint memories the analogy which naturally springs to mind is with things seen in good and bad lights, but we must be careful not to take this too literally. We do not *see* memories in general though we do sometimes talk of seeing memory-images. It may be better to describe faint memories as those which are elusive in the sense that we cannot *fix* them. They seem to flicker through our minds and remain just 'beyond our grasp', as when I have a name 'on the tip of my tongue'. But the elusiveness of such memories does not prevent their being detailed and precise. I am satisfied that the name which 'came and went before I could catch it' was exactly the right name. And, in the same way, the image I now have of a childhood friend and which I have some difficulty in 'holding' seems to be, in itself, a most comprehensive image.

I want now to consider the relevance of vagueness of memories and of memory-claims respectively to the accuracy of memory-claims. On this question Bertrand Russell has some most interesting things to say. He points out that a memory is no less *precise* because it is in fact wrong—'provided some very definite occurrence would have been required to make it true'.[1] And allowing the distinction I have made, what he says is equally true of both actual memories and memory-claims. He continues 'It follows from what has been said that a vague thought has more likelihood

[1] *The Analysis of Mind*, p. 182.

of being true than a precise one. To try to hit an object with a vague thought is like trying to hit a bullseye with a lump of putty: when the putty reaches the target it flattens out all over it, and probably covers the bullseye along with the rest. To try to hit an object with a precise thought is like trying to hit a bullseye with a bullet.' This is a good analogy; it brings out very well the inverse relationship between precision, or wealth of detail, and probable accuracy. But it is important to note that for the purposes of our first question—the effect of vagueness or precision in the actual memory itself upon the memory-claim—we are (to adhere to his analogy) throwing the target at the putty, not the putty at the target, for we are trying to hit a thought with an objective assertion. At this level we are not concerned with whether the memory-claim is in fact true or false, only with whether or not it truly reports the 'remembering state of mind'. There is a greater danger of error in *reporting* a complex and highly detailed 'remembering state of mind' than in *reporting* a vague and sketchy one. The danger is that some of the details, possibly important and relevant refinements, will be left out of the memory-claim or misreported as a result of its complexity.

On the other hand, whilst a vague memory *properly reported* is comparatively immune from the risk of error, it may well be that such a memory is inadequate for the claim I *want to make*, i.e. for the premiss I need for my current train of thinking. And when this happens there is inevitably a tendency to supply the missing detail from imagination. This gives rise to the quite different point—the point which Russell is in fact making in the passage quoted above (though he does not use the expression 'memory-claim')—that the degree of precision of a memory-claim is inversely proportionate to the likelihood of its own factual accuracy. Thus we have two quite distinct 'risks' here: (1) that the memory-claim will fail to report properly the remembering state of mind because of the detailed complexity of that state of mind, and (2) that the memory-claim will misreport the actual event due to the poverty of detail in the memory itself.

However, although these two 'risks' can be distinguished in principle, there may be considerable difficulty in isolating them in practice. For the 'actual memory' is not inspectable, only at best introspectable; the only discrepancy we can demonstrate is that between the event itself and the memory-claim about it.

Let us regard this as the 'total area of possible error' and try to identify the specific points of possible breakdown within it. As this enquiry must hinge very largely on the question of vagueness and precision, our first task is to consider more closely just what it is for a memory to be vague.

Any memory-claim, whether publicly or privately made, tends to give rise to further questions. I claim to remember entering a public bar and talking to a man there. I am then asked, or ask myself, 'Which public house? What kind of man?' and so on. Now, it may be that I am unable to supply answers to these questions at all. In this case my memory is comparatively indeterminate[1] and my memory-claim cannot (legitimately) be augmented. But if I am able to reply—'He was a tall chap with a foreign accent in the King's Arms' further questions will arise: 'What kind of foreign accent? What did you talk about? What did he actually say?'. It is always possible to ask for more precise information which a more detailed memory of the actual experience *could* furnish, and sooner or later we must find ourselves unable to reply. Whatever may be the position at a 'retention' or 'dispositional' level—this is a question for psychologists and physiologists to decide—it seems certain that, as far as occurrent memory goes, we never can remember every detail of every experience. As Stout has said,[2] 'How is it that I can recall in a few minutes experiences which occupied twelve hours? Only by omission. We simply make an outline sketch, in which the salient characteristics of things and events and actions appear, without their individualizing details. Mere forgetfulness in part helps to make this possible. . . .' And it is important to note that the omissions are not generally of 'whole incidents' so much as of precise detail from all the incidents.

We must bear in mind, of course, that something at least analogous occurs in direct perception. We cannot notice every detail and we are obliged, even with what is actually before us, to schematize and classify comparatively indeterminately. What I *see as* simply a group of people *is in fact* ten men, four women

---

[1] I am using the term 'determinate' throughout in the manner exemplified by H. H. Price in *Thinking and Experience*, Chapter I.

[2] G. F. Stout, *A Manual of Psychology*, (revised Mace), London, University Tutorial Press, 1938, p. 143.

and eight children. But the point Stout is making is that the omissions of memory are further imposed, as it were, upon the perceptual experience; we *cannot* remember what we did not in some sense notice, but also *do not* remember a great deal that we *did* notice. So that, although the memory of some small specific event, some particular action or a person's appearance, may be highly determinate, every occurrent memory will tend to fall short to some extent of what in the physical circumstances it *could have* been.

Now, any memory-claim which is more determinate than the memory on which it is based is in obvious danger of being false. Suppose for example that a man claims to remember meeting three Norwegians in the pub when in fact he had met three Danes. There are several possible explanations: (1) he actually remembers meeting three Scandinavians and says 'three Norwegians' simply from carelessness or for the sake of simplicity, (2) he actually has a memory of meeting three Scandinavians but at the time of making his memory-claim he *took his memory to be* one of meeting three Norwegians, or (3) at the time of the encounter he judged them (wrongly) to be Norwegians, and correctly remembered this false judgment.

Whichever of these explanations applies these facts are the same: he actually had a meeting with three big blond men with foreign accents, whom he rightly took to be Scandinavians, and at *some stage* he has increased the determinateness of his claim by moving from 'Scandinavian' to 'Norwegian'—as it happens, wrongly.

There is an obvious similarity here to my earlier example[1] of the boy who remembered an event without realizing that he remembered it. This I held to be possible because every physical event can be described, correctly, in an almost limitless number of different ways. In that case the noises the boy heard were in fact made by an event which could have been described as the delivery of the coal, though, as it happened, he gave a description which was less determinate *within the frame of reference in question*. Remembering loud noises is less determinate than remembering coal-delivery noises—the latter is a sub-species of the former. I say 'within the frame of reference' because for a different purpose or from a different viewpoint quite different considerations

[1] See p. 54.

could apply. Remembering the exact number of bumps, for instance, is more determinate than simply remembering a bumping noise, but for the question in hand it happens to be irrelevant. In the case we considered the memory-claim 'I heard the coal being delivered' would have been justified if it had been made because the noises would have been correctly identified as members of the more determinate class, coal delivery noises. Yet the only difference between this and the 'Norwegians' case is that in the latter the determination of the 'tall blond men with Scandinavian accents' as 'Norwegians' is *not* justified by the facts. In the same way as it was open to us to ask ourselves 'What else could they have been?', it was open to us to ask ourselves what else the coal-noises could have been—and to find alternative answers.

The difference between the two cases seems to be simply in the facts, and if we always had independent evidence of the facts we should not need to trouble ourselves about justifying memory-claims at all. As it is the determination of our memory-claims must be justified, on most occasions, by the nature of the memories themselves. The question is 'What degree of probability *can* ever *justify* a greater determination in our memory-claims than in our actual memories or our original perceptual judgments, and in what sense justify it?

Now, this would be an idle question if such over-determination were in any case *both* illicit *and* unnecessary. But if it is found to be necessary the question of its being illicit simply cannot arise— and consideration shows that it is necessary. We are constantly obliged by mere pressure of time and the conduct of our affairs to 'take a chance' to some extent, in the choice of classification words in both our perception and our memory-claims. I pass in the street a man wearing a grey, air force-ish uniform with what looks like a Polish insignia, and later, when I am trying to recall what sort of people were about, I claim to remember passing a Polish airman. I wake in the morning and I hear twittering noises outside my window. Later, when I am trying to remember what sort of morning it was, I claim to remember that there were birds twittering outside my window. And my memory-claims would be the same *whether or not* I had said to myself at the time 'This is a Polish airman' or 'There are birds about.' When we 'take a chance' in determining any experience we usually do so in the light of what we might reasonably expect to be the case. My identification of the twitterings as bird noises arises very largely from my awareness of the likelihood of there being birds about. Probably our man's assumption that the Scandinavians were Norwegians arose from his knowledge that there were Norwegians in that town. And just as the Scandinavians were in fact Danes, the twitterings *could have* come from a squeaky mangle and the uniformed man *could have* been an elaborately dressed taxi-driver. Yet how hard it would be to protect ourselves against these possibilities of error in our memory-claims. If, at every stage, we confined our reports to what we actually were remembering—the sounds, the sights, the judgments made on the spot—the effect would be quite stultifying; we could never make any effective pronouncement without a full-blown enquiry beforehand.

But the saving factor—and this is terribly important—is that it is *always open to us* on any given occasion to say 'Wait—what am I actually remembering?' We can then exercise the care necessary to avoid over-determining the memory-claim, by focussing our attention upon the points at which it is likely to be over-determined and, therefore, in need of further supporting evidence.

IS WHAT IS REMEMBERED PUBLIC OR PRIVATE?

The question 'What am I actually remembering?' may include in its answer, as we saw, 'judgments made on the spot'—but what if these judgments were in any case wrong? Is there no way of getting past them, as it were, to the event itself? Here we come to the question, foreshadowed in the previous chapter, whether the event we remember is the actual physical event itself or the mental event which was our perception of that physical event—whether we recall the state of affairs or the state of mind engendered by that state of affairs. We have already decided that the memory-claim normally refers to a past event, not to the present remembering of it. And, except in those cases where the subject of memory is specifically a state of mind, e.g. 'I remember feeling depressed yesterday', it refers to a past physical event—a state of affairs. But this decision arose out of the distinction between memory and memory-claim. It does not follow, therefore, that the memory itself is *of* the state of affairs. It may well be that when I claim 'There was a riot here last week' what I am actually remembering is my own past perceptions of certain people, my judgments about these perceptions, and my feeling of apprehension.

This point is raised by Von Leyden who seems to be in no doubt that the 'real object' of a memory of an event is what we could broadly call our state of mind in perceiving that event. He says 'In the case of memory we can never even attempt to recall anything but the way in which we happened to perceive an event in the past; and by the time we remember our past perception of the event it has become something incorrigible, final and irrevocable'.[1] Now, I have argued at length in Chapter III that such judgments are neither final nor irrevocable, the fact is that we frequently *do* amend in memory the errors made in perception. But this does not alter the fact that nothing can *recur* to our minds that has not previously entered our minds. I have heard it argued that there is an equally good case for claiming that what we perceive is always a state of our own minds,[2] but this argument overlooks the 'second event' nature of memory. *Our perceiving it* is a state of our own minds, that is, a mental event, but *what we perceive* is there before us. To put it rather crudely: if we allow that there are minds and there is a physical reality known to them, then perception is a relationship between the mind and that physical reality. But, that relationship having once been established at a present level, remembering can then occur as a relationship between past and present mental events. The present mental event (the remembering) is connected to the past physical event through the agency of the past mental event which was the perception of it. Certainly it is difficult to see what remembering an event could be other than remembering our perceiving that event. And, since the *memory-claim* refers always to the public event, without reference to the perception of it, there is a relationship between claim and physical event parallel to that between memory and mental event. We could set this out in a simple diagram thus:

[1] *Remembering*, p. 61—Von Leyden is not, however, wholly consistent in his position. He says, e.g. (p. 36) 'For instance we can remember one event resembling another event without having been previously aware of their resemblance'.

[2] E.g. This argument is put forward by M. Deutscher in his review of 'Remembering' in *Mind* Vol. LXXI, 1962, p. 278.

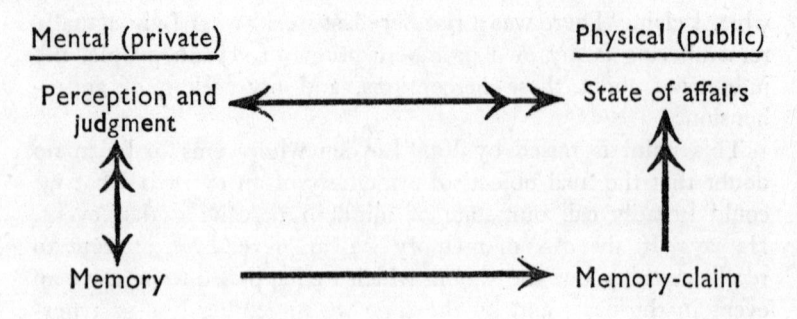

```
Mental (private)                    Physical (public)

Perception and    ⇌                 State of affairs
judgment                                    ↑
    ↕                                       |
Memory            ———————→          Memory-claim
```

(the single arrows show causal direction, the double arrows referential direction)

It may well be objected here that, since despite Von Leyden's assertion to the contrary, we can and do revise our perceptual judgments, as shown in Chapter III, there must therefore be at least some direct connection between the physical events themselves and our memories, there must be some part of these memories untainted by attitudes or judgments. How else, it may be asked, can we justify such revisions, even to ourselves? Surely the diagram ought to be modified thus:

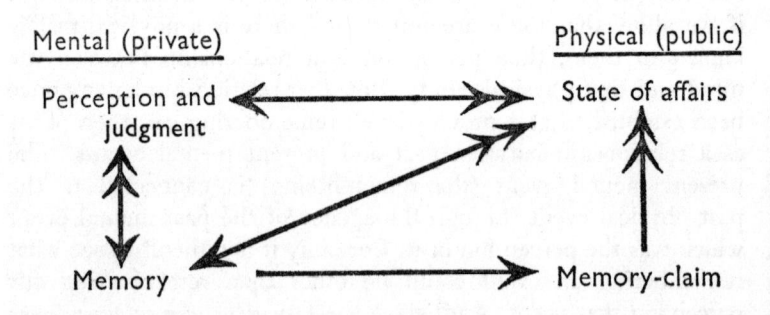

```
Mental (private)                    Physical (public)

Perception and    ⇌                 State of affairs
judgment              ↗                     ↑
    ↕             ↙                          |
Memory            ———————→          Memory-claim
```

(the single arrows show causal direction, the double arrows referential direction)

But, whilst I shall in fact argue for such a modification, this objection, as it stands, is not conclusive. We can make any number of judgments about what we subsequently remember as the same event, and some of these may be found *at the memory level* to be incompatible with each other in the light of facts we know otherwise (i.e. of other remembered propositions). Suppose, for example, that on passing a football ground I make, *inter alia*, the following observations: This is Old St. School football ground; two teams are playing each other; one side is wearing black and yellow jerseys; the other side is wearing red and blue jerseys; black and yellow are the New St. School colours. Old St. School is playing New St. School at football. And subsequently I make the memory-claim 'I saw Old St. playing New St. at football on Old St. ground'. But I *only then* recollect that at Old St. School they wear green football jerseys. I must therefore amend my claim to the less determinate one 'I saw New St. School playing another team on Old St. School ground'. My reason here for amending a remembered judgment is simply my remembering further relevant propositions.

Even so Von Leyden's view would commit us to a conclusion, which is very hard to accept. For if he is right, then *quite apart from the possibility of misremembering we could never be sure that a memory-claim is a true report of an actual past event*. The certainty we feel about our perceptions arises very largely from the fact that, though we can and do make mistakes, we can always look again. The very similar certainty I feel about my considered memories suggests very strongly that in memory also I can 'look again' at least at some element or feature of the remembered event; that within the memory, or as part of the remembering, there can be re-manifested some element of this physical event itself, something below the level of interpretation, to provide a basis of actual contact with the past 'state of affairs'. My own view, which I shall develop in Chapters VII and VIII, is that this 'physical element' can only be our 'brute sensory intake' as retained and reproduced in imagery. But I think we must allow that, in so far as what is remembered is an event as perceptually interpreted, however indeterminately, the direct object of the memory itself is a mental, not a physical, event.

It should, of course, be kept in mind that memory-claims are not necessarily confined to physical events; the proper subjects of memory-claims—let us call them the *ultimate referents* of memories—though usually physical, public events, may in many cases include—and quite properly so—much that was mental and private. If what is being referred to in the claim includes a past state of mind then clearly not only the perception of past physical events, but also attitudes towards them and conjectures about them must enter into the memory. I could, for instance, make the memory-claim 'When I realized what had happened I was just horrified.'

Consider these passages from Furlong:

'When I compare these two events, the original event and the remembering of it, what strikes me is not the difference but rather the resemblance. My state of mind when remembering is extraordinarily like the state of mind I am recalling'.[1]

And a little later,

'On the occasion of recall, there is the sensory, or quasi-sensory, element, but there is also, and this is the important point, the propositional element. I am aware of imaged watchface, and I respond to this datum by thinking, "That was my watch." The proposition is there, though its tense has changed. Similarly as I recall the ticking, I also recall that I wondered whether cleaning was needed. In other words, when we remember a past occasion we do not merely reproduce the sensory data in imaged form, we reproduce or image, more or less completely, our *whole state of mind* on the remembered occasion'.[2]

These passages draw attention to what we might call the subjective element within the remembered state of mind, but they do not make clear the quite important difference between propositions about states of affairs in the world, such as 'This is my watch', and propositions about mental states, such as 'I wonder if it needs cleaning'. Both propositions may belong, as it were, to the state of mind, but, as propositions, they are concerned with quite different sorts of things. One sort of thing is imageable in the ordinary sense; whether or not it is in fact imaged does not matter. The other sort of thing is not. I could have an image of a watch held in my hand, but I do not know what it would be like to have an image of wondering whether it needs cleaning—nor yet of thinking it a handsome watch. Furlong's rather odd phrase 'Image the whole state of mind' obscures this distinction.

But this 'imageability test' is valuable only for distinguishing the 'physical' and 'mental' elements within what is claimed about the past event; it cannot serve to distinguish a proposition which

[1] *A Study in Memory*, p. 74.   [2] *A Study in Memory*, p. 75 (his italics).

correctly reports the physical event from one which reports a mere assumption made about it. Suppose, for instance, I see a group of men enter a public meeting, perceive (quite correctly) that they look like ruffians, and *conjecture* that their intention is to break up the meeting. This conjecture may in fact be quite wrong; these men may be supporters of the speaker; but, assuming that I leave the meeting without learning this fact, I may well subsequently claim to remember that a group of ruffians came in to heckle and break up the meeting. And the proposition 'There were hecklers present' lends itself just as well to imagery as the proposition 'There were rough-looking men present'. The fact that in the latter case the images would (or could) be memory-images whereas in the former they *must* be imagination images can help us only if we have some way of distinguishing between these. Even assuming that we have such a means, quite apart from the fact that we have now shifted from 'imageability' to 'memory-imageability', the test could never be conclusive. For there could well be propositions which quite correctly reported the event as actually presented to us, but which, when remembered, were accompanied by imagination images—or were not accompanied by images at all.

At this stage, then, we must be content to distinguish those remembered propositions which *purport* to refer to physical events from those concerned with other matters, such as how we felt and what we wondered. By subjecting the former group to a careful scrutiny in the light of what we take to be our memory-images and the coherence of the remembered propositions themselves, we can achieve at least some measure of security against confusing remembered conjectures with remembered perceptions.

Before leaving this question it should be pointed out that what I have said applies equally to memories of events, of individuals and of qualities. I may 'remember' the presence of Jones at a particular gathering because in fact *I supposed* at the time that he was there. And the decision I made that a car standing under a greenish street lamp *would* look pale blue in normal daylight can all too easily be remembered subsequently as my seeing the car to look pale blue. Those parts of the remembered state of mind concerned with what things were like, can as easily give rise to this type of error in the memory-claim as those parts of the remembered state of mind concerned with how things were behaving. If I had to give a name to the error of remembering conjectures *as* perceptual judgments, I would call it 'subjective half-truth/objective falsity'. Whilst the memory-claim is false, the memory itself is at least partially true; what is remembered was part of the earlier state of mind, but it was conjecture, not conclusion, about the perceived event. And it is necessary to distinguish this case from those cases where a genuine perceptual error is perpetuated in memory, and which we might call 'subjective *truth*/objective falsity' of memory. Both 'subjective truth', and 'subjective half-truth' kinds of error seem to be always possible in the memory-claim relating to an event or state of affairs. But it is as well to note at this point that these errors are simply not applicable to memory-imagery as such. Only when a judgment or classification has been made can there be a mistaken judgment or misclassification.

Shortly I want to consider how, and to what extent, these errors can be guarded against. But first I want to consider a class of memories in which, on the face of it at least, the memory seems to be identical with the memory-claim.

NEGATIVE REMEMBERING OR REMEMBERING BY DEFAULT

A memory-claim refers to a past state of affairs, not a present state of mind. I am therefore making a memory-claim when I attend an identification parade and claim 'The man I saw yesterday is *not* here'. Perhaps I am remembering the man I saw yesterday, but this does not seem to be necessary. All I need know to make the claim is that he *is not* any of these people before me, or rather, none of these people is him. Thus my memory seems to just be my claim 'He is not here'.

Again, if someone asserts 'Fred's house had a green roof' I may deny this either because I in fact remember that it had a red roof or because I simply remember that whatever colour roof it may have had, it did not have a green one. My memory-claim may be the same in both cases—'it was not green'—but in one case it is supported by an actual memory, the memory of a red roof on Fred's house, in the other case it does not seem to be supported at all; the remembering seems to consist wholly in the framing of the proposition which is the memory-claim.

Let us return for a moment to the 'identification parade' situation which is perhaps the commonest case of negative remembering. It might be felt that this is simply a case of recognizing what *is* present as other than what we are seeking. Yet, to recognize that something is not the one we want, either we must *actually recognize* the presented article, as when I identify and reject my wife's comb in searching for my own, or we must remember the sought article, and fail to find it amongst those offered, as when I reject a number of nondescript and unfamiliar combs in searching for my own. There does not seem to be anything we could properly call 'negative recognition'. On the one hand there is positive recognition, on the other hand failure to recognize. If I wanted to return to a house I had once seen but about which I could recollect little or nothing, I may well walk along the street hoping that when I did come to the right house I *could* recognize it. But if I were successful this would surely mean only that on seeing the house I then remembered things I had earlier failed to remember. So long as something is actually presented for our perception either it is, or it is not, recognized as what it is.

In recollection of the past, however, the question is much more difficult. Nothing is being 'presented to us' independently of our own minds. What I am remembering *as not the case* is in some way an idea in my own mind; but where does it arise from and what kind of idea can it be? How can I remember that Fred's roof is not green or that I did not go to the theatre last Saturday unless I remember what colour Fred's roof *is* and what I *did* last Saturday? In some way I must be entertaining the idea and rejecting it, but it is by no means easy to see how I entertain it nor why I reject it. Perhaps I am able to picture Fred's house and try out a green roof in 'my picture'. But I may be quite competent to make the memory-claim, 'Fred's roof is not green', without being able to picture Fred's roof at all. And even if I can picture it, there are lots of different greens; how can I be sure that I have tried out all of them? In the theatre case this difficulty is even more obvious. I might be able to picture a visit to the theatre, though I do not quite know what this would be like. But it would be quite hopeless to try to run through pictures of all the possible variations of such a visit.

In some cases, of course, we may simply be remembering a

negative observation made in the past. I might for instance observe that the Regal cinema is not showing *Hell's Angels* without observing what it is showing, and subsequently make the memory-claim 'The Regal was not showing *Hell's Angels* last night'. But I do not think we can account for all our negative memories this way. I do not go around making such observations as 'That roof is not green' except in very rare circumstances.

We seem, then, to have two problems with negative recollection: (1) Except in an 'identification parade' situation, where we are deliberately trying to render an indeterminate memory more determinate, where do memories of 'what is not the case' arise from? (2) How can we assert 'This is not the case' except on the authority of a memory of what was the case?

To the first question the only answer I can give is that negative memories *do not* arise except in some kind of 'identification parade' situation. I am satisfied that when we make a negative memory-claim this is always in the course of attempting to answer some positive question, even though we may not consciously have posed that question to ourselves. Always something has reminded us of a past situation and sent out memories in search of details of it.

It may be unwise, however, to be too precise about just how this occurs. Bertrand Russell considers the well-known case of entering a familiar room where a new picture has been hung on the wall and being conscious of a sense of unfamiliarity. He says[1] 'In this case it is fairly clear what happens. The other objects in the room are associated, through the former occasion, with a blank space on the wall where now there is a picture. They call up an image of a blank wall which clashes with the perception of the picture'. Whilst this account is no doubt feasible, I am afraid I find it far from convincing. There is something rather odd in the suggestion that the objects in the room call up an image of a *blank wall*; certainly I personally have never been conscious of such an image on such an occasion. I am more disposed to say simply that the picture itself is unfamiliar to us whereas the rest of the room is not, and we are therefore surprised by our failure to recognize it.

I think Russell's explanation would be more plausible if the room had simply been rearranged and the picture moved. For

[1] *The Analysis of Mind*, p. 178.

then the separate items of furniture would all be equally familiar and the sense of unfamiliarity could attach only to the room as a whole, and we might well feel that some image or memory of the room as it had been must exist to account for the sense of unfamiliarity. But, even here, it could be maintained that no separate memory of the past situation is needed. The recognition of the individual items is not accompanied by the recognition of the room as a whole, and once more there is a clash of the familiar and the unfamiliar. Our recognition of *what was and still is the case*, the appearance of the individual items of furniture, forces our attention to what *was not* and now is the case, the present appearance of the whole room. We then speculate in a vague sort of way about how the furniture used to be arranged, and in doing so set up a series of hypotheses which we can accept or reject.

Or to take a quite different case: suppose I am reminded by an overheard conversation both of the way people talk in South Wales and of the way a former colleague of mine talked. What could be more natural under these circumstances than to remember that my former colleague *was not* a Welshman, whether I do remember where he came from or not? Our thoughts of things and events experienced in the past are usually stimulated by present perceptions or by present trains of thought. It is quite natural, therefore, that these thoughts should include some hypotheses which are disconfirmed, as well as those that are confirmed, by memory. I think it is safe to say that on those occasions (if there be any) when a memory comes to us completely out of the blue, it *must* be a positive memory.

The second question—'How are we able to reject these hypotheses?'—is already partially answered. In remembering that my colleague was not a Welshman I am not necessarily remembering what nationality he was, but I am certainly *remembering him* in some way. And similarly within the memory-claim 'Fred's house did not have a green roof' is the covert memory-claim that Fred *did have* a house, and the implication that, in some way, I *am remembering* Fred's house.

It is apparent, therefore, that negative memory situations can be explained very largely in terms of levels of determinateness. The negative memory-claim arises because we are seeking to further determine our memories. The relatively undermined memory provides the basis for the 'identification parade'; imagination stimulated by our current perceptions and their associations provides the 'candidates'. Thus, even when no successful candidate is forthcoming, there is some positive remembering, however indeterminate, which enables us to say and keep saying 'No, it was not like that'.

Whenever I am remembering how or what a thing was not, I am also remembering, at a lower level of determinateness, how or what it was. Thus, even in the case of negative remembering, the memory-claim is not wholly unsupported by an existent 'remembering state of mind'. My memory-claims about what was *not* the case, *refer*, like any other memory-claims, to the actual event, *what was the case*.

TESTING MEMORY-CLAIMS

In this Chapter I have claimed that: (1) Whether what is being remembered is an event, an individual or a characteristic of an individual, a distinction can be made between the memory-claim and the memory occurrence on which it is based, and (2) It is the memory-claims which enable us to pursue trains of remembering and reasoning; these develop, as it were, according to the statements we make to ourselves, not according to our evidence for making those statements. Our chief concern, therefore, is how the truth of memory-claims can be established—what is to count for and against them.

It must be emphasized here that I am speaking of claims arising from current remembering. Dispositional claims, e.g. that I can remember a poem, or remember how to tie a clovehitch, do not entail that I *am remembering* anything except the propositions, 'I can recite . . .' or 'I can tie a clovehitch'. In these cases I am simply claiming to have a certain dispositional ability; that my having it is rendered possible by memory is an additional, and for our present purposes irrelevant, assumption.

Let us consider an ordinary memory-claim about a past physical state of affairs—'There was a rose growing beside the door'. Clearly the simplest and most obvious test of this is to actually perceive the door and the rose. But if there has been a lapse of time the rose may have withered away or been pulled up; so its absence from the doorway will not falsify the claim. And if there has not been a lapse of time the question hardly arises. We do not trouble about *remembering* what is still there *to be perceived* unless we are playing some sort of memory game.[1]

It does not follow from this, however, that memory-claims can be tested, confirmed, or disconfirmed, only in very rare cases. When a memory-claim refers to a past public event, then even though the subject of the claim may have perished we may find evidence for its having existed both in what we can reasonably assume to be its physical effects—a bomb crater is pretty fair confirmation of the memory-claim that a bomb fell—and in the testimony of other people who also experienced it.

But this is not enough. In many cases we make memory-claims where any such independent confirmation is simply not possible, yet it is still vital to us to be quite sure that they are true. My memory-claim 'I arranged to meet the professor at ten o'clock' may be extremely important to me, but, since I do not keep a diary, it is doubtful whether I can check it by anything but a careful reconsideration of the memories which support it. The fact that a memory-claim refers directly to a public event does not mean that it can be checked only by public events. We can and often do satisfy ourselves that our memory-claims are correct simply by reference to our memories. We saw that one way of confirming memory-claims is by discovering the present events which we believe to be probable effects of the remembered events. And physical events may have non-physical effects. There is an obvious sense in which my perception of an event is an effect of that event—the perception could not have occurred without the event—and in which my memories are effects of that perception, since I can recall only what I have experienced. This being so, my claim to remember any event is at least *prima facie* evidence that it did occur. And it is evidence which I can accept confidently once I have satisfied myself of three things: (1) that my original judgments were well made, i.e. were what any careful observer would have judged from the appearances presented. (2) That my present remembering represents faithfully my judgments and perceptions at the time of the event. (3) That the present memory is adequate to support the claim made.

We must now consider how we might go about satisfying

[1] Like 'Kim's Game', which used to be popular in the Boy Scouts.

ourselves of these conditions. Let us take a concrete case. I make the following memory-claim: On my way to work today I was attacked by a magpie. Now, suppose that this claim is challenged by a bird-lover who is opposing a scheme to get rid of these creatures. It becomes necessary for me, if not to substantiate my claim (this may not be possible), at least to be very sure in my own mind that it is a true account of a past event. We shall assume that there were no witnesses, that I was not in fact injured, and that my only means of checking my claim is by introspection. I therefore ask myself:

What am I actually remembering? Is my 'remembering state of mind' in full accord with, i.e. ample warrant for, the claim made, according to the normal usage of the words and sentences employed in that claim? Perhaps I can satisfy myself that I am actually remembering the following observations made at the time of the occurrence: 'Something whizzed past my head from behind; there was a snapping noise close to my ear; there it is, it's a magpie; the snapping noise must have been its beak; it deliberately attacked me. I may also be actually remembering the fright I got at the time.

In this case, notwithstanding the comparative weakness of the 'must have been', I can reasonably assure myself that no error has occurred between the 'remembering state of mind' and the memory claim. But I would not have felt so sure had I discovered that my actual remembering included only being frightened by something flying past me with a snapping noise as it passed, and that I had *worked out later* that it must have been a magpie attacking me.

However, so far so good; I am satisfied that my memory-claim is in accordance with my remembered judgments. I must now consider those judgments themselves.

On what evidence did I make the judgments I remember? Consider these questions: (1) How did I know it was a magpie? (2) How did I know it was the same bird that had flown past my head? (3) Why did I assume it was attacking me? To answer these questions I must expand my memory to include further supporting propositions, or memory-images of the event itself.

If I am able quite sincerely to answer thus: (1) It was a large black and white bird of the kind I call 'magpie', and I am (and was at the time) good at identifying such birds. (2) Its direction and speed when I saw it correlated well with the direction and speed of whatever passed my head. (3) It is notorious that magpies are vicious at this time of year and I have been attacked before and recognized the snap of a beak as it passed: then I believe that the more I consider the memory the more certain I shall become that the memory-claim was in fact true. If, on the other hand, my actual memory is found to consist solely in propositions, the original evidence for which is quite lost, then the more I think about it the greater will my doubts become—even though the memory-claim may in fact be quite true.

In practice, of course, we do not hold long courts of enquiry on our memory-claims. We become very adept at singling out the vital features of our recollections which justify those claims, and we merely say 'Yes, I am quite certain that I was attacked by a magpie—go ahead and shoot them'. But 'I am certain' is significant only if I know what it is like to be *un*certain. My confidence is justified only by my realization that a careful reconsideration of my memory-claim *could have* shown me that I had assumed more in my perceptual judgments than the appearances presented to my senses could reasonably count as evidence for.

The case I have just considered is a straightforward 'memory of an event'. Now, I have claimed that the memory-claim distinction can be made whether the memory is of an event, an individual, a quality or even a skill. But in the cases of remembering qualities as such and remembering skills as such it does not seem possible to differentiate between error in making the original judgment and error in making the memory-claim. When I make the claim 'I remember his face was flushed', it is important that what I am actually remembering justifies the normal usage of the word 'flushed'. The claim may well be misleading, for instance, if it were made about someone who simply happens always to have a red face. But, as the memory *of a quality*, the particular redness of the face—not of an event, the reddening of the face, there does not seem to be anything which *could* constitute the actual memory except a memory-image.[1] And with images either we have them or we do not. The only explanations we can give of them are causal. The question 'What was the evidence which gave rise to the memory-image?' cannot be asked. The imagery *is* the evidence.

[1] It may be protested here that a suitable quality-word, e.g. brick-red would serve to remember the quality of the face with. For my reasons for denying this see p. 172 ff.

When we consider remembering a skill as such the case may be further complicated by a doubt as to whether what is claimed is that we are remembering something or simply that we possess a dispositional ability to perform something. Let us assume that my claim 'I remember how to make paper boats' is actually based upon some specific occurrent memory. Simply taking up a piece of paper and making a boat of it certainly confirms the dispositional ability claim. But does it prove anything about occurrent memories? Now, clearly there is a sense in which we can be remembering how to do something without actually doing it, but it is hard to see how we could confirm this kind of memory except by actually imaging at least some stages of the proceedings. The mere ability to remember a series of propositions—rules for the successful performance of a task—does not of itself provide any very great assurance that we can in fact perform that task, as those of us who have waited outside examination rooms know. Of course, even my having a complete set of images of the stages involved in making a paper boat does not guarantee that I shall succeed in making one when I try. My fingers may be too stiff and awkward. It is this fact which renders perfectly intelligible the difference between *remembering how* to do something and *being able* to do it.[1]

Considerable doubt may be felt, not without justification, about my use of the expression 'normal usage of the terms employed in memory-claims'. What constitutes 'normal usage' is itself always somewhat arbitrary and indecisive. I must therefore make it clear that by 'normal usage' I mean only non-misleading usage within a particular context and for a particular purpose.[2] We must also bear in mind that what I am calling a memory-claim is not simply, or even primarily, a claim for the edification of other people. It is primarily a claim about the past made to myself—in words in so far as I do in fact think in words—and used as the basis of further remembering and reasoning. Part of my reason, then, for checking my memory-claim against my actual occurrent memory is to prevent myself from making a tacit assumption, as a result of ambiguities in the words I am using, that I actually remember more than I do in fact remember. I am not concerned, therefore, with normal usage in any formal or dictionary sense,

[1] This distinction is dealt with at length in Chapter V.
[2] I frankly admit here that I am committed to the view that words do not mean things; people mean things when they use words.

but with the appropriateness of the terms in the memory-claim to report my memory within my current train of thought and reasoning.

To take a very simple example: I may remember a play I once saw and 'sum up' my memory of it in the claim 'It was thrilling'. This claim may, henceforward, 'stand in for' my memory. If my sole purpose in remembering is to decide whether or not to go to see another play by the same writer for an evening's entertainment, then the memory-claim 'It was thrilling' is a good enough guide for me. If, on the other hand, I am making a study of melodrama as a dramatic form, the claim 'It was thrilling' could very well be misleading without some augmentation by actual memories to show wherein and how it was thrilling. It is always possible for the dispositional memory of a proposition to be replaced, in the course of time, by a dispositional memory of mere words, and for those mere words, when remembered, to be 'taken for' the original proposition.

I specified three potential 'breakdown points' between the event and the memory-claim. So far I have shown how introspective checking, by securing us against the first and the last of these, can narrow the field of possible error. But to *eliminate* the field of possible error we must have some means of guarding against the second 'breakdown point', the fallibility of memory itself. If we are to give an adequate explanation of the certainty we in fact feel about our memory beliefs, or, more specifically, our ability to distinguish our reliable memory-beliefs from our less reliable ones, then we must show that, in some way, there is within the memory an actual recurrence of some element of the remembered event itself. Since this would not admit of error, it could serve as a basis for checking all our remembered judgments.

Now, it is noticeable that in all our attempts to find greater security in our memories of events, of individuals and their characteristics, and even of skills, we have come back sooner or later to memory-images. These have always represented the terminal point of checking. There is a strong suggestion, therefore, that the 'physical element in memory' will be found, if at all, in our imagery. I believe, therefore, that it is vital to consider in detail the nature of imagery and the role which it plays in our memories.

First, however, because so much recent writing has centred

upon them, I shall consider that class of memories which I have been referring to as 'remembering skills' and have found to be a somewhat confusing mixture of remembering in images and propositions, recognition, and mere dispositional capacities. I hope to show that when, and in so far as, public performances *are remembering at all*, they are simply one variety of memory of events and, as such, subject to the same analysis.

CHAPTER V

REMEMBERING HOW TO

ARE SKILLED PERFORMANCES MENTALLY DIRECTED?

It is commonly thought, by quite unsophisticated people as well as by 'traditional philosophers', that when we perform some skilled action which we have learnt to perform we are in fact doing two distinct things: making certain effective physical movements, and remembering past experiences in a way that enables us to make those movements effectively. It is commonly thought that exercising a skill is making our bodies follow the dictates of a mental directive composed very largely of memories of past events and performances. But strong arguments have been produced to challenge this belief both on empirical and on rational grounds, and we must now consider these arguments.

When we say that someone performs a task well or skilfully, we generally mean that he can be relied upon to achieve what we take to be his desired end smoothly, efficiently, without hesitation or deliberation, *as though it were* an automatic process. In fact, the more closely our overt behaviour assimilates that of a well-regulated machine, the further it gets from the fumblings and ponderings we associate with learning, the greater is our skill held to be. As A. J. Ayer puts it,[1] 'Remembering how to swim or how to write, remembering how to set a compass or add up a column of figures, is in every case a matter of being able to do these things, more or less efficiently, when the need arises. It can indeed happen in cases of this sort, that people are assisted by actually recalling some previous occasion on which they did the thing in question, or saw it done, but it is by no means necessary that they should be. On the contrary, the better they remember, the less likely is it that they will have any such events in mind: it is only when one is in difficulties that one tries as it were to use one's recollections as a manual. To have learnt a thing properly is to be able to dispense with them'.

Certainly it would be very strange to say that the man who

[1] A. J. Ayer, *The Problem of Knowledge*, London, Macmillan, 1956, p. 150.

dives into the pool and swims faultlessly to the other side *does not remember how to* swim—simply because his mind throughout the performance is wholly occupied with what he intends to have for dinner. But is it equally strange to say that he *is not remembering how to swim?*

We might, of course, say that he is certainly aware—whatever else may be occupying his thoughts—*that he is* swimming; and that to be aware of what we are doing is, in a sense, to be remembering previous occasions since it is to classify this (the present performance) with that (some past performance or group of performances).

But, though we can be fairly certain that our swimmer knows that he is swimming, we cannot be so certain that he knows that he is swimming sidestroke. We frequently 'catch ourselves' performing tasks quite efficiently, and a swimmer may be surprised to discover that he is swimming sidestroke after he has been doing so for quite some time. But, assuming that he once learnt the stroke, his performance seems to qualify just as well as an example of remembering how[1] as it would have done if he had been giving it his undivided attention. We may wish to deny that a fish remembers how to swim, but a human swimmer is not a fish; he had to learn the skill he is now exhibiting. It could be claimed, therefore, that whether or not he is concentrating upon what he is doing is quite irrelevant. His exercise of that skill *is* his remembering how to swim sidestroke.

Against this we may argue that such efficient actions are simply things we do, things which, because their successful completion is dependent upon our having had some past experience, are analogous to remembering. But they are not, we may claim, a species of remembering, any more than boxing is a species of ballet because it happens to involve considerable grace of movement. I do not want simply to dismiss this argument. On the contrary, I think it merits much greater attention than in recent years it has received. But, at this stage we must not blind ourselves to the fact that swimming, when we have learnt to swim, is much more like remembering an event, when we have witnessed that event, than boxing is like ballet. In one case there is a superficial

[1] Throughout this Chapter 'remembering how' will mean 'remembering how to do something' not 'remembering how a thing looked, felt, etc.'.

resemblance in the performance itself; in the other case there is a formal resemblance in the relationship of past and present events *and* the application of the retention of past events to our present requirements. There is at least the assumption of a causal connection.

In *The Mind and Its Place in Nature* C. D. Broad writes 'We may acquire by practice the power of performing at will certain characteristic sets of bodily movements, such as those that are used in swimming. If we find that we can still swim when we get into the water after an interval, we should commonly say that we "remember how to swim" or "remember the movements of swimming". There is nothing cognitive about "memory" in this sense. To say we remember how to swim is merely to state (*a*) that we can perform the proper movements after an interval, and (*b*) that we believe, or the speaker who observes us believes, that this is due to our having performed them in the past. It would be better to call memory in this sense, "retention of an acquired motor-capacity".'[1]

But even allowing that our arms and legs can, as it were, look after themselves, they do so as the result of prior training *and in a way that is conducive to the end we seek*. There is a sense in which we are both deliberately setting in motion and deliberately *keeping* in motion the performance in question when clearly it is open to us, as intelligent beings, to behave otherwise. If a fish is dropped into water it simply commences swimming; we do not think of it as *deciding* to swim, how to swim, or where to swim to. If a man is suddenly dropped into water (assuming that he can swim) he may to some extent react in the same way as the fish—simply commence swimming. Yet in adapting his mode of swimming to the condition of the water and directing his course to the nearest safe landing place his reactions (if 'reactions' is the right word here) are quite different from those of the fish. His first struggle to the surface may be wholly attributable to conditioned reflexes, but thereafter his performance is always *to some* extent deliberate and purposeful and preconceived. To what extent will vary from man to man.

The question is—'How are we to characterize this deliberateness and purposefulness in our skilled performance?' In most cases they do not seem to be constantly accompanied by any mental

[1] *The Mind and Its Place in Nature*, p. 269.

events of the kind we normally call remembering. When I swim across a pool I do not generally recollect any previous occasion of swimming nor yet any propositions or maxims about how to swim, nor am I generally aware of any images of what my arms and legs should be doing. And on such occasions as I do have recollections—perhaps I am reminded of some previous occasion of swimming—those recollections are more distraction from than directive to my present performance. Normally, so far as I am conscious of anything to do with my present performance it is of what I am doing *now* and I would usually claim that I 'know what I am doing' when what I am doing *happens to be* what I have done many times before.

Yet, as I pointed out in Chapter II,[1] although we do not seem to be remembering anything on these occasions, our performances are of the kind we feel *would have to be remembered*, which suggests that in some way we have a constant memory-disposition always, so to speak, directing our activities so that no specific recollection, either of event or of proposition, is needed for the successful completion of the task. It is something of this sort, I believe, that philosophers have had in mind when they have spoken of memories as 'present in power' though not in fact. They have been driven to making such mystical-sounding assertions because although we are able to discover *retrospectively* that we *were* in fact performing in accord with certain learnt skills and performing to some specific end, after the initial learning period we rarely seem to be conscious *in performing* of any recollections of events or rules with which we compare, or any directives by which we guide, our performance. Although the performance seems to exemplify 'remembering how'—clearly *it is* intentional, skilled, and in some way dependent upon past mental as well as physical performances—those past performances, mental or physical, do not seem to be specifically recalled or in any way 'presented to us' as directives of our present efforts.

We have considered the empirical grounds for holding that to be remembering how to do something is simply to be performing appropriately. Now I want to consider arguments designed to show that it *must be so*, that remembering how *could not* be reduced to a variety or aspect of remembering that.

[1] See p. 47.

If, in every instance, the performance of a skilled act were dependent upon the prior remembering of how to perform it, our lives would be a series of alternate thinkings and doings; before making each move we should have to pause to remember how to make it. In actual fact the occasions when we do proceed in this manner, as, for instance, when we work out very carefully the moves to be made in a game of chess, contrast very sharply with the ordinary conduct of our affairs where we are constantly putting into practice learnt skills of various sorts with never a pause. If we all paused to remember how to perform each operation whilst we were driving a car in heavy traffic (as indeed a novice driver often does have to) the result might well be catastrophic.

Suppose we suggest that remembering how does always take place (as a mental preliminary to action), but is very swift, hardly noticeable at all, always just a fraction ahead of the action itself. This could hardly be disproved on empirical grounds. During the learning stages of any skill we are in fact conscious of such 'mental preliminaries' and it is always open to us to say that *if we introspected more carefully* we *would* catch ourselves mentally rehearsing even when we are fully competent. Furthermore, as we shall consider later in this chapter,[1] it is by no means easy to say when a skill is perfect, nor yet what constitutes *a particular* skill. But to show that something cannot be disproved is one thing; to prove it is quite another. And there are specific objections to this 'solution' which must be considered.

It may be argued that according to this view, since the overt performance is continuous, our minds would need to be attending always to what we were just about to do, to be concentrating upon how to make the next move—never upon the move we were then making. Thus by virtue of remembering how to perform we would be precluded from giving any attention to how we were in fact performing. However 'swift' the decision, there would always be a further decision to be made as soon as it was completed.

There have also been attempts to demonstrate logically that no prior mental directive can be entailed by the skilled performance of any action. The argument usually runs thus: Remembering

[1] See p. 115.

and planning are activities which, like any other activities, can be done well or badly. If no skilled performance can be given until a prior remembering has occurred, then that remembering cannot occur until a prior remembering has occurred, and so on *ad infinitum*. Thus we could never even commence the overt performance itself.

I do not, however, attach great importance to this argument as it begs the point at issue. Unless we are already agreed that remembering is a skilled performance of the same kind as swimming or driving motor-cars the argument does not hold. And if we *were* agreed upon this the demonstration would be redundant. Further, as I shall argue later in this chapter, doing a thing well or badly is a quite different thing from doing it intelligently in the sense of that word which is relevant to remembering.

In *The Concept of Mind* Ryle produces two closely connected arguments designed to show that 'remembering how' and 'remembering that' are different in a way which would make it impossible to reduce the former to a mere sub-species of the latter.

He says[1]

'We never speak of a person having a partial knowledge of a fact or truth, save in the special sense of his having knowledge of a part of a body of facts or truth....On the other hand, it is proper and normal to speak of a person knowing in part how to do something, i.e. of his having a particular capacity in a limited degree.'

And Ryle claims that this means only that the person knows how to do the thing fairly well, i.e. that he performs fairly well—not that he is conversant with only some of the maxims governing its successful performance. Remembering that is necessarily a closed affair—either we remember or we do not. Remembering how is always an open affair—we can perform the task in question with a greater or lesser degree of skill.

Furthermore, he maintains—remembering that A was B is always traceable, in principle, to discovering that A was B at some exact time, whereas remembering how to perform some task can never

[1] *The Concept of Mind*, p. 59.

be traced to an exact moment when we *knew how for the first time.*

'Learning *how* or improving an ability is not like learning *that* or acquiring information. Truths can be imparted, procedures can only be inculcated, and while inculcation is a gradual process, imparting is relatively sudden. It makes sense to ask at what moment someone became apprised of a truth, but not to ask at what moment someone acquired a skill'.[1]

It is noticeable that Ryle does not explain how we can *improve* an ability unless we have already acquired it, i.e. learnt how.

The importance of Ryle's claims is that, if they are true, then it simply does not make sense to talk of remembering how to do something except as being able to do it more or less effectively. And the test of 'being able' is the performance on demand of the task in question. On the other hand, if it can be shown that it does make sense to talk of remembering how as distinct from the giving of public performances, then it follows that these claims, however convincing they may seem, simply cannot be true. We shall now consider some arguments which might lead us to deny that remembering how *just is* performing appropriately.

If I am asked 'Do you remember how to drive a motor cycle?' I may well reply 'Yes' notwithstanding that there is no motor cycle for me to drive. On what authority do I make this reply? It could be that I recall some occasion on which I drove a motor cycle and I assume that I could do so again. Or it could be that what I recall is not any specific occasion, but simply the proposition, formed at some time in the past (when does not matter) 'I can drive a motor cycle'. In these cases the claim 'I am *now remembering how* to drive a motor cycle' would not be justified. What I am remembering is, in the one case a certain event, and in the other case, a certain proposition *from which I am inferring* that, given opportunity, *I could* drive a motor cycle.

But suppose I am remembering, not a single event, nor the single proposition 'I can drive a motor cycle', but a set of propositions which constitute the rules for driving a motor cycle. And suppose also that I have clear kinaesthetic images of balancing and directing a motor cycle. Could we then deny that I am

[1] *The Concept of Mind*, p. 59.

remembering how to drive one? The point is that we frequently do feel justified in claiming to remember how to do something as distinct from claiming that we are able to do it—or even that we ever have done it. No doubt there are many old-world Japanese gentlemen who remember how to commit Hari-Kiri.

Consider the question 'Do you remember how to play tennis?' addressed to a man now confined to a wheelchair. Must he reply 'No' simply because he is incapable of getting up and demonstrating? If a man is asked 'Do you remember how to swim the crawl?' when he is sitting at home he may rehearse in his mind the movements involved and consider images of performances he has seen and answer 'Yes, I do', whereas, if the same question is addressed to him when he is in the swimming pool he may simply execute a few strokes by way of reply. The two ways of answering the question are quite different; but it is the same question which is being answered. The effective difference between the answers is that the one given in the water tells us more than we asked. By his demonstration our man is showing us not only that he *remembers how* to swim the crawl but also that he *can* swim it, whereas the verbal reply would still be justified if he remembered how only in the sense that the man in the wheelchair remembers how to play tennis, e.g. he could instruct other people. It is worth noting that many dramatic producers are very unsatisfactory actors—but we should hardly say that this is because they do not *know how to* act.

Now, why do we say that the man showed us *both* that he can swim *and* that he remembers how? If a small boy picks up a stone and hurls it into a pond this is evidence enough that he *can perform* this 'task'. But it is surely not evidence that he is remembering how to do anything. The boy could be doing something quite clever, throwing a stone in a particular way that he has been practising. But, equally, he could be acting quite carelessly and thoughtlessly and have never thrown a stone before. Our swimmer's performance counts as an affirmative answer to our question only because (*a*) it follows the asking of the question and (*b*) we presume it is the application of a skill he has learnt. We accept it as an example of remembering how only on the assumption that he is aware that his demonstration provides the answer to our question, i.e. that his present performance has certain essential resemblances to an indefinite number of past performances which have been classified as swimming the crawl. We are in fact assuming, as the condition of our granting that he is remembering how, some association by him of his present performance with other performances he has given or witnessed. Part of what we are attributing to him is the ability, should he make a wrong stroke, to realize that it is a wrong stroke and correct it. But how can he realize that this is a wrong stroke unless he has some present idea of what constitutes the right stroke? To argue here that it simply 'feels wrong' is simply to make this into a 'negative memory situation'. And, as I have argued,[1] such situations have always a basis of positive remembering. In his claim to be remembering how the man in the water is adopting at least some of the same criteria as the man on the land.

It may be instructive to compare the extents to which conscious activity is involved in (*a*) breathing (*b*) walking (*c*) riding a bicycle and (*d*) playing Bridge.

(*a*) Breathing (though not deep-breathing) is something we just do—we do not need to be conscious at all.

(*b*) To walk we usually need to be conscious—but not conscious *of our walking*. Although it is something we have had to learn, and is to that extent a skill, it has become almost as automatic as breathing. The difference is principally that we can and do decide to start and to stop walking. But only if we have not walked for a very long time do we *need* to pay attention to the performance itself.

(*c*) In contrast to this, riding a bicycle does require a lot of attention. We can think of other things while we are riding, but unless we are aware to some extent of what we are doing *and how* we are doing it we shall soon meet with disaster.

(*d*) in playing Bridge we are constantly 'telling ourselves' what to do next. Our minds do the real work, our hands and lips are just the labourers on the job. Here there is generally very little about our performances that we would call automatic—only such things as the actual holding and handling of the cards.

Let us allow, for the sake of argument, that walking (notwithstanding that we once learnt how) is for most of us a wholly automatic affair, and that playing Bridge is a wholly intelligent affair. Riding a bicycle, which is a fairly standard example of

[1] See p. 97.

remembering how, might then be called a quasi-automatic affair since it patently includes a great deal of conscious (deliberate) and a great deal of unconscious (motor-responsive) behaviour. In the preceding section I described the 'conscious part' of 'remembering how' as the association of what we are now doing with—and its guidance by—what we have done or witnessed in the past. The question we must now consider is how we are to regard the unconscious part of the performance, and what, if anything, this has to do with remembering.

One maxim that may fairly go unchallenged is that whatever we can remember we can forget. What does forgetting how to do something amount to? Suppose we say it amounts to not being able to do it any more. But (regarding walking as a wholly automatic performance) if I quite suddenly *could not* walk we would not normally say that I had *forgotten how* to walk. Even if no physical defect could be discovered to account for my inability we should be more inclined to assume some undiscovered physical defect than to attribute it to a breakdown of memory. I have forgotten if I do not know something I previously knew—and what in this case did I know previously that I do not know now? There seems to be a certain oddness in saying I knew how to walk; I simply walked. And this would surely be true of the automatic part of any performance. One of the things we mean by calling a performance automatic is that it does not make sense to say we have forgotten how to do it, though we might for other reasons cease ever to do it.[1] And, if remembering how to ride a bicycle were simply being able to ride a bicycle, what could forgetting how to ride a bicycle be but not being able to ride one? But this would be no proof of having forgotten. It would be quite reasonable, if I could, nonetheless, state things about how a bicycle should be ridden, to say 'I remember well enough how to ride a bicycle, but nowadays my legs are not strong enough to do it'.

There is naturally a close association in our minds between remembering how and being able, so close that we often treat the concepts as interchangeable. But the vitally important point is

---

[1] I am not, of course, claiming that walking *is necessarily automatic*. Although we would always tend to attribute the failure to walk to some muscular defect it is still intelligible to say that the defect is not muscular at all, simply 'mental'.

that, whilst the exemplifications of the two concepts so frequently overlap in practice, there is no *necessity* for them to do so. A child told to draw a picture entitled 'Earthquake' would almost certainly draw a scene of devastation—but this does not mean that the concepts 'earthquake' and 'devastation' are identical. It is our ability to differentiate 'remembering how' from 'being able' if and when the occasion arises that has led to the use of the expression 'remembering how' even if it is not always used in a way that makes the distinction obvious.

Since 'remembering how' is so evidently connected with the exercise of acquired skills, it is strange that so little attention has been paid by writers on memory to two crucial questions: What constitutes *a* particular skill? and—By what criteria is a performance judged to be skilful?

Suppose I mount my bicycle after many years of driving cars and promptly fall off. Does this show that I have forgotten how to ride a bicycle—or only that I have forgotten how to *balance* a bicycle? I may still remember how to do a great many other things which come under the general heading of riding a bicycle. Let us look again at Ryle's claim that knowing in part how to do something is not a matter of being conversant with only some of the maxims governing its successful performance.[1] It certainly does seem possible to maintain that, just as balancing is part though not the whole of riding, so other activities, sub-skills let us call them, are parts of balancing; that every 'imperfect performance' may contain within it many 'perfect' ones. Now, I am not going to suggest that every such 'sub-skill' could necessarily be contained in a verbal maxim so that if each maxim is followed the balancing (the 'major skill') must be successful. On the contrary the point I am making is that there is no such thing as a 'basic unit' of skill; there are simply greater or lesser sets of effective activities, and it is perfectly legitimate to regard any of these as *a* skill which *could be* the object of a maxim. As I argued in Chapter II, we remember a great many 'propositions' without words at all, and some of these could well be concerned with muscular feelings in our bodies. I grant that by the time we are competent cyclists balancing a bicycle has become a wholly automatic affair. But there seems nothing absurd about the

[1] See p. 110.

suggestion that, at the learning stage when we are in fact *remembering how to* balance, balancing should not be regarded as one single skill but as a complex mass of skills, each with its own corresponding memory-directive.

Under this analysis, 'improving a skill', as Ryle calls it, becomes a matter of developing from lesser skills to greater skills. And the fact that 'a skill' is developed over a long period of time no more proves that its exercise is not dependent upon 'remembering that' (or a complex of 'remembering thats') than the fact that a complicated piece of information is gleaned over a long period of time proves that the remembering of it is not the case of 'remembering that'. I feel that having come to a decision as to what constitutes *a skill* or *a fact or truth* we can ask with equal intelligibility at what time, or during what period, the skill was acquired or the truth was learnt.

I have argued that we should talk of remembering only such things as it makes sense to talk of forgetting. The skill that we remember is, therefore, something that it is possible to forget. It is in some sense an intelligent performance. This, so far as I know, nobody has openly denied. But there is a tendency in recent philosophy to slide from statements attempting to reconcile this fact with the apparent absence of 'mental directive' in the exercise of skills, to statements which, though similar-sounding, pay lip-service to the 'intelligence' of skilled performances while in fact rendering impossible the application of any effective criterion of intelligence. Compare, for example, these two short passages from *The Concept of Mind*. Ryle allows that there is a difference we are all aware of between an action done accidentally or automatically and one done deliberately and carefully, and he writes:

(a)[1] 'But such differences of description do not consist in the absence or presence of an implicit reference to some shadow-action covertly prefacing the overt action. They consist, on the contrary, in the absence or presence of certain sorts of testable explanatory-cum-predictive assertions.'

(b)[2] 'But to admit, as we must, that there may be no visible or audible difference between a tactful or witty act and a tactless

[1] *The Concept of Mind*, p. 25.   [2] *The Concept of Mind*, p. 32.

or humourless one is not to admit that the difference is constituted by the performance or non-performance of some extra secret acts.'

It is not wholly clear what Ryle means by 'the absence or presence' and it has been suggested to me that the 'explanatory-cum-predictive assertions' are to be made, not by the agent, but by an observer of the act. But if this interpretation is correct then surely Ryle's claim loses all its plausibility. We do not need the testimony of an observer to assure us that our actions are careful and deliberate. I feel that we must allow that the 'absence or presence' is in the agent himself, even though there may be a sense in which he is merely an observer of his own action. So understood assertion (*a*) says in effect that although something is going on in the mind in accompaniment to what is going on in the body, it is not in the form of a rehearsal prefacing the actual performance, but rather of attention to that performance, its nature and purpose. With this we may very well agree—and still go on to consider what constitutes the difference between attending to our performance simply as to any object of observation and attending to it as our means of achieving certain desired ends.

But assertion (*b*) goes much further. It not only denies the existence of any *prior* mental directive of the action, it denies in effect that there is a distinguishable mental element involved at all. I feel that Ryle has deliberately selected words which evoke a certain emotional reaction: 'extra' suggests 'extraneous' and 'secret' suggests 'kept secret', and we may well wish to deny the existence of any such goings on. If we substitute the more neutral expression 'additional private factor' we shall be able to approach the question much more dispassionately. Now, it may be protested that I have no right to substitute the neutral word 'factor' for 'act'. A mere 'mental existent' is no more a 'mental act', it may be claimed, than a physical existent is a physical act. But, whereas, in considering the physical there is a clear distinction—we can all say which physical factors are acts and which are entities—there is no such obvious distinction when we consider the mental. Any terminology which suggests that 'mental acts' are distinguishable from 'mental entities' in the way that physical acts and entities are distinguishable is bound to be misleading.

Now, if there is no 'additional private factor' in the skilled performance, wherein can the difference between it and the automatic or accidental performance lie? It has been conceded that we are all aware of the distinction and that there is no visible or audible difference, so any factor *present in one performance and not in the other must be private in the sense of being knowable only to the agent*. It may be argued that the distinction is simply a matter of whether or not the performance can be repeated. But what does 'can be repeated' mean unless it *is* repeated? And surely we do not have to perform everything twice in order to know that the first occasion was an exercise of skill. Apart from which an overt act done once accidentally may well be repeated intentionally.

The problem is precisely to know what doing something intentionally is. Ryle speaks of acts done 'on purpose' but he seems to suggest that the agent may not know what he does on purpose and what he does 'not on purpose'. This I find very queer. I would say that I am doing something on purpose when I am aware as I do it of my aims and intentions, and because of this it is reasonable for me *to take it* that you are doing something on purpose when you express your intentions before or during the activity or when your activity has every appearance of being intelligently directed to what I believe to be a reasonable goal for you.

It is true that people are sometimes accused of doing things 'on purpose'—and perhaps rightly so—when they have not been 'aware of their intentions'. But the making of such *accusations* presupposes that people do normally know their own intentions. These cases (which are in the province of experimental psychology rather than of epistemology) show only that a predetermined action may be taken by the agent to be an accidental or automatic action. They do not set up a separate group of deliberate acts which are not predetermined. When children slide along the floor and fall down on their bottoms we have to *ask them* whether they did it on purpose or not. We mean—was it an accident or did they decide to do it? The choice remains the same whether they are able to tell us or not. Because 'on purpose' is contrasted with 'accidental' there is an obvious sense in which a lizard catches flies on purpose, simply in that it does not do so accidentally. But plainly this sense of 'on purpose' is too limited to make the distinction Ryle does in fact allow to exist. Assuming that the lizard does not *decide* to catch the fly, his catching it is a purely automatic response.

It is worth noting that where we are concerned with cases we *do* want to call remembering how the claim that these can never be reduced to or explained in terms of 'remembering that' seems to run counter to the assumptions that most of us make, apparently quite successfully, whenever we give instructions. When my little boy calls to me that he cannot remember how to do up his football boots, I call back to him *that* the laces must go through the eyelets in such and such order, *that* they then go through the loops at the sides and back, and so on. It is true that there are elements of most performances which we may find difficult, if not impossible, to describe in propositions of this kind. But to me and, I think, to most 'common men' this seems to reflect the limitations of our existing language rather than any mysterious indescribability of those elements themselves. There is also (as we shall presently consider) in every performance some motor-responsive behaviour which, though it forms an essential part of the 'remembered performance', is not itself remembered in the ordinary sense of that word.

If we are employing someone to do a job for us then clearly our only concern is that the job be done. We are pleased to concede (that is, we have no wish to deny) that he 'remembers how' so long as the job is done properly. In such a case we can fully endorse Ryle's assertion[1]: 'Our enquiry is not into causes (and a fortiori not into occult causes), but into capacities, skills, habits, liabilities and bents.' It is when, not as employers but as epistemological enquirers, we turn our attention to what his remembering how amounts to that we seem obliged to attribute to him all sorts of 'memories that'. It is one thing to observe success and quite another to attribute skill. We observe the success of the lizard which never misses the fly it aims for, but our attributing skill to a marksman who repeatedly scores bull's-eyes (though not to a child who lets off a rifle and just happens to hit the bull's-eye) seems to rest upon our ability to explain his repeated success in terms of his *knowing that* the sights must be in such and such a position, *that* his breathing must be controlled in such and such a way, and so on. It is more natural to say

[1] *The Concept of Mind*, p. 45.

'I remember how to hit the bull's-eye' than to say 'I remember that bullets hit bull's-eyes when the sights of the rifle are so and so, and my finger squeezes so and so, and allowance is made for the wind'—and etc., mainly because it is so much more economical of words, and because, as I pointed out above, we do not always have the words to express everything we would need to say. Nevertheless 'He remembers how to' must 'stand for' all these unexpressed, and perhaps unexpressable, assertions. The lizard can catch flies all day but we do not want to say it remembers how to. The marksman need display his prowess once only and we grant immediately that he remembers how to hit bull's-eyes.

It may be helpful to consider under what circumstances I would ask anyone whether he remembers how to do something. Not, surely, while he is actually doing it. But, if 'remembering how' is in fact quite distinct from being able, why should it be unreasonable to ask the man performing the task whether he remembers how?

My answer is that it is not unreasonable; it is simply an odd and confusing way of putting the question. We could, for instance, ask such a man whether he was exercising a learnt skill or attempting the task for the first time. But we would have to make it quite clear what 'task' we were referring to; even if he is experimenting in the 'major task' he is almost certainly exercising his learnt ability to perform certain 'sub-tasks'.

In fact we do not generally ask the question in these circumstances, not because it would be absurd but simply because it would be uninteresting to us. What does interest us is whether he can carry on—whether he can master the next stage in the performance with the same apparent ease. 'Do you remember how—?' is always in some sense appropriate—but it is in fact asked only when the performance in question is not being given—though it may be pending. And if the reply is, as it may well be, 'I'm not sure—but I dare say I would remember if I had to' this need not mean that the man we have asked is *identifying* remembering how with being able. The assumption behind the reply *could* be that under the stimulus of actually attempting the task the 'memories that' which now elude him would come back to him.

It is sometimes held that we cannot know how to do certain things *because* we remember certain events and propositions, since remembering is never a *source of knowledge*. Now, there is a sense in which this may well be true—but is completely trivial. Assuming that I cannot remember anything until I have already known it, I must come to know it in the first place by some means other than memory.

But, quite apart from the possibility (discussed at length in Chapters III and IV) of making factual discoveries from the re-interpretation of our memories, there is a very real sense in which memory is one of two main sources of our present knowledge. I may be said to know, in the dispositional sense, a great many things which I am not at present thinking about. But this is only on the assumption that I shall think about them, and think truly about them if and when the occasion arises. We do not generally speak of occurrent knowing but there is occurrent true believing about states of affairs, and this occurrent believing occurs either because I am presently perceiving them or because I am presently remembering them.

It is interesting that Ryle, in discussing the question of the allocation of praise and blame, decides that a boy is blameworthy if 'knowing how to tie the knot, he still did not tie it correctly'.[1] There is no suggestion that the boy deliberately tied the knot wrongly. We must assume therefore that by 'knowing how to tie the knot' Ryle means knowing in the dispositional sense. Most of us would say here 'He could have remembered how to do it but he didn't bother'. And what he did not bother about could only be knowing (or remembering) *in the occurrent sense*. And to those who protest that knowing how in the occurrent sense *just is* tying it correctly, I once more point out that the lizard *just does* catch flies correctly. And the boy *could* tie the knot correctly entirely by accident.

INTELLIGENCE AND INTELLIGENT BEHAVIOUR

We may say that in doing something we remember how to do we are giving an intelligent performance, but we must be quite clear what we mean by this. For we feel a certain natural reluctance to say that the child who deliberately falls on his bottom is giving an intelligent performance however 'memory-directed' it may be.

[1] *The Concept of Mind*, p. 71.

I believe that a great deal of the difficulty about what constitutes remembering how, arises from the confusion of quite different senses of the word 'intelligent'. We want to say that remembering how to do something is always an exercise of intelligence (whether the remembering is 'public' or 'private'), but the word 'intelligent' is sometimes used as a term of approval, and at other times simply to mean thoughtful as distinct from automatic or motor-responsive. Clearly these two uses are by no means the same—even though both frequently apply to the same instances of behaviour. It is most important that we see clearly in which sense we are using the word when we say that remembering how to do something is always an intelligent performance.

Some recent philosophers have made great use of the concept of paying heed. We are paying heed when we are fully aware *what* we are doing, *how* we are doing it, and *why* we are doing it. But none of these guarantee that our activity will be effective. The boy who is busily misapplying a mathematical formula is paying heed to what he is doing, but he will not get the answer right.[1] On the other hand the man who is thinking about anything and everything but what he is doing while he climbs a ladder will still get to the top if he carries on as he is going. Now, clearly we regard the performance of the boy as ineffective and that of the man as effective if we believe that their respective aims are answering the problem and surmounting the ladder. But, if we equate intelligence with attention, or 'paying heed', then the boy is giving an intelligent performance whilst the man is not, for the boy is heeding what he is doing. We shall be forced into the position of claiming, paradoxical though it may seem, that a dull man is *exercising* more intelligence when he is puzzling over the completion of an operation than a bright man who achieves the required end with a minimum of mental effort.

Here you may well object that the second man is obviously the more intelligent man simply because he does not need to puzzle over the task. But already you have shifted to the other (and, I grant, more common, though perhaps derivative) use of 'intelligent'. What we are now speaking of is a capacity for *effective*

---

[1] Note H. H. Price's observation that the mark of intelligence is the ability to make mistakes—*Thinking and Experience*, p. 87.

behaviour. Indeed the building up of such a capacity is an excellent thing, but with it comes a lessening, not an increase, of intelligence in the performance of the task in hand in the only sense of that term in which intelligence could be used as the mark of 'remembering how'.[1]

For, as allowed at the outset of this chapter, the better we get at doing anything the less we need to think about it. Exercising any acquired skill is largely a matter of repetition. In the early stages it may be conscious repetition; in the later stages it will tend to become unconscious repetition. But, to an observer, this difference shows up simply as an improvement in effectiveness. We must never forget, however, that a well-regulated machine may be a greater improvement still—unless and until it breaks down.

Ryle cites the case of a chess-player developing this kind of competence.[2] 'Very soon he comes to observe the rules without thinking of them. He makes the permitted moves and avoids the forbidden ones; he notices and protests when his opponent breaks the rules. But he no longer cites to himself or to the room the formulae in which the bans and prohibitions are declared. It has become second nature to him to do what is allowed and avoid what is forbidden. At this stage he might even have lost his former ability to cite the rules'. But 'second nature' is a very vague sort of term, suggestive somehow of being aware in a non-occurrent kind of way of the thing to do, a situation much easier to suggest than to analyse. Playing chess is not the most fortunate example since it involves both the formal rules which constitute the game itself and also what we might call the 'informal rules' which constitute good playing, and it is not altogether clear to which Ryle is referring. But either way, if the player *really had* lost the ability to cite the rules by which he was in fact playing, (we are concerned here with the propositions—not just the forms of words) would it not be fairer to say that he had reached a stage of physiological conditioning which enabled him to carry on by motor-responses alone; that he had in fact become a kind of human chess machine? This need not, of course, be to his discredit. A human chess machine, like a real chess machine, may play a very effective game of chess. The point I am making is

---

[1] This seems less paradoxical when we consider that by 'perfecting a skill' we free our 'intelligence' for other tasks.
[2] *The Concept of Mind*, p. 41.

that if ever this stage were reached it would not be a case of remembering how so well that he need no longer bother about 'mental states'. On the contrary, it would be a case of reaching a stage of physiological conditioning where he need no longer bother to remember how.

I want now to look again at the use of 'intelligent' in which it is applied to persons and contrasted with 'stupid'. Although this is not the sense of the word in which remembering how is an intelligent performance (we can remember how to do stupid things as well as clever ones) some further consideration of it may nevertheless throw light upon the relationship between remembering how and remembering that. Intelligence in the laudatory sense is not measured by our ability to remember things but rather by our ability to make good use of the things we remember. Indeed we often contrast intelligence with the mere possession of a good memory. But, as H. H. Price has pointed out, we must be careful not to push the 'contrast' too far.[1] 'Without memory' he says 'there would be no primary recognition; without primary recognition, no abstraction, and therefore no basic concepts; and without basic concepts there would be no derivative concepts, which are acquired by intellectual operations directed upon these basic ones'. Inventiveness is the mark of the intelligent man. As Ryle says[2] 'He has to meet new objections, interpret new evidence and make connections between elements in the situation which had not previously been co-ordinated. In short he has to innovate. . . . ' But it is his memories which provide the basis for his inventiveness—and indeed it may well be that much of the 'inventiveness' is itself simply the reapplication of certain kinds of memories, the recognition of similarities which are not obvious to less lively minds.

In so far as we are conscious of how to achieve some end, whether this be a slow, deliberate performance or a spontaneous realization which seems to occur along with the action itself, we must in some way classify the situation before us and predict the outcome of our actions accordingly. This, I am presuming, is what Ryle means by 'the presence of certain sorts of explanatory-cum-

[1] *Thinking and Experience*, p. 59.
[2] *The Concept of Mind*, p. 47.

predictive assertions'.[1] And these classifications and predictions certainly involve operations of memory; the recognition of kinds and the memory of cause-effect sequences. Thus *discovering how* is in part a matter of remembering how—which in this case is very clearly a matter of remembering *that* certain kinds of things behave in certain ways in certain kinds of situations. Our 'inventiveness' rests upon our ability to observe relational similarities in past and present situations and so make predictions about the achievement of our present needs, and the more extensive our memories the greater opportunity we have to make such observations. If we remembered, and appreciated the full predictive implications of, every cause/effect sequence we had ever witnessed we should indeed be well equipped to tackle any problems which confronted us.

I agree with Ryle's assertion[2] 'Often we deplore a person's ignorance of some fact only because we deplore the stupidity of which his ignorance is a consequence'. But, as we have seen, what we praise and what we deplore is a totally different question from what we do and do not consider to be instances of remembering how. And the reason for our disgust in such cases is that we are assuming that the person remembers certain facts which constitute premises and yet is incapable of moving from these to an obvious conclusion. Classification and prediction cannot operate without memory; thus we can hold the man to be stupid only *on the assumption* that his memory is sound. If he were proved to be suffering from amnesia (and therefore ignorant of the 'premises' in question) we should not then think him stupid. Even in normal conditions 'I forgot' is often the best defence against a charge of stupidity.

It would undoubtedly be wrong, a misunderstanding of the language, to equate lack of intelligence with lack of knowledge. A man is not unintelligent because he does not know something he has had no opportunity to learn—nor yet because he has forgotten something he once knew. On the other hand it would be equally wrong to overlook the very real connection, *for the purpose of the question we are considering*, between *intelligent behaviour* and knowledge of facts, for the current awareness of, and guidance by, *certain* facts—those proposed in our 'explan-

[1] *The Concept of Mind*, p. 25. See also p. 117, (of this work). [2] *Ibid*, p. 28.

atory-cum-predictive assertions'—is the only factor we have been able to find to differentiate intelligent performances *both from automatic and from accidental* ones.

In Chapter III we discovered that 'remembering by doing' involved at least the recognition of our present situation as similar in some vital respect to some past situation. It is not enough that a situation 'looks familiar'; it must look familiar in a particular, informative way. We cannot expel 'remembering *that*' from the situation simply by concentrating our attention upon the present perception. Thus when my remembering how to go home is manifest simply in my going home, in so far as it *is* remembering how and not just 'sleep-walking', it is in part dependent upon my knowing, i.e. remembering, a great many facts of the kind 'this is the street which has led me to such a place—the turning I took on those occasions is just past the gasworks', whether I recite these propositions to myself or not. Intelligence, as it is involved in remembering how, is not a matter of *knowing a great many* facts, but its exercise is wholly dependent upon knowing the relevant facts.

Thus, whilst we do not hold a man to be ignorant because of the things he cannot do, we may be justified in suspecting that he cannot do them because he is ignorant. If a man cannot write down the English for a passage of Greek prose this is more likely to be because of his ignorance of Greek or English than because of an inability to manipulate a pen. And although it might well happen that a man could recite every instruction a good teacher had given him but still not be able to ride a bicycle, his failure *could* be the result of his ignorance of certain facts which his teacher had been unable to tell him. There are elements in most performances which defy description within the framework of our existing language.

'Remember' is a transitive verb; when we remember we always remember something. And when the *something* we remember is 'how to cycle' the quotation marks must always be implied even if they are not shown. Unless we use 'remember how' simply as a synonym for 'be able'—and this, if my arguments are sound, would render impossible the distinction between intelligent and non-intelligent performances—then it is hard to see what remembering how to do something could amount to unless it involved the occurrent remembering of at least some of the rules, maxims and propositions which may be held to constitute 'how to do it' or some past occasions of doing it. How else could we characterize the distinction we are all aware of between 'remembering how' and 'being able'?

CONCLUSIONS

After that long, but necessary, account of the distinction between 'intelligent behaviour' and commendable behaviour (the behaviour of 'intelligent people') I can return to the main problem of this chapter which is:

We are satisfied that many of our performances are intelligently directed towards some specific end in the light of our experience of similar performances in the past. We therefore view them as instances of remembering how. Yet, in performing, we do not generally seem to be relying for guidance upon any memories of past events. We can appreciate the difference between purely automatic responses and intelligent performances, and also between accidental and intentional performances, yet most often we cannot find by introspection that series of directive memories which is the only differentiating factor we can conceive between them.

To solve this problem we must, I believe, recognize that *every* performance includes a great deal of automatic motor-response whether or not the performance counts as an instance of 'remembering how'. We must also be prepared to broaden considerably our view of what constitutes remembering events.

The point I made in Chapter II, that the distinction between disposition and occurrence, though applicable to memory, is not peculiar to memory, is here very important. We develop dispositions (how we do so is the concern of physiologists) to give certain effective bodily performances as well as to recall certain past events, both mental and physical, when stimulated in the appropriate ways. In the dispositional sense, therefore, it is possible that I both *can perform* the bodily activities which are essential to my driving a car and *do remember* those rules, maxims and propositions which may be classified as 'how to drive a car'.

While I am sitting at my desk, I may run through in my mind all these rules, maxims and propositions. To do this would be to actualize my disposition *to remember how* to drive a car. On the other hand I may, on a long, straight, lonely road, sit back at the wheel of a car allowing my mind to wander while my hands and feet respond automatically to the feel of the car beneath me and the sight of the road ahead, and then I would be actualizing my dispositional ability *to make the efficient physical manoeuvres* which constitute the overt performance.

But, when I am driving through the town, easing the clutch, touching the brake, marking to whom I must give way and who must give way to me, making signals, anticipating traffic jams and avoiding one-way streets (all of which operations come under the general heading of 'driving a car') then, unless I am an extremely practised driver, I am actualizing both dispositions together. Or perhaps it would be better to speak of actualizing a whole complex of variously acquired dispositions grading up, so to speak, from mere muscular abilities to the conscious entertaining of directive propositions. I do not want to suggest that each little facet of the performance could be unequivocally allocated to the *motor-responsive* or to *mentally-directed*. My argument is simply that my performance still includes much that is purely automatic and much that we might call *quasi-automatic*, but it also includes much that is planned and considered, the conscious application of those rules and maxims which constitute 'how to drive'. There is no harm, of course, in our speaking of a single disposition to drive carefully—provided that we bear in mind that driving carefully includes *both* remembering how *and* being able, just as working happily includes both working and being happy about it.

When we appreciate that the body can retain the capacity for effective activity just as the mind can retain acquired knowledge, and further, that with the continued repetition of any task what we might call the 'motor-response dispositions' become adequate to account for an ever increasing part of the efficient performance of that task, there is no longer any mystery about those performances which we feel to be both wholly effective and completely 'unconscious'. There is no reason why they should not be both. What makes these performances seem mysterious is only our insistence upon calling them 'remembering', without acknowledging that we are using the term in a very 'extended' way. And we do this simply because there was once a time when similar performances *were* remembering, in the quite ordinary sense and also because as overt performances (even when the observer is also the performer) they are indistinguishable from consciously planned performances.

By showing that within an effective performance there are both 'automatic' and 'intelligent' elements, we simplify, but do not solve, the problem. The fact remains that the 'mental factor' of which we are conscious, even in what I am treating as the 'intelligent part' of our behaviour, does not seem to be a series of memories of past events running through our minds, but rather, to use Ryle's phrase, 'certain explanatory-cum-predictive assertions'. Yet how are we able to make these explanatory-cum-predictive assertions, and know them to be explanatory and predictive, except by virtue of being apprised in some occurrent way of past situations and events?

It is true that we can become physiologically conditioned to utter (or sub-vocally speak) certain sounds in response to certain stimuli just as we can become physiologically conditioned to act in certain ways with our hands and feet. In fact we often 'catch ourselves' giving a muttered commentary on our activities and plans as we go about our business. But it is noticeable that on these occasions we are generally engaged in routine tasks which demand little of our attention, tasks which we frequently do perform quite automatically, like washing up dishes or sorting a pack of cards into order, and the commentary is simply an extension of the automatic performance; it could be said to be 'directing' our activities only if we were to attend separately to it as we might to any independent instructing agent—a gramophone for instance—and obey its dictates. But this re-introduces deliberate intelligent behaviour, the following of the instructions, and the problem breaks out afresh.

It does not seem possible to avoid the conclusion that, in so far as we are actually remembering how to perform some task—are predicting the outcome of our conduct and shaping it accordingly—we must be basing our predictions upon our occurrent remembering of similar tasks performed in the past or on maxims formed in the light of past experience. That is, we must be relying on our occurrent remembering of events in some sense of that expression. We must therefore consider what sense of remembering events this can be.

What constitutes one particular event must always be an arbitrary matter. It can be misleading to talk of remembering *an* event as though there were certain fixed limits to this achievement as there are to eating *an* apple. One event is whatever we choose to regard as one event, *and it may be remembered in more or less detail.* My remembering sitting down on this chair a moment ago is no more remembering *an* event in any essential way than my remembering a football match which lasted an hour or, for that matter, my coming to this room nearly every day last year. Each memory *could be* augmented by greater detail and each 'event' *could be* sub-divided. Further, the temporal location of events is not an essential part of the memory of them.[1] It is possible, therefore, to allow that in remembering how to swim sidestroke I am not actually recalling some *specific* previous occasion of swimming sidestroke in the past. I may well be recalling, though not necessarily in verbal propositions, my exercise of the skills and 'sub-skills' involved on an indeterminate number of past occasions, and being guided accordingly in my present performance.

Now, I contend that, unless and until our 'motor-response dispositions' develop to the point where we no longer *need* to remember how, the effective performance of tasks *is* dependent upon our occurrent remembering of this kind. And, further, that since there is an obvious thread of connection between all these past performances, the recollection of any of them, with or without specific location in time, can quite properly be described as the memory of an event (or of events—there is no real difference), even though the event in question may have spread over a considerable period and be of too indeterminate a character ever to be thought of as 'an event' in normal contexts.

At this point I feel obliged to say something in support of my claim that these events may be remembered 'though not necessarily in verbal propositions'. In Chapter III, I distinguished between remembered propositions and the forms of words which

[1] This point was made in Chapter III, p. 57.

are used to convey them and gave my reasons for believing that we must accept the existence of non-verbal thinking and remembering. The separation of memory-claim from memory in Chapter IV and the conclusion that the memory, as distinct from the memory-claim, is *of* our private experience in perceiving the event, not *of* the public event itself, shows how a non-verbal memory can play its part in the production of a verbal claim. The memory-claim when it is made must (qua claim) be made in verbal propositions, but there is no reason why the memory on which it is based should contain anything verbal.

Now, in the case of 'remembering how', instead of an uttered (or otherwise formulated) claim we have a deliberate activity. The memory is manifested not in an expressed belief but in a piece of purposeful behaviour. And the memory which gives rise to this piece of purposeful behaviour need not itself be a verbal memory. It *may*, of course, take the form of a verbal proposition (an ordinary memory-claim), as it tends to in our hesitant 'learning' performances. But here no problem arises.

Suppose that whilst I am swimming I am aware that a certain muscular movement of my body has produced on previous unspecified occasions a particular thrusting effect through the water. It is very doubtful that this could be expressed precisely enough in words to be of any directive value to me, yet it does not seem at all doubtful that *I am remembering* a certain relationship which I have observed in the past, and whilst I may not be able to describe this to myself in words I can exemplify it in action. It seems to be a matter of complete indifference whether we say that the actual 'subject of memory' here is an event or a series of events or a belief formulated non-verbally to myself at some past time as the result of my observation of a series of events. The important point is that my failure to make specific memory-claims to myself does not entail that I am not in fact remembering *in the occurrent sense*.

Thus, whilst Ryle is no doubt right when he says[1] 'A well-trained sailor boy can both tie complex knots and discern whether someone else is tying them correctly or incorrectly, deftly or clumsily. But he is probably incapable of the difficult task of describing in words how the knots should be tied', he is wrong in supposing this to show that the sailor boy is not in fact *remembering*

[1] *The Concept of Mind*, p. 56.

how the knots should be tied *in order to* tie them. It shows only that his remembering is not in the form of verbal propositions.

In the case of this sailor boy, assuming that he is not performing by motor-response alone (which he could be), much of the remembering may well be in the form of imagery. If he is able to perform the task without watching what he is doing, there would be a good case for denying any visual imagery.[1] But not all imagery is visual. There are certain bodily feelings involved in the performance of tasks, and the memory of these feelings, as distinct from the memory of any propositions about them, would be one kind of imagery—kinaesthetic imagery. And he *could* remember how to tie the knot by rehearsal, as it were, without an actual rope in his hands, *and* without the recitation of any rules. His remembering could be in a series of visual or kinaesthetic images of the stages of the performance, and he may also twist his hands in a kind of mime, possibly, though not necessarily, accompanied by a stumbling verbal account based on his imagery.

The manner in which we learn a skill must to a great extent determine the way in which we remember it. When we learn by instruction we tend to remember by recitation; when we learn by attempt we tend to remember by imagery, together with half-formed dictums made to ourselves during the attempts. Since most often we learn by a combination of both, our way of remembering will depend largely upon the relative effectiveness for ourselves of the two ways of learning the skill in question. This is why some men can tie bow-ties (usually a very 'conscious performance') only upon themselves, whilst others can tie them only upon other people or on themselves with the aid of a mirror.

Since the tasks we think of ourselves as remembering how to perform are mainly of the muscular kind it is reasonable to suppose that any imagery involved in the remembering is mainly of the kinaesthetic kind. This makes it particularly easy for us to overlook the occurrence of imagery when we retrospect. Thus, in his article 'Remembering' B. S. Benjamin wrote[2]:

'Anyone who assigns the memory-image a central role in the analysis of remembering must explain the connection or lack of

---

[1] Though not a perfect case. A man who has lost his sight may well perform a number of manual tasks with the aid of visual imagery.
[2] *Mind*, Vol. LXV, 1956, p. 317.

connection between our rememberings when memory images naturally are likely to occur, as in our memories of places and faces, and those where they are not, as for instance when we remember how to tie a running-bowline. . . . '

Since tactual or kinaesthetic imagery would be very likely to occur in our remembering of how to tie a bowline, once it is allowed that the tying and the remembering are not one and the same thing, it seems clear that Benjamin is regarding memory-images as visual images—which for a very obvious reason play only a minor part in remembering how to perform physical tasks. It should be noted however that not all recent writers have fallen into this trap. E. J. Furlong writes[1] 'This stress on the visual has given a handle to those who for one reason or another are ill-disposed to imagery. Perhaps impotent to visualise themselves they write off "mental images" in any form'. And H. H. Price[2] attributed his own poor performance at golf to his weakness in kinaesthetic imagery-powers.

We are now in a position to answer the argument that if we were occurrently remembering past events and directive propositions and acting in accordance with the dictates of our memories whenever we performed intelligently, we could not then achieve the smooth continuity which characterises our overt behaviour. Our attention would be absorbed by planning to the exclusion of any doing.[3]

Let us suppose that I am building a wall, and that my performance is an instance of 'remembering how'. It would clearly be absurd to suggest that I must therefore remember every detail of how to build it before commencing operations. I do not have to 'remember how' and *then* build—nor yet do I have to remember how to lay a brick and then lay it. It is enough that my remembering keeps, as it were, always one jump ahead of my performance, that each 'task' (and what constitutes one task is what we choose to regard as one) be considered with a degree of determinateness suitable to its complexity and, *in so far as it*

[1] E. J. Furlong, *Imagination*, London, Allen & Unwin, 1961, p. 70.
[2] *Thinking and Experience*, p. 237.
[3] This argument was put forward in the first section of this chapter. See p. 109.

demands direction, planned accordingly in the light of my memory of how similar 'tasks' have been accomplished. Many such 'tasks' are wholly contained within other 'tasks'; the merest flickings of the wrist, straightenings, smoothings, settings, *may* each be regarded as separate tasks. Thus the remembering how need not precede the building of the wall, or the laying of the brick—it may accompany it.

I say 'in so far as it demands direction' because much of the actual performance does not; it is simple motor-response to a physical stimulus. That it may be a learnt ability like walking, and not an inherent ability like breathing, is here quite irrelevant. It is the ability of our bodies to carry on, so to speak, with the job in hand which smooths out and renders continuous our overt performances. Our motor-responses, by filling the gaps between our planned activities, allow our overt performances to continue uninterrupted.[1]

In my account of what it is to remember how to do something, I am not disputing that we can and sometimes do perform with complete efficiency tasks which we once learnt to perform and that, in A. J. Ayer's words,[2] 'such exercises need not be accompanied by anything that anyone would be even tempted to call a memory-experience'. I am claiming simply that in such cases we are concerned, not with memory in the normal sense of that word, but only with acquired physiological capacities of a muscular kind. When those capacities were developed, and whether they might someday collapse, throwing us back upon the resources of our memories, is beside the point. I also claim that notwithstanding this, there are activities which can properly be called 'remembering how', which are quite distinct from 'being able', and which can occur whether or not we are actually performing the task in question. They are, however, more likely to occur whilst we are performing the task, both because their occurrence may then be demanded and because the performance acts as a stimulus to the memory.

It is intelligible to talk of remembering only when there is

[1] Compare Russell *An Outline of Philosophy*, London, Allen & Unwin, 1927, p. 198, 'In talking, words suggest other words, and a man with sufficient verbal associations may be successfully carried along by them for a considerable time.'
[2] *The Problem of Knowledge*, p. 153.

something which we remember—and conceivably could forget. If none of the performances people commonly speak of as remembering how fulfilled this requirement my arguments in this chapter would be tantamount to a plea for dropping the expression from the language. But since many of these performances do—in my opinion by far the greatest proportion of them do—my plea is only for the more careful application of the expression, at least in an epistemological enquiry.

CHAPTER VI

IMAGES—THE SUBJECTS OF IMAGERY

KINDS OF IMAGERY

When we speak of the graven image of a god the assumption is that the statue copies or reproduces the physical characteristics of that god, so that by looking at the statue we learn how the god is alleged to look. But the term 'image' is often used to mean a strong resemblance or suggestive likeness rather than an exact likeness. When someone says 'Our Fred is the image of our Arthur' he does not usually mean that he cannot tell them apart. He does mean, however (though he may, of course, be wrong) that nobody could fail to see the resemblance. 'Image of' is much stronger than simply 'like'. 'Image', in its most basic and general sense, sometimes means an exact copy and sometimes not, but always it means an unmistakable likeness.

A mirror-image or reflection *is* an exact visual copy, but for the reversal of right and left. (The colour photograph is perhaps the most exact visual copy).[1] But it is not because of its exactness that I take 'mirror-image' to be a special sense of 'image'; it is because I feel that a mirror-image is something we can examine, it is itself an observable entity in the ordinary sense. We speak of the statue as an image but it is also, and primarily, a statue, and we see the image of the god, as it were, *in it*. The mirror-image is *nothing but* the mirror-image. To speak of a statue as the image of a god is to speak of a *relationship between two entities*, the god whose existence is assumed as the statue, as when we speak of Fred's being the image of Arthur. But to speak of a mirror-image does not seem to be to speak of a relationship, a likeness between a man and something else, his replica; nor yet between a man and the sheet of glass or polished steel, or pool of water, or whatever else the image is 'in'. Rather it is to speak only of the visible image itself. We could claim that it is just one way of seeing the object— but it is a mediate way of seeing it, and I feel that the mediating entity is not the mirror but the actual image in it. Although I do

[1] I am ignoring the fact that both mirror-image and photograph are usually smaller than the subject imaged.

speak of 'seeing myself in the mirror' I would be prepared to allow that I can never see myself, only my reflection.

Whether or not we regard a mirror-image as an entity, something that is there to be seen *simply as an image*, there can surely be no doubt that we do so regard after-images.

When I close my eyes after looking fixedly at a sunlit window the 'picture' of that window remains before me as though it had been photographed onto my retina. Except by such mechanical means as pressing my eyeballs I can neither remove it nor change it; it is just as much outside my control as is the view of the window itself. If the light has been particularly bright the after-image will remain superimposed on my visual field even when my eyes are open, partly obscuring the normal view from a section of that field.

The study of after-images, including the 'reversal' of their colours in some cases and not in others, lies within the province of physiology—but that does not necessarily mean that it is philosophically uninteresting. Being a common and easily identifiable experience, the after-image provides a useful contrast to the memory-image. There may also be a strong connection between after-imagery and eidetic imagery. For eidetic images seem to have both some characteristics normally associated with after-images and some normally associated with memory-images and imagination.

In discussing eidetic imagery I am at a considerable disadvantage in that I cannot recall having ever experienced it myself. I must rely, therefore, on the reports of those who have. I understand that an eidetic image may occur immediately, or some considerable time, after the perceptual situation which gave rise to it. It resembles an after-image in that it is seemingly 'there, before the eyes', in a way that permits us to study it as we might any external object. It is claimed that an eidetic image can be 'projected' on to a blank surface and can then be *examined* much as we might examine a painting or a photograph. Normally it is a faithful reproduction of the scene perceived.

It would seem possible, then, to explain the eidetic image as simply a delayed positive after-image, a mere photograph on the retina, provided that the reproduction *always was* exact and that the 'picture' remained always wholly outside the control of the 'viewer'. But experimental psychologists suggest that neither of these conditions is in fact fulfilled. Apparently eidetic images are often found on 'examination' to be imperfect reproductions of the scenes perceived, and the people 'viewing' them can sometimes be induced by suggestion to make them change, or even 'come to life'.[1] If we accept their testimony we must allow that eidetic imagery is not simply a physiological process of 'photographing' like after-imaging. The alternative is to assert that those people who have reported inaccuracies and changes in eidetic images were unable to distinguish the point at which normal memory-imagery or imagination-imagery came in to augment or replace the eidetic imagery. I find this second alternative very difficult to reconcile with my own experience of memory-images, for these do not seem to be substantives in any sense at all, and would hardly seem likely, therefore, to be confused with the kind of phenomena I understand eidetic images to be. We can, perhaps, draw comfort from the fact that most of the reports of such changes come from young children, and it is notorious that children are sometimes carried away by their imaginations. I do not wish to give any definite opinion on the question, firstly, because as I have admitted, I have no experience of eidetic imagery, and secondly, because the eidetic image does not seem to play any vital part in memory. People who do have eidetic images usually allow that they also have other images, distinguishable from these, which they call memory-images.

At this juncture we need say of memory-images only that they are our means of being aware (or our actual awareness)[2] of our own past sense-perceptions. It is not essential that they be exact reproductions of these past sense-perceptions. Leaving aside for the moment the question whether it is proper to speak of seeing or hearing our memory-images, it is sufficient that in having them we are recalling some past sensory experience of our own, as it were directly, not through the medium of verbal description. We need no command of language in order to have memory-images; on the contrary, psychologists claim to have considerable evidence that the occurrence of mental imagery diminishes with the development of linguistic habits. Let us say, then, at this stage, that

---

[1] See I. M. L. Hunter—*Memory—Facts and Fallacies*, (revised edition) Harmondsworth, Penguin, 1964, p. 146 ff.

[2] The significance of this distinction will become apparent in the following chapter p. 157 ff.

memory-imagery is the *direct* linkage of our past sense-perceptions with our present awareness. The experience of imaging is similar, in a way that seems quite impossible to describe and yet which those of us who habitually remember in images must know, to the sensory experiences of seeing, hearing, and so on, though it does not involve the present use of any sense-organ; there is no reason why a man who has gone blind should not still have visual memory-images. Memory-images, unlike after-images and eidetic images, can often be induced and dismissed at will—though at other times they 'appear' as if from nowhere and seem to linger when we would be rid of them. In this their behaviour is no different from that of any other form of memory.

Sometimes we have images which are not, and which we know full well not to be, of any particular object we have ever experienced by sense-perception. Just as I can have an image of my friend sitting on the bicycle he habitually rides, so I can have an image of the same friend riding a donkey, a thing I have certainly never seen him do. And, it may well be felt that, *as images*, the two can be different only in their subject matter. I in fact distinguish between them simply because I know one to be a memory-image and the other to be merely a figment of my own imagination; but *how* I know this is no small problem. The extreme difficulty which has always been found in demonstrating how memory-images can be distinguished from imagination-images by their own intrinsic qualities or their 'modes of presentation' is one of the factors which have led so many philosophers to assert that we distinguish them only by their compatibility with other, non-image, memories—and to relegate the memory-image to the status of a mere *aide-memoire* accordingly. But I myself am quite unprepared to abandon the belief, arising in part from my own experience of in fact being able to distinguish them without the aid of additional propositional memories, that there *must be* inherent distinguishing marks. I want now to suggest that the failure of so many people to put their finger on these distinguishing marks is largely the result of a misunderstanding about the kind of differences they are trying to discover. They are seeking efficient criteria for a difference of kind, when the difference in question is one of degree only.

However wild or grotesque our imagination-images may be there is at least some sense in which they arise out of actual past experience. I can visualize my friend on a donkey because, though I have never seen this sight, I have seen my friend and I have seen a donkey. I am not in the position of the Prince in one of Anthony Armstrong's stories, who, when given a magic wish, wished for a blue rumped gnurgle because he wanted to know what one would look like. Imagination imagery can be likened to those cards with heads and middles and rumps of animals on them that we used to play with as children; the creatures we 'made up' were quite fantastic, but the individual parts did all belong somewhere. In the same way our imagination-images *are* memory-images—but not of any single past perceptual occasion. To accept them as re-presentations of our own past perceptions would be wrong—but not altogether wrong.

And, conversely, in taking memory-images to be re-presentations of our own past perceptions we are right—but not altogether right. For an image does not have to be perfect to rate as a memory-image; if my memory-image of the friend I lunched with today included a white shirt whereas in fact he wore a blue shirt, this alone would not be grounds for holding that I am not having a memory-image at all but an imagination-image. It would be a memory-image with some of the detail inaccurate, that is, including some detail recalled from a different perceptual occasion from the one I consider myself to be remembering. Where, then, should we draw the line between memory-images and imagination-images? The answer is, I believe, that we do not need to 'draw a line' at all.

Once we cease to think of memory-images and imagination-images as two distinct kinds of phenomena we can point to at least three different criteria for 'allotting marks' on the side of memory or on the side of imagination—in the act, as it were, of actually having the images. I do not mean that we consciously judge the image to be 'memory-like' or 'imagination-like', only that there are different factors which prompt us to accept it *as* memory or *as* imagination. I shall call these factors 'firmness', 'controllability' and 'expansion into context'.

FIRMNESS

There is about my image of my friend on a bicycle a unity and 'firmness' that is lacking from my image of the same friend on a donkey. In the one case there is a single whole, man on bicycle, a single focal point of attention. In the other case there are two separate focal points; it is almost as if I were imaging a man and then imaging a donkey and trying to 'clip them together'. The bicycle image, though it may be sketchy, is still constant and steady. The donkey image, though more detailed (as detailed in fact as I want it to be), tends to be constantly blurring and changing; details come and go and only in the face of my friend does the detail seem to be set and firm.

It could well be that Hume was thinking of this difference when he spoke of the 'vividness' of memory-images as compared with imagination-images. But 'vivid', as that word is normally used, is certainly not the best description. 'Self-sufficient', 'unitary' and 'constant' are perhaps better terms. I realize that a particular imagination-image *may be* unitary, self-sufficient or constant, but since we are considering only one means of 'allotting marks', not a rigid distinction of kinds, so long as these qualities are *generally* characteristic of memory-images and not of imagination-images, the exceptions are not disastrous; we still have other yardsticks to apply. And when exceptions do occur their nonconformity can often be explained as something peculiar to a particular case. They might, for instance, be *images of images*.[1]

CONTROLLABILITY

Our imagination-images come and go and change quite freely. The donkey beneath my friend can be turned into an elephant, his hair can be turned bright green and made to stand on end; the image is at the disposal of my every whim. As Hume said[2] 'A man may indulge his fancy in feigning any past scene of adventure'. But surely the reason we speak of feigning is that we are aware of our own control over what is being postulated. Feigning and shamming are intelligible only on the assumption that the performer knows this is not 'the real thing'. And I suggest that it is the feeling of being in control of the imagery which makes him so aware.

Of course I *can* make the *bicycle* beneath my friend 'turn into'

[1] See p. 144.
[2] L. A. Selby-Bigge, A Treatise of Human Nature, Bk. 1, pt. iii, p. 85 of *Hume's Treatise*, Oxford University Press, 1897.

an elephant—but in doing this I am immediately aware of having 'taken charge of' my image. The bicycle will tend to re-assert itself as soon as I discontinue my deliberate fantasy, and there may even be a sense, which we shall consider later,[1] in which it is 'there' all the time.

EXPANSION INTO CONTEXT

Closely connected with 'controllability' is the third criterion, what we might call the natural development or expansion of images. The memory-image I have of a friend on a bicycle leads on naturally, quite involuntarily, to an expanded image which includes the trees and buildings behind him, and to further images of his getting off his bicycle to greet me and of the sound of his voice as he did so. And all this additional imagery has something of the 'firmness' and the 'involuntariness' of the original image.

There are, of course, occasions when I remember so much and can remember no more, when the context simply refuses to 'expand' further—a stage which is bound to be reached eventually. But the feeling of 'expandability' still persists—I seem *compelled* either to enlarge my image, to expand its context—or else to shift my train of thought to something altogether different. So long as my attention remains, the 'next move' is both demanded and to some extent predetermined. At the conclusion of his book *Remembering* Bartlett says, 'Always it is the material from some specially organized mass which has to be central, and about this the constructions and reconstructions of memory cluster'.[2] This certainly seems to be true of memory-imagery.

The imagination-image does not so much expand as simply change. We have no feeling of predetermination or compulsion; the development, if any, is haphazard and voluntary (unless it follows some pre-arranged pattern of associated ideas).[3] To quote Bartlett again: 'With constructive imagination this is not so. The central "scheme" is not, so to speak, predetermined by the initial orientation. There is a freer range from setting to setting and from interest to interest.'[4] Memory-imagery, on the other hand, is always felt to be an integral part of the greater whole.

[1] See p. 152.
[2] F. C. Bartlett, *Remembering*, Cambridge University Press, 1932, p. 313.
[3] Cf. 'metaphorical imagery', p. 168. [4] *Remembering* p. 313.

It 'belongs in context', and this may well be the basis of the 'feeling of familiarity' of which Russell speaks. The familiar is the firmly set; that which is felt to form part of an established, integral whole. To say of any sight that it is familiar is generally to say that we know from a glance what to expect on close scrutiny. It 'strikes a chord in us', and I submit that the chord it strikes is precisely this expectancy. Certainly such an account of familiarity enables us to give an answer to Holland's objection that an imagination-image entertained many times is more *familiar* than a memory-image of an experience had but once.[1] The imagination-image, however often it occurs, will not normally develop a contextual setting into which it naturally, almost compulsively, expands. It has been pointed out to me that dream imagery has a natural development of context, may be completely firm and not felt to be within our control. But this counts in favour of rather than against my choice of 'distinguishing marks'. For this is precisely why we do not recognize dreams as such when we are having them.[2]

Since I have argued that the difference between memory and imagination imagery is one of degree reather than one of kind, it may be better to speak not of memory-images and imagination-images, but rather of the memory-elements and imagination-elements in imagery. We can then say that, on any given occasion, the memory-elements are those 'parts' of an image which derive from a single past perceptual occasion, whilst the imagination-elements are those 'parts' which derive from past perceptual occasions other than the one we take ourselves to be remembering. Or, at the level of 'unidentified images', when everything in an image derives from the same past perceptual occasion it is a memory-image, i.e. composed wholly of memory-elements, and when the content of the image is derived from more than one past perceptual occasion it is potentially *either* an 'imagination image' or an incorrect memory-image—the part which is incorrect being dependent upon *what we subsequently take it* to be the image of.

I have been speaking of 'past perceptual occasions' but there is

[1] This objection was referred to in Chapter II, p. 42.
[2] Dreams are 'felt', of course, not as memories but as the 'real thing'. This follows from my later arguments for a 'single scale' of perceiving/remembering/imaging. See p. 202 ff.—See also B. Smith 'Dreaming', Australasian Journal of Philosophy, Vol. 43, No. 1, May 1965, p. 48.

really no reason why 'remembered experience' should be limited to 'remembered perceptual experience'. Just as I can remember perceiving things so I can remember imagining things. And if my imagining took the form of imagery, my memory of that imagining may well take the form of imagery too. In his article 'The Empiricist Theory of Memory' Holland considers the possibility of someone amusing himself repeatedly by contemplating an image of Magdalen Tower standing on Magdalen Bridge.[1] Such an image, when first entertained, would be 'taken as' imagination. The memory-elements and imagination-elements would be equally balanced (whether we thought of the image as *of* the bridge or *of* the tower) and would be discordant with each other, with a consequent lack of 'firmness'. The image would be completely controllable and detached from any single context. But subsequent occurrences of the same image *could be* memory-images—memory-images of the imagination image—and the image would tend to become more 'firm' and less controllable. What would still be seen to be the image of a fantasy in the light of other extraneous knowledge, could well, in time, come to have many of the inherent characteristics of an ordinary memory-image. It could not, however, acquire *all* the characteristics of memory-imagery. For the only 'context' it could acquire would be one which would show it up immediately as the contrived fantasy it is. We could, if we wished, avoid any assumptions about 'entity images' by speaking of a habit of forming a particular image rather than of the occurrence of memories of a previous image, but the effect would still be the same.

This, incidentally, provides us with at least one possible explanation of the 'fixed idea', the wrong belief to which we return even after we have been shown that it is wrong. I myself got it into my mind at an early age that a certain schoolmaster was cross-eyed (why I cannot say) and so often entertained an image of him with cross-eyes that on meeting him much later I was astonished to find that his eyes were in fact quite straight. Notwithstanding this I still image him with cross-eyes, and only by a considerable effort can I make myself image him otherwise.

I have been talking rather as if imagination-imagery was just bad remembering. But this, of course, is not so. Imagination plays a

[1] *Mind*, Vol. LXIII, 1954, p. 468.

part, and an important part, in our thinking and our remembering as well. For instance I may have a memory-image of my father riding a horse down a country lane and then, just to amuse myself, 'turn the horse into an elephant', and so create an imagination-image. But suppose I then become interested in the elephant. The image may re-orient itself, as it were, about the elephant, so that instead of a country lane there is a Zoological Garden with an elephant being ridden through it—just as I saw it on my last visit. The rider fades and becomes nondescript, and once more I have a memory-image. In this case the imagination has re-kindled a different memory, but sometimes imagination may serve to augment, rather than to distort, the original memory. This is how I am inclined to interpret a private 'experiment' reported by Furlong.[1]

He tells how once he groped, with his eyes closed, from his chair to the door in a familiar room. A little later, recalling the experience, he was surprised to find that his memory of it was in *visual* imagery. Now, no doubt he had made the same journey many times with his eyes open. What then is more natural than that he should *imagine* the visual perceptions which would have been involved had he had his eyes open, and take this to be his remembering of the event? For the imagining in question is simply the transposition of true memory-images to another, *and essentially similar*, occasion.

He himself explains it by saying that in the remembering his whole state of mind at the earlier time was reproduced. But this seems to entail that *as he groped* he had imagined the visual experience he would be having if his eyes were open and that subsequently he remembered these imaginary visual experiences. Furlong does not mean of course, that he thinks he *is* moving across the room. The state of mind, as reproduced, is modified to the status of a memory. But, even so, unless visual presentations of some kind, actual or imagined, entered the original state of mind it is hard to see why they should enter the 'reproduction'. Now, whilst it is certainly *possible* that such an imaginative performance did occur during the actual crossing of the room, it does not seem here to be *necessary*. Imagination-imagary quite often 'fills out' our memories where memory-imagery is weak or altogether lacking and so long as it is correct in essentials we are not

[1] *A Study in Memory*, p. 76.

likely to be misled by it, though clearly, we *could* be. Had Furlong claimed from memory that he passed the cat on the way to the door, we should have felt obliged to enquire whether he touched it or only 'saw' it.

It is notorious that people who write about imagery often become so preoccupied with visual imagery that they write as if no other forms of imagery existed. I am myself so dominated by visual experience that such examples as spring to my mind are nearly always of the visual kind, and it is as well to remind ourselves as often as possible that memory-images can be of many kinds—as many in fact as there are kinds of sense experience. I want, therefore, to make it quite clear that whatever I may claim for visual imagery I am claiming equally, where it is not patently inappropriate, for every other kind of imagery as well.

It is not necessary here to settle the question of how many different kinds of sense-organs we have. We need only state that whatever can be regarded as one class of sensations can give rise to what may be regarded as a corresponding class of images. We have sight and visual imagery, touch and tactual imagery, smell and olfactory imagery, hearing and auditory imagery, taste and gustatory imagery. If we claim that there is a separate kinaesthetic sense, sense of motion and/or sense of heat, we should also claim that there is separate kinaesthetic, motion and/or heat imagery.

It is sometimes felt that there is a special problem about images when the corresponding sensations are, as people say, localized. We know the difference between seeing something and having a visual image of it, but could there be the same difference (or the same sort of difference) between feeling something, say, a pinprick, and having a tactual image of it? I can see no reason at all why there should not be. The people who raise this problem are overlooking the fact that what is seen is also 'localized', though not in our own bodies, and if it is possible to have a visual image of an 'external object' without thereby having an hallucination, it is equally possible to have a tactual image of a pinprick without thereby having an hallucination. There is no better reason to suppose that the tactual image of the pinprick must be painful than to suppose that the visual image of a car's headlights must be dazzling. In principle every sensory experience is recallable, and according to the view which I shall develop in this and the following chapters, to *recall* a sensory experience *is* to have an image. Recalling a sensory experience is not to be confused with recalling *that* we had the experience, which may take the form simply of a verbal proposition.

Now, here I want to give a word of caution about a frequently encountered, and potentially misleading expression—verbal imagery. Words, like images, often function in trains of associated ideas and when what we are considering is the association of ideas, words and images are genuine alternatives at the same functional level. Bartlett, for instance, says: 'A person who uses visual cues more readily and frequently than other cues can also, as a rule, use other cues—verbal, kinaesthetic, auditory, and so on—if he is forced or encouraged to do so'.[1] This is quite unexceptionable as it stands, i.e. within a discussion of memory-cues. But the listing of 'verbal' with 'auditory', 'kinaesthetic' and 'visual' *may* lead us, if we are not careful, to think of it as 'another of the same kind' in our consideration of imagery—and this would be very wrong.

Again, we find G. F. Stout saying 'There are some people, especially people who are much occupied with abstract thinking, who are inclined to deny that they have mental imagery at all. They are almost or quite unable to visualize objects, and their general power of mentally reviving auditory or tactile experiences may also be rudimentary. The images which with them mark the successive steps in a train of ideas are mainly or wholly verbal'.[2] This too is perfectly all right—so long as we bear in mind that these 'verbal images' are images *of* words and are in fact *either* visual *or* auditory *or* kinaesthetic images. 'Verbal imagery' belongs at the classificatory level of 'tree imagery' or 'people imagery' —it is not a mode of imagery; it is a class of subjects of imagery.

Just as perceptual experience can involve a number of different sense-organs, so the recall of that experience can involve a number of different kinds of imagery. My seeing an apple does not prevent my simultaneously tasting it, smelling it, feeling its surface or hearing it when I tap it to test its hardness. And my subsequent visual imagery of it need not in any way conflict with my tactual, olfactory, auditory or gustatory imagery of it. As I. M. L. Hunter

[1] *Remembering*, p. 109.   [2] *A Manual of Psychology*, p. 149.

writes[1] 'Not only may we see again the high green hills, the blue sky, the light-flecked waves breaking on the rocky shore, but we may also hear again the cries of the sea-birds and the sound of the ship's hooter. We may smell again the odour of the wrack on the shore and the perfume of the rose in our lapel. We may taste the chocolate we ate on that day, and feel again the warmth of the sun in our faces, our movements in walking along the heaving deck, and the sinking experience of oncoming seasickness'. And, of course, it is not necessary that we have these experiences one at a time.

The somewhat lyrical style of Hunter's example draws attention to the richness of image-memory as compared with the somewhat sterile memory of propositions. Only in imagery can we 're-live' a past perceptual experience, and it is not surprising that those of us who are much given to imaging regard people who cannot or do not image, if indeed there really are such people, as greatly to be pitied.

IMAGEABILITY

What sort of things are images of? I can have an image of a tree or of the smell of a railway train, or of a sentence if it was written or heard or spoken, but it just would not make sense to talk of an *image of* a proposition or a fact. I have said that to have an image is *to recall a sensory experience*. We must consider, therefore, what class or classes of 'objects' we can be said to experience by or with our senses.

It is natural to think first of sensible qualities, but we must be very careful here not to confuse image with concept. To say that I have a sensation or an image of blue is to say that I have a sensation or an image of an instance of blueness, i.e. *as of* a blue surface or expanse. It may be that in recalling the colour of the sky on a particular day I have a memory image which includes nothing but a blue expanse of no very definite size and shape, but it still is the image of that particular blue of that particular sky. I may be able to have a general idea or concept of blueness but I cannot have a general image of blueness[2] (for what shade of blue would this be?), though I may have a series of images of

[1] *Memory—Facts and Fallacies*, p. 135.   [2] Cf. Chapter VII, p. 183.

different shades of blue. It is possible to image instances of any particular sensible quality, but to do so is always to image the sensible quality *of something*, the appearance (or part of the appearance) presented by something.

By 'an appearance' I mean a certain combination of sensible qualities in a certain relationship to each other as presented to an observer. So defined it follows that *whenever we perceive a thing we sense an appearance*. R. M. Chisholm has pointed out with great clarity that from 'He sees a boat' we may infer 'A boat appears in some way to him' or 'A boat presents him with an appearance', but not 'He sees an appearance'.[1] However, I believe that it is important here to preserve the distinction between seeing and visually sensing. The former is a perceptual experience which involves *both* the use of our eyes *and* the classification or identification of what is presented to them. The latter is not in itself a perceptual experience at all though it may well be both a causal prerequisite and an integral part of any such experience. By 'visual sensing', as distinct from 'seeing', I mean the mere physiological response of a living creature to what Berkeley called 'a diversity of light and colour'. Thus sensing is epistemologically prior to any classification; it provides the classifiable. To speak of the experience of sensing is to speak of a part—the 'content' or 'presented stuff' part—of the experience of perceiving. It is very hard to avoid speaking of sensing as an experience but to do so could be misleading if it suggests a separate mental activity from perceiving—the same kind of thing but at a different level—for I am quite sure that no such separate *mental* activity exists. So long as the role of sensation *within* perception is borne in mind it seems to me both proper and instructive to say that when the boat presents an appearance to me I *see* the boat as a result of my *sensing* that diversity of light and colour which constitutes the appearance.

My mental reaction is, of course, to a boat, not to an appearance or mere aspect of a boat, in normal perceptual cases. And later, when I image what I previously sensed, my mental reaction is, on most occasions, to a remembered boat, not to a remembered appearance or aspect.

[1] R. M. Chisholm, *Perceiving*, Oxford University Press, 1957, p. 151. See also R. Wollheim 'The Difference between Sensing and Observing', *Aristotelian Soc.*, Supplementary Volume XXVIII, 1954, *Belief and Will*, p. 219 ff.

This may seem to render useless the distinction I have made between the thing and its appearance, but it does not. There are three important differences:

(1) The boat goes on in time; it is a thing in the world—the appearance (as the appearance it is) is contingent upon the existence of an observer or group of observers. For the observer the appearance is simply a momentary sense-experience.

(2) The boat has many other sensible qualities which we know about but which do not enter into the appearance. Therefore if these enter into the memory they must do so by means other than imagery of the event or occasion in question.

(3) The boat is what it is; the appearance is whatever we take it to be. So that if the appearance were such as to suggest to us a whale rather than a boat, then our interpreting the memory-image as of a whale would reflect well, not badly, upon our powers of imagery.

Since I have defined 'an appearance' as 'a certain combination of sensible qualities in a fixed *relationship*' it is necessary to say something of the imageability of relations. Whilst what we image must carry relationships within it (since it is a 'diversity of colour', not merely 'colour') it is important to be clear that, just as an imaged quality must be a particular instance of that quality, so an imaged relation must be a particular instance, a mere exemplification, of that relation. To have an idea of the relationship itself is always to have an abstract idea or concept, and belongs to an intellectual stage involving interpretation and classification.

My reference to the appearance as a momentary experience may call to mind a phrase used by Russell, 'the total momentary experience'. This is the term he applies to any compresent set of mental constituents forming for the man who experiences them a single unit.[1] But it is not clear to me whether he means a compresent set of sensory experiences or of any experiences at all. If he means the former, then a 'total momentary experience' would be very like what I have called an appearance. (Though the appearance, as recalled, may be of any part of the total momentary experience, nor would I be willing to characterize an appearance as 'mental'.) But if he means the latter, then the total momentary experience may include elements—memories, judgments,

[1] Bertrand Russell, *Human Knowledge, Its Scope and Limits*, London, Allen & Unwin, 1948, p. 315.

thoughts, emotions—which are neither sensible nor imageable in the ordinary way. Only that which is presented to us via our sense-organs is recallable by us *in* imagery, as distinct from being recallable *with the aid of* imagery.

It would be generally allowed that, as sensations of the different sense-organs do not exclude each other, neither do their images. But it seems to have been widely assumed, on the other hand, that the sensations related to any one sense-organ come necessarily one at a time, and therefore so must the images derived through any one sense-organ. However, I can find no justification for such an assumption; it may well be that this is a case where pre-occupation with the peculiarities of sight has led to error.

We *can* smell several smells, taste several flavours, hear several sounds, at the same time; and I see no good reason why anyone should claim that on such occasions our experience is *always* of one composite smell, sound or taste. Now, but for the accidental fact that our eyes look the same way—if for instance they were so spaced that their fields did not overlap—we would be able to see two views at the same time, not one superimposed on the other but two quite distinct views. And visual imaging is not an operation we perform with our eyes or any other sense-organ. There seems, therefore, to be no reason why we could not experience several totally different visual images simultaneously. Images do not occupy space. There may, of course, be excellent reasons why we do not generally do so. Even where there are 'external stimuli' it is difficult to give our attention to two distinct sounds at one time, and in imagery there are no 'external stimuli'. Nevertheless, we cannot deny the empirical possibility of the simultaneous occurrence of two or more visual images. I could not attach any sense to an assertion that we may be *having* images but not (to any extent) *attending to them.* Having images implies some degree of attention, but divided attention is by no means an unknown experience. What, for instance, prompts us to 'correct' an image? A. D. Woozley gives an account of his visual memory-image of a cricket umpire, and says[1] 'Even while having the image, I am sure that the bow-tie, the shirt, and the coat are right, I am sure that the trousers are wrong, and about the shoes I have no very clear idea at all'. It could be that he had an independent

[1] A. D. Woozley, *Theory of Knowledge*, London, Hutchinson, 1949, p. 61.

propositional memory that the trousers were, say, striped, whereas those in the image were checked. But Woozley does not give this explanation—he seems in fact specifically to discount it—and certainly such situations do seem to arise in the absence of any relevent propositional memories. If we grant the possibility of different simultaneous visual images we have immediately one possible explanation. In Chapter IV,[1] I claimed that in all negative memory situations there is a positive element. In the case of imagery not supported by any propositional memories that positive element may well take the form of other, fainter, co-existent memory-images, which, though not 'replacing' the image under consideration, show wherein it is wrong, or at least inhibit our acceptance of it as right.

The problem, how an image can persist and nevertheless be known to be inaccurate, has puzzled philosophers for a long time. I have suggested one explanation—that an 'imagination-image' known as such can become habitual[2]—but clearly this would not meet all cases. In *The Problems of Philosophy* Russell wrote 'We are certainly able, to some extent, to compare an image with the object remembered, so that we often know, within somewhat wide limits, how far our image is accurate; but this would be impossible unless the object, as opposed to the image, were in some way before the mind'.[3] There is obviously something very queer about this suggestion. How could any one have an object 'before the mind' except by having imagery? He could have a description of the object *in* the mind, but this is a different thing. It seems that Russell realized this, for, some fifteen years later he wrote:[4] 'Suppose you call up an image of Waterloo Bridge, and you are convinced that it is like what you see when you look at Waterloo Bridge. It would seem natural to say that you know the likeness because you remember Waterloo Bridge. But remembering is often held to involve, as an essential element, the occurrence of an image which is regarded as referring to a prototype. Unless you can remember without images, it is difficult to see how you can be sure that images resemble prototypes. I think that in fact you cannot be sure, unless you can find some indirect means of

---

[1] See p. 97.   [2] See p. 144.
[3] Bertrand Russell, *The Problems of Philosophy*, Oxford University Press, 1912, p. 180.
[4] Bertrand Russell, *An Outline of Philosophy*, London Allen & Unwin, 1927, p. 189.

comparison. You might, for example, have photographs of Waterloo Bridge....' But the fact is that very often we *are* sure, and rightly so. And it could be that our certainty *is* based upon a comparison—the comparison of many simultaneous images of slightly different appearances presented by the bridge, all of which support and confirm each other.

I have spoken of the causal relationship between organic sensing and 'mental imaging' in a way which assumes the two to be so utterly distinct that no confusion could possibly arise as to which was which. But am I justified in making this assumption? Hallucination is a well-known phenomenon but whether it should be characterized as sensation or mental image is, to say the least, highly debatable. And, even under normal conditions, it is sometimes impossible for us to say whether we really heard or just imagined the faint noise in the next room, whether we really saw or just imagined the flash of light on the horizon. Few philosophers have ever faced up to the fact that what we call images *are very like* what we call sensations. Hume spoke of the greater 'liveliness' of sensations; but when we attempt to define this 'liveliness' we are ultimately reduced to saying that it is the distinguishing feature between sensations and images. There can be little doubt that Hume realized this, but it did not perturb him greatly because as he says on the very first page of the *Treatise*—'Every one of himself will readily perceive the difference betwixt feeling and thinking'. Yet every one of himself will readily perceive the difference between a square and a triangle—but in doing so he does not perceive any distinction between the individual straight lines which make up the square and those which make up the triangle. It is hard to find any way to describe images other than as a 're-seeing' or 're-hearing' of some event, and when we are asked wherein this differs from an actual re-seeing or re-hearing what can we say except that the event is not really before us? When the next question is asked, 'How do you know it is not really before you?', we see the trap and are at a loss for a reply. For this reason I find quite unsatisfactory Russell's conclusion that the distinguishing feature by which we tell sensations from images is that the former arise wholly from external stimuli whilst the latter arise from internal stimuli also.[1] Russell is simply

[1] *The Analysis of Mind*, p. 145 ff.

providing formal, i.e. verbal, definitions *on the assumption* that the phenomena to be defined are already known to us, that we already have some means of distinguishing between internal and external stimuli. But such means *could exist only* by virtue of an inherent detectable difference between the experiences we call sensing and imaging in an overwhelming majority of cases.

I find it strange, therefore, that recent philosophers have paid so little attention to the one really outstanding difference between images and sensations, although it was suggested by Ward[1] and stressed by G. F. Stout.[2] It is that images never compete with sensations. My image of a red sky neither obliterates nor becomes superimposed upon my view of the blue sky. Thus two distinguishable experiences 'exist' at the same time quite independently of each other. And whilst I can, if I wish, change one (the image) from red to green, the blue of the actual sky remains steadily before me quite outside my control. I can look away, but so long as I keep my eyes directed upon it the sensation of blue persists. Now surely this persistence is the feature which distinguishes sensing from imaging. When we say that the sky is 'actually there' we are saying (at least) that there is a continuity of stimulus which *cannot be rejected*; it forces itself upon our attention whether we wish it or not. This is why the sudden sound or flash of light does not have the same distinctive character; we feel obliged to ask our companions whether they too heard or saw it. This is also why, if one particular image so monopolized a man's attention as to exclude from it even present external stimuli, he would be liable to hallucination.

If hallucination were a common experience we might well reach a stage where we were able to distinguish our sensations (and thereby the 'external world') from our imaginings only by constantly checking our experience against the testimony of other people. If groups of people suffered the same hallucination together then it seems doubtful whether they could ever finally decide whether the thing they 'witnessed' really happened. On the one hand there would be the inductive improbability, and on the other hand the confirming testimony. But in fact (and this is a very important fact) hallucinations are in any case very rare,

[1] J. Ward, *Psychological Principles*, Cambridge University Press, 1920, p. 171 ff.
[2] *A Manual of Psychology*, p. 148.

and then almost invariably confined to a single person. It is possible for us, therefore, to write them off as odd exceptions for which psychological explanations must be sought and coin the special name 'hallucination' to cover them.[1]

My claim is that there is simply *no need to seek any distinguishing feature between sensing and imaging other than the compulsive continuity of the one which is lacking from the other*. This alone enables us to divide the real and present from the imagined and remembered, to develop concepts of what is normal perceiving and normal imaging, and to frame definitions by which we can decide, after the event, that certain cases were not normal.

Thus we do in fact distinguish our imaging from our sensing, not by their respective subjects, nor yet by any difference inherent in a single momentary experience itself, but rather by a difference found in a sequence of such experiences. In Chapter VIII I shall accept the conclusion to which this view commits me that what we call a sensation simply is an image, but one stimulated by external causes and thereby rendered 'persistent'. Now, is it reasonable to make this reduction and at the same time to go on talking, as I have done very freely, about wrong or inaccurate imagery? For it does not seem to make sense to talk of a sensation being wrong; a sensation is simply what it is. Certainly we can misinterpret our sensations, and in the same way we can misinterpret our images. But the fault then lies not in them but in ourselves. And if it is meaningless to speak of a sensation's being wrong, it is equally meaningless to speak of its being right.

H. H. Price makes this point very clearly in reference to 'primary recognition', recognition at what we might call the sensory level. 'Shall we say then that primary recognition is infallible, or as near to infallibility as we can get? This might be misleading, because it might suggest that mistaken primary recognitions are theoretically possible, though by a fortunate dispensation of Providence they never in fact occur. It will be better, perhaps, to say that primary recognition is non-fallible, because the notion of fallibility does not apply to it'.[2]

---

[1] There have been cases of strange 'appearances' to groups of people—some of the 'miracles' for example—which could not be explained away as mass hypnotism. And in these cases we simply do not know what to say; it must remain an open question whether the event 'really happened' or was hallucinatory.   [2] *Thinking and Experience*, p. 86.

Against this view Russell has argued that there is such a thing as error at a pre-intellectual level. When we are stimulated to action, albeit in a purely motor-responsive manner, by some sensory occurrence, then if that action is inappropriate there is error. 'There is error when a bird flies against a pane of glass which it does not see'.[1] But surely this is very much a reconstructed error. We can say that the bird did the wrong thing; but can we say that it did a foolish thing? Error presupposes some sort of option. We might say that the bird *behaved as if* it thought there was no obstruction, but surely it would be truer to say that the bird *did not* behave as though it thought there *were* an obstruction. To attribute error to the bird we should have to claim that it did see the obstruction but believed that it did not—which is simply absurd unless we are using 'see' in two quite different ways—once as 'visually sense' and the other time as 'perceive'.

But, allowing that 'sensations' are non-fallible, does it follow that all imagery is non-fallible in the same way? It may perhaps be felt that, since an image is already a re-presentation, it comes into being, so to speak, with a criterion of accuracy that cannot apply to a direct sensory presentation. But the 'imagination-image' is wholly composed of misplaced or ill-assorted memory-images, and that misplacement or ill-assortment is itself a form of initial error—*only provided that the image is taken to be unitary*, i.e. provided we regard it as the image of some specific past occasion, not as the assortment of images from different occasions which it in fact is.

To this extent, at least, there must be interpretation for the question of error to arise; and wherever there is interpretation there is the possibility of re-interpretation.

The only circumstances, then, under which we could hold the imagery itself to be wrong or false, would be if something were presented to us in imagery without *any* basis in past perceptual experience. Thus, granted the single assumption that all mental imagery is basically the re-presentation of past sense experiences, however jumbled these experiences may be in their sequence and complexities, then all imagery *is* non-fallible in the same sense as sensation is non-fallible.

[1] *Human Knowledge, Its Scope and Limits*, p. 201.

CHAPTER VII

IMAGES—
THE FUNCTION OF IMAGERY

ARE IMAGES INSPECTABLES?

In Chapter VI we were principally concerned with what imagery is *of;* we must now consider what imagery *is*. It is taken very much for granted in some quarters that the substantive term 'image' is only a courtesy title. I. M. L. Hunter, for example, writes:

'Strictly speaking we ought not to talk of the image of a scene but rather of imaging the scene or experiencing the scene in the absence of any appropriate external stimulus such as exists in perceiving. In the interests of easy expression, we may talk of images as things instead of as processes provided we always bear in mind that such language is more metaphorical than precise'.[1]

Whilst I certainly agree with the view he expresses, I cannot agree with his manner of expressing it, as though it were an obvious truth which needed no supporting argument. A great many empiricist epistemologists still talk of images in 'entity' terms without any apology, and one authority of considerable weight, H. H. Price, has specifically defended their right to do so.

In *Thinking and Experience* Price specifically rejects the view that there *is imaging* but there are *not images*, that the relationship is two termed, between the public thing imaged and the private act of imaging without any intermediate 'entity' being involved. Although he admits that there *could be* a danger of being misled by the substantive term into thinking of an image as 'a persistent intramental *thing* or continuent', he holds this danger to be so slight as to be of no account, and he counter-charges that the upholders of the 'two term' view 'do not scruple to talk about *words* as if they were entities. If they insist that there are no images, but

[1] *Memory—Facts and Fallacies*, p. 137.

only imaging, ought they not equally to insist that there are no words, but only speaking and writing? Indeed a token word is far less "like an entity" than an occurrent image is'.[1]

But the two cases are parallel only on the assumption which Price himself makes that images are symbols. When we talk about words we are talking about symbols—furthermore, about publicly observable symbols, e.g. sounds and marks on paper. My seeing or hearing the word 'Napoleon' may prompt me to think of Napoleon. But if I have an image of Napoleon there is a very real sense in which I am already thinking of Napoleon even though I may not name or otherwise identify him. All that is necessary is that I am aware of imaging *some man* and that man is in fact Napoleon. I am not, of course, claiming that I cannot think about Napoleon without having an image of him—clearly this would be possible. I am claiming only that having an image is itself *one way of thinking about him*, whilst merely reading or hearing his name certainly is not.

We are all agreed that imaging is not a public procedure. But since it must, in any case, involve some private mental performance (which is quite clearly understandable) why need it also involve some kind of private mental entity (which is very difficult indeed to understand). To think and to have thoughts is exactly the same thing. The thoughts are not 'there' to be thought about. And when I remember an event in propositions I do not remember those propositions *in* propositions. Why, then, when I remember an event in imagery, should what I am imaging be *an image of* the past event rather than the past event itself? The usual reply: 'Because that event is no longer existent', is entirely pointless. If it were existent we should perceive it, not image it. What *is* now existent is the 'act of imaging'. And it is the kind of 'act' which can be directed only to past, not to present, objects.

Imagery is, in fact, simply one way of remembering things; the way of remembering which is applicable to perceived appearances. It is not something that helps us to remember things the way that notes in our diaries do. I agree that it is more natural to think of *an image* which eludes us when we want it and obtrudes itself when we do not, than to think of an inability to control our imaging, but this simply reflects the natural tendency to have to 'substantify' our activities, especially those activities which seem

[1] *Thinking and Experience*, p. 248 (his italics).

to be involuntary.[1] It is just as natural for us, in the same way, to think *of a nervous tic* in the leg rather than of an inability to control our legs. And our thinking this way does not make a nervous tic in my leg the same kind of thing (only invisible in some way) as a sheep-tick in my leg.

'Modern philosophers', Price says, 'are never tired of telling us that mental images are not at all like pictures. But they are'.[2] He is quite right, they are—but only in the way that perceived views are like pictures; likeness is a reciprocal relationship and pictures are like mental images. Having a mental image is in many ways like looking at a picture, but it is a good deal more like looking at the 'real thing'. And it certainly is not like looking through a picture at the scene it represents.

It is comforting to turn from the work of those philosophers who treat imagery as little more than an amusing pastime for the simple-minded to an unequivocal assertion like that by Furlong: 'We do also visualize, and when we visualize there is something presented to us, something having the properties we have stated, and this is an image'.[3] But why 'presented'? Why not simply 'There is something present to our minds (though not to our senses); and when this occurs we are imaging?' It is clearly not within my competence to deny any man's account of his own experience. And so I must accept that H. H. Price 'cannot help noticing that in imaging we seem to be confronted with something, to have something over against us or presented to us—and something other than the material object or physical event, real or fictitious, which we are trying to envisage',[4] though I might well ask how he distinguishes ordinary memory-imagery from eidetic imagery. I can only assert that this is not my own experience, nor that of other people I have questioned on the subject, and attempt to show that, though some of our memory-performances do demand that *there is imagery*, none of them demand the existence of any such 'extra entities' as images are sometimes held to be.

The 'three term' view of imagery arises from the assumption

---

[1] It is noticeable that we are more inclined to talk of 'imagining a flying elephant' than of 'having an image of a flying elephant' and we say 'I just can't imagine it', rather than 'the image of it eludes me'.

[2] *Thinking and Experience*, p. 249.

[3] *Imagination*, p. 81.

[4] *Thinking and Experience*, p. 248.

that we observe or inspect our images, as we might a newspaper, in order to gain factual information from them about the sensible appearances of things seen in the past. Russell, for instance, could certainly be taken to be making this assumption when he writes:[1] 'Suppose, for instance, you want to remember whether, in a certain room, the window is to the right or the left of the door as viewed from the fireplace. You can observe your image of the room, consisting (*inter alia*) of an image of the door and an image of the window standing (if your recollection is correct) in the same relation as when you were actually seeing the room'. Now, I do not want to deny that imagery can remind us of, or even, in some cases, enable us to discover, the spatial relationships which existed between the things we have observed. What I do deny, and what Russell seems to be suggesting, is the existence of two distinct 'stages' in the memory of the room's appearance: the 'calling up' of a 'picture' of the room, and the inspection of that 'picture' in order to ascertain how the room looked.

An image is not something we carry about with us like a map (though the capacity to have a certain image may well be part of our present physiological make-up); we actually have the image only in so far as we are remembering the appearance in question. I do not mean that we must first remember and *then* have the image. I mean that, since what we are remembering is an appearance, our remembering of it is in imagery; what is being recalled is not a perceptual observation but the original cause of making that observation. *In imaging the room we are remembering its former appearance*, which includes the relative visual positions of the window and the door. So that what we are observing is the past appearance of the room with the window and the door, not an image or replica of it. Only 'observe' is not the right word here, because the things we observe are present to our senses, they are 'really there'. The word we want is 'remember'; and in this case the remembering is *in imagery*.

I do not deny that if we genuinely could not remember the relative positions of the door and the window, imagery may help us to do so. We might, for instance, 'call up' images of various alternative window/door relationships, and one of these 'called-up images' might then develop the characteristics of a memory-image, become more 'firm' and harder to control, and

[1] *An Outline of Philosophy*, p. 207.

tend to expand in context.[1] But all we are doing here is imagining in imagery in order to stimulate ourselves into remembering in imagery. Having the memory-image, if and when we did have it, would again *be* remembering.

I am convinced that we cannot, as it were, get anything from an image that we have not already put into it. And our ways of 'putting something into it' are by imagining and remembering. We can, of course, interpret our images; we can draw inferences about factual relationships from appearances presented in imagery which we did not draw when those appearances were presented to perception, or which we did draw but have subsequently forgotten. And to this extent we do, in a metaphorical sense, 'read off' information from our images. But this 'reading off' can only be some further interpretation of the appearance we already are remembering—not an addition to it.

Furlong considers the case of a gate of which we had noticed the colour but not the number of bars. In the subsequent image of it, the colour and general shape are clear and distinct, yet though the gate as imaged is barred, it does not have any definite number of bars, only a barred 'look'. And he says:[2] 'If we are in any way acquainted with the past when we remember, then it is hard to see why ... we cannot read off the number of bars in the gate, as we could have done on the original occasion'. But, in the first place, to be *acquainted with* the past is not to be *in* the past. And, in the second place, the past with which we are acquainted is our own past experience, and this happens to have been limited to observing the general 'look' of the gate. People would be far less puzzled by the 'vagueness and sketchiness' of memory-imagery if they realized how very 'vague and sketchy' most of our sense-perceptions are. When I look at a corrugated iron roof I am aware that I am seeing 'stripes', but I am certainly not aware of the number of these. To ascertain their number I must move my eyes along the roof, inspecting the 'stripes' one by one. And this is precisely what I can never do with my memory-image of the corrugated roof. Our imagery can contain, at most, only that degree of detail that the sensory experience re-presented in it contained. Thus we can 'read off' an image only such information

---
[1] The 'memory characteristics' of imagery, as described in Chapter VI, p. 140 ff.
[2] *A Study in Memory*, p. 38.

L

as it *would have been possible* to have 'seen at a glance' at the time of the perception. This may be more than was in fact 'seen at a glance'. The 'look' of a three-barred gate is quite distinctive, and so the fact that a gate was three-barred could be learnt from the memory of that 'look' (the memory-image) even though we had not remarked this fact when we saw the gate, or, having remarked it, had subsequently forgotten it. But, for most people, this would not be so with a twelve-barred gate. So there is a sense in which we 'notice'[1] the three-barred character of the gate although we do not actually count the bars, whereas it is not possible to 'notice' a twelve-barred character in this way. Noticing the twelve-barred character, as distinct from the multi-barred 'look', necessarily involves counting the bars.

IMAGERY AND RECOGNITION

We sometimes speak of recognizing images, and also of recognizing by means of imagery. Both these are suggestive of an 'entity' view of imagery, and, in the light of my argument that images *are our memories of the appearances* previously presented by events and things, but not extra inspectable 'entities', we must now consider whether, and in what sense we can be said to recognize images and/or to recognize *by* imagery.

I have a visual image which I recognize to be of the man who lives in the flat below mine. What does this amount to? I have a certain image, i.e. remember a certain appearance. The image is 'involuntary', 'firm' and 'unitary'; it is a memory-image. It is of the upper half of a man, and this is not something I work out or infer; in having the image I am conscious that I am imaging a man whose appearance is familiar to me. I may then wonder 'Who is this man?', which generally amounts to 'Where and when did I see this man?' And, as the result either of a 'broadening' of the image or of the stimulation of certain propositional memories, the answer comes to me: 'Yesterday, coming out of the flat downstairs'. The recognition may come immediately, or it may take time, or it may not come at all. It may be incomplete; I may, for instance, remember where I saw him but not when.

[1] I feel, however, that this is doing some violence to the word 'notice' as it is normally understood. Perhaps 'register' would be a better term since it has less 'mental' association.

This all seems exactly similar to what would have happened had I passed him in the street instead of having an image of him—except, it might be objected—that what is being recognized is an image and not a man. But is this really so? In both cases the person I am identifying is the man who lives in the flat below mine. The only difference is that one time he is within my sight, the other time he is not. If we are to call one of these cases recognizing an image (which amounts, on the view I have expressed, to recognizing an imag*ing*) then what are we to say of the cases where what *is* recognized is an image or imaging? I might, for instance, amuse myself by imaging an elephant with wings, and be aware as I do so that I have produced a similar image on a previous occasion. Here I *am* recognizing an image.

Suppose we draw a distinction between recognizing and 'recognizing that'; in recognizing the man in the street I also recognize that he is the man who came out of the flat below mine yesterday. We might then say that in having the image I *recognize that* it is of this particular man.

I do not think that such a distinction would help us because it simply robs 'recognize' of any special force, and in any case it is wholly arbitrary. For what is my original recognition of the man but the recognition *that* I have encountered him before? And wherein is this different from the initial familiarity of my memory-image? If we maintain that recognizing a man is something prior to any 'recognition that' about him, then, to be consistent, we would have to allow that knowing an image to be a memory-image is a basic recognition of this kind. And since it is not the recognition *of an image*, it could only be the recognition of the subject imaged.

It seems, then, that we can recognize images if we have had them or others very like them before—but only in the sense that we may recognize any of our performances when we have performed previously in the same way. We may also, if we wish, speak of recognizing things and events in their absence by means of imagery. But to do so is to destroy such distinction as there may be between 'cognize' and 'recognize', and it is much less confusing to talk simply of remembering things and also remembering further propositions about them.

We must now consider the part played by imagery (if any) in recognizing things in their presence. In Chapter III, I claimed that recognition entails some form of comparison between present and past. My claim 'This is the dog that bit me' or 'This is the same kind of car as my father's', shows me to be simultaneously aware, in some way, of both present and past instances. Now, as we have seen,[1] present sensations and memory-images do not compete, so that a simple and obvious explanation of recognition is that an appearance presented to us is found to be like an appearance we remember, that is, an image we are having of a certain past perceptual situation.

The catch in this simple explanation is that it does not seem to accord with our common experience. In most of the cases which we would tend to regard as recognition we simply name things or act in some other manner appropriate to them. This does not mean, however, that the 'explanation' must immediately be abandoned. We discovered in Chapter V that a great deal of our activity can be accounted for in terms of developed motor-capacities to respond appropriately to given stimuli; and this applies to the great bulk of our recognitions and recognitional behaviour in our daily lives, including, incidentally, our 'recognitions in absence'[2] if these are to be classed as recognitions at all.

And what of those cases where recognition is not immediate? Quite often we pause and ponder before deciding that this wool is the same colour as the socks our wives are knitting for us, or that the cat outside the window is not our neighbour's cat after all. And here, although we *could* in some cases be reciting to ourselves descriptive catalogues which we check against the present object,[3] there seems little doubt that, sometimes at least, we are comparing the perceived object with a past object remembered in imagery in exactly the way suggested.

Now, if we do in fact behave in this way when recognition is considered or deliberate, there is at least a good case for suggesting that this is the basic mode of recognition which renders possible the development of language habits and other 'motor-capacities'. I find it surprising, therefore, that Price refers to this theory as

---

[1] See Chapter VI, p. 154.
[2] i.e. recognising that this image is of so and so.
[3] This possibility is considered later in this Chapter, p. 174.

an 'extreme imagist view' and doubts whether anyone has in fact ever held it.[1]

Price supports his condemnation of the theory with a claim that it is logically impossible for recognition ever to 'depend upon' the presence of imagery. He argues that when we recognize, say, aircraft by means of a silhouette chart, the identification is valid only because we have independent grounds for believing the chart to provide accurate models. But if our exemplars are simply images in our own minds no such independent grounds for accepting them are possible. Their acceptability as 'models' must depend, then, upon their being themselves recognized as 'true copies' of the objects we are remembering. And if recognition demands the existence of a prior image for comparison, their recognition could be achieved only by comparison with some pre-image, and so on *ad infinitum*.

Now, on the view of imagery which I have put forward the 'regress' cannot ever get started. For there can be no question of 'checking the copy'; the imagery *is the memory* of the past perceptual situation itself.[2] In Chapter VI we discussed the manner in which, and the extent to which, we can know it to be a past perceptual situation and not just a 'piece of imagination'.[3] It is true that we can be mistaken about what it is we are imaging. And, equally, we can be mistaken in our recognitions. Price seems to overlook this, to talk as though our recognitional abilities were somehow infallible, and clearly they are not; we have all had the embarrassing experience of 'recognizing' somebody and finding that he is a total stranger. But so long as recognition (or what we take to be recognition) is a two-termed relationship betweeen a present object and a remembered past object, although there is always the possibility of error, there can be no question of an infinite regress. As I have pointed out, objects may be 'recognized' when we image, but only under special circumstances do we ever *recognize images*, i.e. when we recognize them *as previous images, not as previous perceptions*.

[1] See *Thinking and Experience*, p. 277.
[2] In so far as anything is recognized in the mere act of imaging it is the subject imaged. And the 'recognition' in such cases can only be of the 'motor-responsive' kind.
[3] See p. 140 ff.

I am not here claiming that we *must* accept an 'imagist theory of recognition'. Our behaviour *could be* accounted for without it—I have admitted that most of our everyday recognition is simply motor-response and there is no logical reason why the motor-response dispositions, the capacities we have for recognizing things in this immediate sense, should not have developed like any other purely physiological capacities. But I do claim that it is not a silly theory. It appears to be so only when it is taken in conjunction with the 'entity' view of imagery. I also claim that most people are capable of what I have called 'considered recognitions' and that in such cases we seem bound to admit that they are in fact comparing a remembered appearance with a presented appearance. The final decision that something is, or is not, the same shade of colour as something else was, could be made only in the light of a knowledge of the past appearance as well as the present one. Price allows that 'Recognition is only possible to a being with the capacity of *retentiveness*, whatever the right analysis of that capacity may be',[1] and in this case the only analysis which can meet the demands of the situation is a dispositional knowledge *of the appearance*. And if I have a dispositional knowledge of an appearance it is always at least empirically possible that I shall have a memory-image of that appearance. From the definition I have given of imagery as the direct memory of appearances it follows logically that a capacity to recognize *from a direct appearance* is also a capacity to have the appropriate memory-image. For the dispositional knowledge *of an appearance* can *only* be the dispositional memory of that appearance. Thus a dispositional ability to recognize A in its presence in the non-motor-responsive sense entails a dispositional ability to image A in its absense.

In stressing the fundamental importance of recognition, Price says:

'Having made my generalization, having learned to expect milk (in my actions at least) whenever tea is observed, I cannot apply what I have learned or use it as a guide to my future behaviour, unless I can also recognize further instances of tea when I meet

[1] *Thinking and Experience*, p. 58 (his italics).

them; even though I may be as incapable of conceiving tea *in abstracto*, as the cat is in Locke's opinion'.[1]

Now, if we *do* conceive something *in abstracto* then we may be able to recognize an instance of it, as it were, by description—much as the aeronautics students may 'recognize' a helicopter the first time they see one.[2] But, apart from cases of immediate motor-response, it is hard to see what the recognition of an instance *could* amount to in the absence of any such abstract concept, *except* the noting of similarities between a present appearance and a remembered past appearance.

Once we grant that we can distinguish between immediate, motor-responsive recognition and what I have called deliberate and considered recognition, and grant also that the occurrence of the latter entails at least *the capacity to have* the appropriate image, then the only really strong objection to the 'imagist theory of recognition' is that we are not generally aware, even in our most deliberate recognition, that we are having images. But imaging, like any other remembering, requires a stimulus to 'set it in motion'. And in the case of recognition, the stimulus is a present perceptual experience. It is hardly surprising, therefore, that we think of the object of our attention as not an image, but its prototype, the actual object which is persisting before our eyes.

Nobody thinks it terribly strange that in the 'helicopter case' we are at once seeing the machine and remembering a past description of it. Why then should it seem strange that in another case we may be at once seeing an object and remembering a past appearance of it? On the other hand it would be very strange indeed if, under what must be the strongest possible stimulus, the actual appearance before us of the thing itself, an image for which we have the 'capacity' failed to occur; and in fact it *is* surprising when we fail to recognize something or someone we 'ought to' recognize.

Further, the fact that we often at once recognize a man and notice that he is in some way different—has shaved his moustache for instance (though we had never 'noted to ourselves' that he

---

[1] *Ibid*, p. 43 (his italics). Price is considering the case of a cat which has come to expect milk when it sees people preparing tea.
[2] Price uses this example in *Thinking and Experience*, p. 53.

had a moustache)—suggests that such images must be occurring even when the recognition seems to be entirely spontaneous.

There is a tendency amongst philosophers to refer to images without apology or explanation as symbols. Thus A. J. Ayer writes: 'As in the case of any other symbol, it is the use we make of its qualities that matters, the construction we put upon them, not these qualities themselves',[1] and in his description of what he regards as 'the Imagist Theory of Thinking' Price writes: 'Mental images are the primary symbols, and all other symbols are secondary and derivative'.[2] I want to suggest that an image is not, and cannot be, a symbol. If it be protested that it is a 'natural symbol' in that it symbolizes by resemblance, not by any set of rules, I would suggest that 'natural symbol' is, in any case, a contradiction in terms as the words are normally used. There is a distinction which can be drawn between symbols, phenomena specifically (and arbitrarily) made to stand for other phenomena, and signs, phenomena which simply lead us to think of or expect other phenomena. But I am not here concerned with this distinction. My argument is that both symbolising and signifying are three-termed relationships—A signifies or symbolizes B *to C*— and once we reject the 'entity' view of imagery we simply cannot maintain that *an image* is a symbol or a sign either of a past event or of a kind or class of entities. What we contemplate when we image is the appearance presented by the past event itself (though we may take it to be some other past event, i.e. we may make an error in 'locating' the image). This is not to deny that an image can be *made to act* as a sign (and thereby made into a symbol)— *anything* can be made to act as a sign. But when this occurs it is a sign for one thing, an image of another.

Price speaks of such cases as 'metaphorical imagery', his assumption being that it is the imagery which 'stands for' something other than what is being imaged. 'An example of a *metaphorical* image would be an image of a lion which is used, not for thinking about lions, but for thinking about courage. It is possible that some of our verbal metaphors, even some which are now *cliches* like 'the ship of state' may have originated in this way'.[3] The only

[1] *The Problem of Knowledge*, p. 158.   [2] *Thinking and Experience*, p. 239.
[3] *Ibid*, p. 295 (his italics).

thing I wish to object to here is the suggestion that it is the image which is a sign or symbol of courage, whereas in fact it is *the lion which is imaged* which is the symbol of courage. To think of courage we think of a lion, and our thinking of it may take the form of imagery.

But according to Price the 'Imagist Theory' holds that in all cases images are the only true symbols, and that, although words do have a meaning, 'they have it only indirectly, as substitutes for images. These substitutes are needed because words can be manipulated more quickly and easily than images can'.[1] But they have, so the theory is said to maintain, only a temporary licence—they are meaningful only so long as they *could be* cashed for the images of what they stand for.

Now, the most damaging criticism of such a theory would be that many words stand for concepts which are simply not imageable because they are wholly relational, and therefore derived *through* rather than *in* sense-perception. This difficulty being well known and widely accepted, Price does not elaborate it. Instead he develops at length an argument designed to show that even for the consideration of 'qualities' and 'entities' the traditional imagist theory is not tenable. But he is arguing *only against* this 'traditional theory' which treats imagery as a combination of 'entity symbols' (like words) by which we identify and classify objects.

Now, I do not want to claim that he is arguing against a 'straw man' of his own creation. There may well be some philosophers against whom his arguments are most damaging. But I do claim that his argument in no way affects the 'imagist theory of memory' (if it should be so called) which I am here putting forward. When Price maintains that the imagist is wrong to assume that 'thinking can only be in touch with reality if it is a kind of inspection',[2] he is taking this to mean an inspection *of* images, not an inspection of past reality itself *in* imagery. And his argument quite fails to take account of the distinction between the appearances presented to us and our perceptual interpretations, definitions, and descriptions of those appearances, (although this is, in effect, the distinction he himself has made between 'primary' and 'secondary' recognition).[3]

[1] *Thinking and Experiance*, p. 239.
[2] *Ibid*, p. 262.
[3] See Chapter II of *Thinking and Experience*, p. 44 ff.

The claim central to his argument is that an image cannot be essential for thinking of what is absent since we can exemplify a concept in many ways other than by imagery—by making a model or a drawing for instance. And 'if it be objected that one has to have a mental image first, in order to produce the model or drawing, we must reply that this is both false and vicious in principle. It is false in fact. If I am asked to draw a hexagon, I may have an image first, especially if I am somewhat uncertain what a hexagon looks like. But it is not true that I *must* have one. . . . And if such comparison with an image blueprint were indeed indispensable, how about the production of the image blueprint itself? Should we not be driven to say that it too could only be produced if we have a super-blueprint to copy it from, and to guide us in detecting and correcting any defects it may have?'[1]

Let us look at the 'false in fact' claim first. If Price means that, being unable to remember what a hexagon looks like, he may, (though he need not), consult his image of a hexagon to find out what it looks like, then clearly he is simply wrong. If he did not remember what it looked like he *could not have* an image of it.[2] It would be like saying 'I couldn't remember his name so I consulted my memory of it'. If he means only that one way, though not the only way, of trying to remember it would be trying to image it, then, in the case of the hexagon, I agree with him. In fact, if I did remember what a hexagon looked like, i.e. had a memory of its 'look' in imagery, this may (though it may not—compare the barred gate case) assist me to remember that it is a six-sided figure. But there is a confusion here between remembering a 'look' and remembering a proposition. I agree that I can remember the fact that a hexagon is a six-sided figure without any image at all—and, remembering it, can draw a hexagon—but this is only because what I am remembering is not the appearance of an individual but a formal relationship quite simply definable in words. If I were to set out, instead, to draw from memory a picture of my friend John, with a certain peculiar facial expression he sometimes has, the story would be very different. For then I *would* be concerned

---

[1] *Thinking and Experience*, p. 256 (his italics).
[2] I am assuming here that 'looks like' is being used in its popular sense, not in the special sense (as distinct from 'how it looks') in which I use it later in this chapter.

with a particular appearance which would defy any attempt at 'complete description', not simply with an instance of a particular quantitative relationship. Price fails to make this important distinction. He seems to assume that since the occurrence of imagery is not essential for *all* thinking and remembering it cannot be essential for *any* thinking or remembering.

When we turn to his argument that it is vicious in principle the charges made simply do not apply to my view that imagery is indispensable for a certain kind of remembering, the remembering of appearances, however damaging they may be to the 'traditional imagist theory'. My reply is the same, in effect, as I made to similar charges against the 'Imagist Theory of Recognition'.[1] There can be no question of an infinite regress of the images; our imaging simply is our remembering the appearance that was presented to us by the thing or event. To the extent that the image is 'imperfect' our memory is imperfect as to the past presented appearance, however perfect it may be at the propositional or descriptive level. And, in so far as we are concerned with appearances, it must remain imperfect—unless and until the imagery itself is 'perfected'.

We now come to the distinction which is central to my view of imagery, and thereby to my view of memory, a distinction which has been foreshadowed, I trust, in everything that I have said to date. This distinction is that between *how a thing looks*, smells, sounds and so on, and *what it looks like*, smells like, sounds like and so on. To quote William James: 'The best taught blind pupil ... yet lacks a knowledge which the least instructed seeing baby has. They can never show him what light is in its "first intention"; and the loss of that sensible knowledge no book learning can replace'.[2] It is this 'first intention' which is *how* a thing looks. And the extraordinary difficulty in talking about it is that, whilst we *know* how it looks, in the sense of experiencing its 'look', we can describe it only in terms of *what it looks like*.[3] But, whilst the car standing opposite looks like thousands of other cars in many respects, and unlike them in others, *how it looks* is something quite peculiar to itself. Or rather, it is peculiar to a

---

[1] See p. 165.   [2] *Principles of Psychology*, Vol. 2, p.4.
[3] Cf. Wittgenstein—*Philosophical Investigations*, Pt.1, para. 78, p. 36c—We can know, but cannot say, how a clarinet sounds.

relationship between itself and myself, the viewer. How something looks refers only to the appearance *it* presents; what it looks like refers to its resemblances to countless other things. And, quite plainly, there must be *some* registering of how a thing looks in order that the thing's 'looks' can be assimilated to those of anything else.[1]

Price is quite right when he says 'One man can describe his visual images to another. He may describe them in great detail, and he may be understood'.[2] But when he continues 'You cannot be acquainted with my visual images; but you may know them by description if you have images yourself' he is obscuring a very important distinction. He should say 'You may know *about* them'. For it is not simply a matter of your not being able to be acquainted with my images because they happen to be mine and not yours. In this sense you cannot be acquainted with my visual perceptions, but if you and I stand successively in the same place facing the same motionless scene, then we may well be satisfied that we have enjoyed effectively similar visual perceptions. It is reasonable to assume that since we both have equivalent sense-organs which were stimulated by the same external causes in viewing the scene, we each learnt independently *how it looked*. And, under these circumstances we *would* subsequently 'know each other's imagery' if we agreed that we were both imaging that scene as we had seen it. But this is not a common situation. The 'absolute privacy' of most imagery arises from *two* facts; remembering how a thing looked, like perceiving how it looks, is a unique experience quite distinct from any catalogue of descriptive terms; and remembering, *unlike perceiving*, is not dependent upon any present public object. Philosophers have not altogether ignored the distinction between how a thing looks and what it looks like—the ways in which its appearance can be classified. Chisholm, for instance, writes:[3]

'The man in charge of the stage lighting will be concerned not with the actual colours of the settings but with the ways in which they appear under certain conditions. And philosophers and psychologists, studying perception, may be concerned with the

---

[1] This does not mean, however, that the 'registering' is itself necessarily a 'mental activity'.
[2] *Thinking and Experience*, p. 154.
[3] *Perceiving*, p. 161.

nature of the appearances rather than with the objects which appear'.

And von Leyden asserts that 'self-centredness ... is implicit in every recollection, at any rate in those cases where we remember *how* something took place, though not perhaps always in those where we remember *that* something took place'.[1]

Yet no-one seems to have observed, or if observing to have felt it worth remarking, that this 'how it looks' is, at the memory level, the peculiar province of imagery.

No descriptive catalogue can ever give direct knowledge of how something looks. But it does not follow from this that such a catalogue can never serve to *identify* that thing for all practical purposes. It would be wrong to suppose that the ability to describe some past event is *prima-facie* evidence for the existence of an image of it. Benjamin seems at least to be attributing this view to others when he says: 'It is a genuine puzzle sometimes to know what is to count as an image. For instance, what the writer *presumes* is his memory-image of the High from Magdalen Bridge is so fleeting, blurred and thin that, if, as it were, it could be captured for the requisite time, it would undoubtedly prove impossible to draw it; yet he can describe the view to himself and others. Would this count as an image, a reliving? One tends to put an end to such a question, I think, by wearily agreeing that it *must* be an image'.[2] I agree that if he has an image he has an image, albeit a fleeting, blurred and thin one. But his ability to describe the view in no way entails his actually having an image of that view at the time, and few, if any, imagists have ever maintained that it does. It entails only that he has *either* a good memory for descriptive propositions (which might have been learnt from any source, not necessarily his own experience) *or* a memory-image of the view.

Thus Russell, who states that he is a poor visualizer, says: 'When now I meet a man and wish to remember his appearance, I find the only way is to describe him in words while I am seeing him, and then remember the words'.[3] He admits that this method is unsatisfactory if 'Two men having these characteristics are present at once'. 'In this respect', he says, 'a visualizer would have

---

[1] *Remembering*, p. 78 (his italics).
[2] 'Remembering' *Mind* Vol. LXV, 1956, p. 320 (his italics).
[3] *An Outline of Philosophy*, p. 195.

the advantage of me'. But he claims: 'Nevertheless, if I had made my verbal inventory sufficiently extensive and precise, it would have been pretty sure to answer its purpose'.

Of course, if the description *were sufficiently* extensive it *would* answer the purpose. But how extensive must that be? As the police know well enough, a couple of good photographs of a wanted man may be worth more than a description a mile long of his visual appearance. A great many men might still answer the description, but the chances are that one man, and one only, would match the photographs. And why does Russell say 'unless two men having these characteristics are *present at once*'? We do not use our memories of people only for identifying them when we meet them. Furthermore, if we take seriously what he has said of himself, even when one of the two men answering the same description appeared by himself, Russell would still not know who it was, even though he might have known the man well for a considerable time.

Since it seems improbable that Russell is in fact incapable of distinguishing between his acquaintances, either when he meets them or when he just thinks about them, we must suppose either that he makes very careful descriptions indeed to himself and is fortunate in that these never coincide, or that verbal descriptions *augment* his imagery rather than that they *replace* it—despite his claim, 'I do not think there is anything in memory that absolutely demands images as opposed to words'.[1] Of these two possibilities the latter seems to me to be the more probable.

I must grant, however, that wherever distinguishing relational features exist it is possible, in principle at least, to isolate and describe them, however difficult this may sometimes be in practice. But what of the case where the distinguishing feature is a quality rather than a relation? (What Locke would have termed a secondary quality). To take the obvious example: How is it that I can now remember that the car which stood outside my window a while ago was a different shade of green from the one that stood there yesterday? I did not note this fact at the time, and I do not know any names for either of the shades. Even without names for the shades I could have noted, say, that one was like the colour of peas and the other was like the colour of yew trees, and I could

[1] *An Outline of Philosophy*, p. 196.

now be reasoning that they were not, therefore, the same shade. But this only moves the problem a stage further back; for how was I able to note these likenesses when there were neither peas nor yew trees present to my senses? And how do I know the different shades of peas and yew trees in the absence of these objects *in a way that enables me to compare them*?

Surely we cannot seriously suggest that, unless I have noted to myself the names for two different shades of colour at the times of perceiving them, I cannot ever compare them in memory except by means of a complex network of propositions of the kind 'A is the same colour as B', 'C is a different colour from D', 'D is rather like B', which I have framed on various occasions when two or more coloured objects were present together for my inspection. Yet this seems to be the only way in which shades of colour could be remembered by describable relational features. The only alternative I can conceive is that I know that the two remembered shades were different, or that they were the same, simply because I now remember *how* each of them looked, i.e. I now have memory-images of them both.

If we accept this last alternative, then it seems to follow that images of the same (organic) kind *are* entertained simultaneously.[1] Perhaps I *could be* forming some propositional description of the relationship of one imaged colour to some presently perceived colour, and then checking the other imaged colour against this description; but in fact I am satisfied that I am not doing this. If, then, as I have maintained, *how* the colour looked is knowable *only in imagery*, the two images *must* be simultaneous. For if I had the images in chronological succession, then, as soon as I had one, and thereby knew how *it* looked, I should have ceased to have the other and thereby ceased to know[2] how *it* looked. This would render impossible any comparison of the 'look' of the one with the 'look' of the other. The two 'looks' could, of course, combine in a kind of composite image. But I would still have to be conscious of having two distinct memories, not a single 'imagination-image'.

I have claimed that there is a large and important area of our memory (and our imagination) which is solely the province of

[1] This question was discussed in Chapter VI. See p. 151 ff.
[2] In the 'occurrent sense', which is what we are here concerned with.

imagery. This is the memory of presented appearances as such, and, at the introspective level, it is the final court of appeal for all our memory-claims. What are we to say, then, about these people, including many of Galton's correspondents, who seem to be quite normal in every way, and yet simply deny that they ever have images at all? There seem to be three possible alternatives:

(1) They lead what would seem to be strangely empty mental lives (in the way that we might feel that congenitally blind and deaf people must lead empty mental lives). And, further, they can achieve only a very poor degree of certainty about matters of past fact in the absence of supporting testimony or 'cause/effect' evidence, since their memories, being all propositional, would not permit of any individual reinterpretations. If their remembered propositions were wrong—that is, if they were formed as the result of misjudgments about perceptual situations—they would have no means of setting them right so they would have to remain wrong for ever.[1] Or

(2) They are lying in order to pose as 'superior intellects' or simply to be perverse. Or

(3) They have misunderstood the nature of imagery, and their denial that they have images is the result of their misunderstanding, much as the denial by a respectable housewife that she has erotic impulses would be the result of her misunderstanding.

I discount possibility (2), and I am naturally loath to accept possibility (1). I shall therefore begin with the third possibility. Now, I myself have no experience of eidetic imagery, though I am happy to believe that others have. And if I conceived of imagery as necessarily the same kind of thing as eidetic imagery—in Price's words, 'something over against us or presented to us—and something other than the material object or physical event, real or fictitious, which we are trying to envisage'[2]—then I should have to place myself in the ranks of the non-imagers. This is exactly the misunderstanding which A. J. Ayer seems to be guilty of when he says 'I remember that a moment ago I ran my hand over the surface of my writing table: I remember *how it felt* in the sense that I can give a description of the feeling, but I do not

[1] The reinterpretation and 'correction' of memories is dealt with in Chapter III, p. 55 and Chapter IV, p. 99ff. I say *individual* reinterpretations' to allow for the 'football team example' given in Chapter IV, p. 91.

[2] *Thinking and Experience*, p. 248. Note that Price is referring to ordinary memory-imagery, not to eidetic imagery.

have any tactual image of it'.[1] Now, unless he accompanied the gesture, Russell fashion, with a catalogue of descriptive phrases—which seems at least highly improbable—his assertion *must* be false according to my definition. For to remember how it felt in a way that makes possible a *subsequent* description *is* to have imagery, and in this case the imagery would be tactual.

It may be protested here that I am simply applying my own definition in order to convict Ayer of error. But the only point I am interested in making here is that we do have a unique experience, the direct memory of appearances, the memory of *how* things looked, felt and so on, and that this does play a central role in our remembering of events, *and in our achieving certainty that we are remembering events*. I call this kind of remembering 'imagery' because this seems the natural thing to call it: if someone else wants to reserve the term 'imagery' for something like eidetic imagery, well and good. Subject to this reservation Ayer can make his denial without contradiction; but he must find some other term to cover what I am calling imagery. He must not ignore its existence. And he can call it simply 'describing' only if he is prepared to claim that he *never has* perceived, or remembered, *how* anything looks, sounds, and so on, without actually describing it to himself or to somebody else—and that his ability to distinguish remembering reported events from remembering witnessed events rests wholly upon independent evidence and testimony about his own past history, or the highly unlikely inclusion of the proposition 'I am here' in what is being remembered.

For obvious reasons it is hard to see how we could 'demonstrate' or 'ostensify' this unique experience to someone who denied having it. Suppose a man, blind from birth, knew and used the word 'smile' but claimed that he himself never smiled. To convince him that he was wrong you would have to say to him each time you caught him smiling: 'That's it, you're doing it now', and in time he would probably get the idea of what a smile is; not the impressive affair he had imagined it to be, merely a very mild (for him, kinaesthetic) experience he had hardly even noticed.

But with the man who claims that he never images the position is more difficult. Not only can he not see *our* imaging; we cannot see his either. The best we can do is to say to him something like: 'Think of your wife—think of her smiling with that particular

[1] *The Problem of Knowledge*, p. 136 (*my* italics).

quizzical expression she sometimes has', or even: 'Remember the colour of your new curtains—not the manufacturer's fancy name for the colour, or a catalogue of other things the same colour, or whether you like it or not—the actual colour itself'. And if he says 'Yes, I am doing that' we can tell him that he *is imaging*. His reaction may be like that of the blind man—'Oh, if that's all it is, then of course I image'.

However, if he stoutly maintains that he is having no experience which he can distinguish from the construction of descriptive propositions, or if he finds himself simply unable to perform the tasks asked of him, then we must, however sadly, revert to the first alternative. We can allow that his propositional memories are, in general, adequately supported by further propositional memories, and that in most cases, if challenged, he can look to testimony or cause/effect evidence to support his claims. But we should nevertheless be well advised before accepting his memory-claims about past events to check very carefully his reasons for making those claims—especially if they contain any wealth of detail.

THE ACTUAL CHARACTERISTICS OF MEMORY-IMAGES

In Chapter VI we considered what kind of objects images are of, and we have now discussed the functions imagery performs. But before concluding this chapter we should look at imagery itself and consider certain questions about what kind of experience imaging is.

Images do not occupy places. Since we have decided that what we call an image is just a particular kind of memory, the memory of how things looked, sounded, and so on, it makes no more sense to ask 'Where are images?' than to ask 'Where are memories?' Our insistence upon the existence and importance of imagery does not involve us in any mysterious speculations about other dimensions of space, nor are we obliged to make any such empty assertions as 'an image is where it is'. Imagery 'occurs in' our minds, and something correlated with it no doubt occurs in our brains, and the event imaged occurred, if at all, in physical space at a past physical time. But, even though imagery is a performance rather than a set of entities, there are still some questions about its characteristics which we may reasonably ask. What are the relationships of size and position between the scene as imaged and the scene as originally perceived? Do we necessarily image the *whole* scene as it was perceived? Must the original colour, or any colour at all, be reproduced in the imagery?

Ideally, when we remember a scene in imagery the parts of that scene as imaged are in the same spatial relationship to each other as they were in the scene as perceived. There is, however, as we considered in Chapter VI, an imagination element in nearly all imagery,[1] and this may well manifest itself as a disproportion between the parts as imaged, especially if some particular feature is the focal point of our attention.

It has been held by some philosophers that there must be a spatial relationship of some kind between an image and a presently perceived scene, since it is possible to 'project' an image into an actual view (although this neither becomes nor obscures any part of that view). For instance, it is claimed that I could image a cat *as* sitting on the mat which is now before me. Now, there is no doubt that we often talk as if such 'projection' were a possible and quite normal activity. But 'projecting images' is certainly nothing like projecting a picture of a cat on to the mat with a cinematograph. Indeed there is really nothing to be projected. When we attempt an analysis of what is happening there seem to be two possibilities only, neither of which involves anything we would wish to call a spatial relationship between an image and a present perception. It is possible that:

(1) I have an image of a cat and I conceive the possibility of this cat being on the mat which I am in fact looking at; or

(2) In addition to my perceiving the actual mat on which there is no cat, I am also imaging an exactly similar mat (together with its visible surroundings) on which there sits a cat.

Now, in the second case, would the mat, as imaged, be the same size as the mat as actually perceived? It is clear that we *can be* talking only of 'visible size', and since in this case it is my perceiving the mat which has stimulated me to image it, the chances are that it will be 'the same size'. A memory-image may be said to be as visibly large or small as its object as originally perceived, even though it does not occupy, as does an after-image, any part of the

[1] See p. 140.

total field of vision. There is nothing deep or mysterious in this. It simply means that if I saw my friend twenty paces away from me, I image him *as if he were* twenty paces away from me. To test this, try to remember a favourite snapshot in imagery; you will find that it is always imaged as if it were about eighteen inches away, the distance at which we normally look at snapshots. By an effort it may be possible to 'enlarge it', but once we do this we are immediately conscious of the entry of 'imagination elements' into the imagery; we feel ourselves 'in control'.

Thus, a memory-image 'covers' only that portion of the possible visual field which was covered by the object imaged in the original perception of it. And since it is possible, in principle, to have a visual memory-image of a complete visual field, a thing we rarely if ever in fact have, it follows that there generally is, as it were, a 'blank surround' to the image—much as there is to a particular object looked at through a telescope. Now, when a particular area or object is detached from its setting, we are aware of the 'blank surround' and of its potential occupants, and I suggest that it is this awareness which provides the spatial element (there is also the temporal element) of that 'context' which is distinctive of the memory-image, known as such, and determines the 'expansion' of the image.

Now, what is visible is, *ipso facto*, coloured, and it seems to follow that visual imagery must likewise involve colour. In *The Mind and Its Place in Nature* Broad asserts:[1] 'A visual sensum must in fact have some perfectly determinate shade of colour; and so must a visual image'. It would be very difficult to deny this claim, but nevertheless it raises certain questions: Need a memory-image include the same colours as the perceived scene? Need the image include any chromatic colour? Can we make a distinction between colour and mere visible variety?

Of course imagery *can* include exact shades of colour; I have argued that to remember a particular shade of colour *is* to image it. But, if what is being remembered, or our particular interest in what is being remembered, is the shapes and relative sizes involved in the appearance, colour seems to be no more necessary than in a newspaper photograph. We do not feel that the picture in the paper is not a true representation of the Prime Minister because

[1] *The Mind and Its Place in Nature*, p. 258.

it shows his face as grey and not pink, though we might well do so if the rest of the picture were in colour. Whether or not our visual imagery always does involve chromatic colour is an empirical question we should each have to answer for ourselves; there seems to be no reason why it must do so.

This does not, however, count against Broad's claim that an image must have some perfectly determined shade or shades of colour. The 'black and white' picture is intelligible only so long as it is a kind of 'translation' of the multi-coloured appearance, and blacks, whites, and greys must themselves be 'perfectly determinate'. It is true that our concern is with the relationship between the shades rather than with the shades themselves, but whatever is related must be one shade or another. Notwithstanding this, it seems to me that I can image in considerable detail a framed photograph of my father in military uniform, yet I would find it very hard to say whether I am imaging it as 'black and white' or as 'sepia'. Possibly I am imaging it as both simultaneously.

In another odd case, I remember a particular man's voice, i.e. remember in auditory imagery *how* it sounds, yet without remembering it as making any specific utterance. There is at least an initial puzzle about both these cases; the 'voice case', I feel, is simply an extreme case, and an auditory one, of 'remembering the "look" of the gate'.[1] But in the 'photographic case' what is vague is the 'look' itself, not the relationships disclosed by that 'look', and this seems to demand for its explanation an investigation of what is usually called 'generic imagery'.

Thinking and remembering in imagery, as this performance is traditionally understood, seems to demand that the image be at once sufficiently like the original perception to be identifiable, and sufficiently unlike it to be productive or reminiscent of the concept or idea of a continuous thing in the world. This problem is often magnified by the assumption that an image is a kind of symbol for a class-concept, an assumption which I have denied. Having an image of a dog *may* lead us to think of dogs in general, but there is no reason why it *should* do so. And certainly I do not 'use the image' to think about the concept dog, although I might well regard my having an image of Rover as my thinking about Rover as a creature in the world, especially if the image I have of

[1] See p. 161.

him is not specifically identified by me with any one occasion in his life. In practice I find that my own 'standard images' do tend to be of 'fixed instances'. Thus the images I have of people are frequently in fact images of their photographs. For obvious reasons these photographs can more easily be 'imprinted on the memory' than can any single fleeting appearance of the people themselves. Similarly, the images I have of places are most frequently of the oft-repeated views of those places from certain vantage points: houses from their front gates, valleys from the nearby hills we climb to look at them, and so on.

Nevertheless, we do have memory-images of sights seen only once and only for a moment (else our memories of events would necessarily be wholly propositional). We also *do seem* to have images of particulars which have been built up over a series of different, *and differing*, viewings, and it is these that are felt to be at once both like and unlike any one single 'viewing'. We might want to say that such images are vague in a peculiar way. But we have to decide what this peculiar way is. We have discussed the way that one kind of vagueness permits us to remember the 'look' of the gate without knowing the number of its bars.[1] Now we must consider how another kind of vagueness may also permit us to remember the 'look' of the gate open, half-open or shut, all seemingly at once. For we do seem able, in some way, to do this.

Russell seems to treat vagueness as a very simple and obvious concept when he contends that *the* vagueness of imagery not only fully explains this strange ability, but also 'supplies an answer to Hume's query: Could you imagine a shade of colour that you had never seen, if it was intermediate between two very similar shades that you had seen? The answer is that you could not form so precise an image, even of a colour that you had seen, but that you could form a vague image, equally appropriate to the shade that you had not seen and to the two similar shades that you had seen'.[2]

I believe that, in so far as this is a statement of fact, it is wrong. Unless we beg the question by making precision an empirically unattainable ideal, then why does Russell assert that you *can not* form a precise image of the required shade of colour? It would be most surprising if many painters and other people whose job it is to match colours do not do so regularly, and I am satisfied

[1] See p. 161.   [2] *Human Knowledge—Its Scope and Limits*, p. 125.

that I not infrequently do so myself. If we rephrase the question as 'Could you form *as precise* an image of a colour you had never seen as you could of a colour you had seen?', my own answer would be an unequivocal 'No'. What we *can* have is a *concept* of such a shade; the use of the word 'intermediate' shows this to be possible; but we cannot have an image of it for the very reasons which led Hume to regard the 'possibility' as a puzzle. The problem only arises because people have overlooked the fact that colours, like sounds, form a natural scale. The missing shade is not, therefore, a completely unknown quantity like the blue rumped gnurgle.[1]

I said 'in so far as it is a statement of fact', because 'vague' is itself a vague word.[2] If we are to decide what, if anything, permits us to image 'all the positions of the gate at once' we must seek some much more specific explanation.

There are several possibilities and they are generally classified together under the heading 'Generic Imagery'. Firstly, there is the notion of a composite image, rather like a composite photograph, that is, a number of photographs taken on the same film and superimposed on each other. Clearly we cannot take this too literally, for unless the separate objects were extremely similar in outline the resultant picture would be simply an undecipherable mess. The appearances involved must be at least sufficiently alike to be compatible, e.g. if the composite image is of a man's face they must be all frontface or all sideface; a combination would not be possible. And if they were sufficiently close—say, several shots of the same face with just slightly varied expressions the need for the composite would be lost. For any one of the pictures would serve equally well—except as regards the expression—and this would be the one point wherein the composite would be blurred and useless. With colour the position would be just as bad. A yellow surface superimposed on a blue surface would give a green surface, not a surface that was somehow both yellow and blue at once.

Suppose we suggest that instead of superimposing each entire image upon the others, we 'select' and combine parts of each to make up a composite which is, as it were, a single image drawn from many sources. This seems quite possible. But the image

[1] See p. 140.
[2] This point is made by J. L. Austin. See *Sense and Sensibilia*, Oxford Clarendon, 1962, p. 125.

itself would still be specific and, being drawn from many sources, it would lack the authority of a memory-image; whereas what we want is an image which is *not* specific and yet *has* that authority. Nor would this composite be representative of the continuous object except in the way that a piece of china made up from bits of different articles in a teaset would be representative of the teaset.

There is however one other possibility which Price, amongst others, has advanced. 'When I think about some object or class of objects in an imagy manner, I am not restricted to using just one single image. I might use a series of different images. Again, the images which I use need not be static'.[1] Thus by a series of different images of the same object, drawn possibly, but not necessarily, from a perceived sequence of events, we can image, as it were, all round the object in both space and time.

I would also add that it is by no means certain that this would have to be a series in the chronological sense. We could find no reason to deny (and some empirical reason to assert) the possibility of having several simultaneous images; why then should we not have several simultaneous images of different 'aspects' of the same object?

From this analysis of 'generic imagery' it follows that '*a* generic image' is a misleading expression. What we have is a number of complementary images or imagings which act jointly to exemplify or bring about in us a general idea or concept of a continuous individual entity or a set of characteristics. The images are, as Berkeley and Hume held them to be, the particular re-presentations to us in memory of associated sets of particular past sense-experiences. Out of them concepts can arise, and by means of them concepts can be checked and defined. I suggest that, because of this, people have been led to use the expression 'generic image' for what is in fact a concept in the old-fashioned, Lockean sense.

A memory which consisted wholly of imagery would not be so utterly meaningless as a 'perception' which consisted wholly of sense-experience, since it *would be possible* to form concepts, with the aid of present perception, from series of occurrent images. It would nevertheless be a very limited and strange memory—the kind of memory we are disposed to attribute to 'lower animals'.

[1] *Thinking and Experience*, p. 272.

On the other hand, a memory with no imagery would be, as we have seen, both sterile and inconclusive. Language assists the development of complex forms of thinking; imagery provides the constant link between that development and our own past perceptual experience, our actual apprehension of the world about us.

CHAPTER VIII

CONCLUSIONS

RECAPITULATION

It may be remembered that in Chapter I I made the point that the question to be answered is not: Should we trust our memories? but: How is it that our memories are in fact trustworthy when they seem, at every stage, to be open to error? At all times we are aware of a great deal of the experience we have had in the past, and aware of it in a way that gives us confidence in every way as great as the confidence we feel about our present surroundings. Yet in no case, it seems, can we prove to ourselves, or to other people, that things did occur as we remember them to have occurred, in the way we feel that we can prove our assertions about our present surroundings—by pointing to them, knocking against them, measuring them, or tasting and smelling them.

Of course, one of the ways by which we prove the existence of our present surroundings—the prediction of effects which will arise out of them—is open to us, on some occasions at least, for establishing the truth of our memory-claims. But here we are not really proving anything about memory, only about matters of fact: the rose which is evidence for the accuracy of my memory-claim that I planted a rose could have been put there by somebody else, or could have grown wild; the crater which reassures me that there was an explosion could have been made by an excavator. In any case confirmations of this sort do not generally create memory-beliefs, they merely reinforce our confidence if we are doubtful whether we really are remembering, and assist us to convince other people who may be inclined to doubt our memory reports.

The 'memory-experience', the certainty we feel about matters of past fact whether or not there is any 'objective evidence', suggests very strongly that in some way we actually 'look at' past events or re-live our past experiences as part of our present experience. But the difficulty is to give a sense to this which is not purely metaphorical. When we look at something we are directly acquainted with it, and in this direct acquaintance lies our authority to make confident assertions about it. Our task, therefore, is to show that in memory, or in some kinds of memory, we have the same authority. In short, we must explain how, and when, we are directly acquainted with the past when we remember.

Firstly, the past with which I am directly acquainted must be my own past. It would be blatantly absurd to suggest that when I remember that the Battle of Waterloo was fought in 1815 I am somehow directly acquainted with that battle itself. It is not so absurd, however (though it may well be false) to claim that I am directly acquainted with the occasion of my learning this piece of history. I am maintaining that there is a distinction we must allow between our actual remembering in the sense of reproducing or reporting something learnt or discovered in the past, and our knowing what is so produced or reported to be a true account of a past happening. I have therefore endeavoured to show that although it is perfectly natural and intelligible to talk of remembering individuals or remembering propositions or remembering how to do things as distinct kinds of remembering, the *memory authority* of all these rests upon, and must ultimately be explained in terms of, remembering past events in our lives, events which we ourselves experienced or witnessed, so that the citing of such experienced and remembered events provides the terminal point of effective challenge to all our memory-claims.

I have argued that to remember an individual is either to remember a particular appearance or a series of appearances which *we regard as being* of the same individual, or else to remember an event or series of events in which that individual figures.[1] Thus to say that what I am remembering is an individual, not an event, is only to say something about my point of interest in my memory. The same memory which I now regard as 'of my uncle' I *could equally well* regard as 'of the time my uncle fell down the steps' or 'of the time my uncle wore a bowler hat'.

When we turn to 'propositional memories' it is vital to bear in mind the distinction I made between remembering propositions and remembering *in* propositions.[2] All our remembering, in so far as it is expressed in memory-claims, is *in* propositions. To *remember propositions* is to remember the beliefs we have held in the past about matters of fact—whether we announced them publicly or

[1] See Chapter III, p. 52.   [2] See Chapter III, p. 60 ff.

not—as distinct from remembering the events, our perception of which led us to hold those beliefs. (And as distinct also from remembering the sentences in which the propositions were expressed.)

Clearly, a proposition is not an event in the world. Thinking—producing propositions—is, of course, a mental event, and mental events as well as physical ones may be remembered. But in remembering them we are not acquainted with a past public event; we are only presented with evidence that we *have been* so acquainted. And the past public event with which we were acquainted *need not be* the event which the proposition is about. It may simply provide evidence for the truth of the proposition. It frequently happens that we remember a proposition though we have forgotten, or are not presently recalling, or never even witnessed, the event to which it refers, though it is always possible, of course, if we *did* witness the event, that we may remember it, or some part of it, along with the proposition. For instance, I remember that as an infant I lived in West Hartlepool; I can remember several occasions of producing a Birth Certificate which showed West Hartlepool as my birthplace and several conversations about my having been born there. And but for these memories my claim—I remember that I once lived in West Hartlepool—would be quite unconvincing, even to myself. For *I cannot remember living in West Hartlepool*.

I spoke of reporting *or reproducing* something once learnt, or discovered, and it is the reproducing, the remembering how to do things, which, above all, has traditionally been regarded as a special case of remembering, not to be fitted into the 'perceptual mould'. My argument here is that, although it is normal practice in everyday speech to identify 'remembering how' with 'being able', there is nevertheless a distinction between them which we are all conscious of, and which we are sometimes obliged to make in order to be intelligible. And though 'being able' may well be, in many instances, a case of retentiveness, it is not the kind of retentiveness which gives rise to the remembering part of our performances. I endeavoured to show that when we use *intelligence* as the criterion of remembering how we are using that term in its basic sense—mental or mind-directed activity—not in its popular sense—effective activity. The confusion about *what is remembering* arises, as does the extension of the use of the term 'intelligent',

CONCLUSIONS

only because in fact mentally directed (memory-directed) actions are *generally* effective actions. 'Use your head' is not a pointless instruction. My claim is that remembering how to do something *is remembering* at all only in so far as it involves remembering that—remembering events and propositions. And, as we have seen, remembering propositions is itself dependent for its authority upon the memory of events.

In Chapter IV, I distinguished between our memory-claims—the propositions we produce about our past experiences—and our actual memories—the remembered propositions and occurrent imagery which constitute the 'remembering state of mind' on which those claims are based. I pointed out that, whilst it is by the former that our memories are judged to be true or false, it is from the latter, and only from the latter, that what I called the initial authority of memory can arise. *The memory-claim may refer directly to a past state of affairs in the world; the memory is always of a past state of myself—my own perceptions and judgments when confronted with that state of affairs.* Thus it is always possible, in principle at least, to amend a memory-claim in the light of a re-assessment of the memory itself without recourse to any 'external evidence'. When a man is relating what happened on some past occasion which he witnessed it is always sensible to ask him 'But what are you *actually* remembering?'.

We have already come some way towards the solution of our problem. If it be allowed: (a) that all memory-claims must be or rest upon memory-claims concerning perceived past events, and (b) that these memory-claims are based upon occurrent memories of our past states when we were confronted with these events; then, the authority we attach to all our memory-claims must derive from our ability to remember our own past states. And since these claims are always open to revision in the light of a closer scrutiny of our occurrent memories, it may well be that many of our so-called 'false memories' are not *memories* at all; they are merely false inferences from our memories of our own past states.

It may be recalled that I distinguished two kinds of error which could be avoided, or at least guarded against, by introspection. We can avoid claiming more than is warranted by the occurrent memory. We can also re-check the remembered propositions to ensure that, at the time of the perception, we were not misinterpreting the event we witnessed—provided only that we have memory-imagery of the event against which to check.

Thus our memories are open to 'checking' and reinterpretation at two points. But unless that which is being reinterpreted, the memory-image itself, is a re-presentation to us of the actual past event, and not itself an interpretation of that event, then all our reinterpretations are pointless and vain. Before we could decide whether, and in what way, our imagery does constitute such a re-presentation—a direct acquaintance with the past event—it was necessary to consider the nature and function of imagery.

I claimed that the function of imagery is to provide a direct contact with how things looked, sounded and so forth. I defined imagery, accordingly, as the direct memory of appearances, an appearance being what is presented to the senses by a physical event or object irrespective of any perceptual judgment or classification (or, in case the word 'what' should be misleading here, perhaps I should say an appearance is *the way that* or simply *how* a physical object is presented to the senses). I also claimed that we may have a disposition or capacity to image a particular appearance (whatever the physiological explanation of this may be) just as we may have the capacity to make any overt muscular movement, in response to an appropriate stimulus. The appearances 'given to us' in imagery are the same appearances as were previously 'given to us' in sensation. The objects which presented those appearances are no longer here; but the appearances never were 'here' in the sense that the objects were, so the absence of the objects does not entail that the appearance is not the same appearance.[1]

'Sensing an appearance' is not itself a cognitive operation, though it may be a pre-requisite of certain kinds of cognitive operation, e.g. perceptual judgments. To perceive is always to perceive *that* something is the case, to note a factual relationship. Because they wish to acknowledge this and still maintain that

[1] By 'same' I mean qualitatively same. On p. 195 following I argue that the notion of numerical sameness and difference cannot be applied to appearances, as distinct from 'appearings', since they are neither spatially nor temporally located.

'sensing appearances' *is something* philosophers have attempted to distinguish between 'knowledge of' and 'acquaintance with' the objective world. But the danger of making this distinction is that, having made it, there is a tendency to then apply it as though it were between two 'kinds of knowledge', when in fact it must be between knowledge and something else. For 'acquaintance with' something as a separate state, can be characterized only as a particular condition of a sentient *and conscious* being. We do not want to say that a sunflower is acquainted with the sun in this sense although it undoubtedly responds to it. And since consciousness is necessarily consciousness *of* something, 'acquaintance with' cannot occur without at least some 'knowledge of'. So, however valuable and necessary the distinction may be, for a causal explanation of perception, it has no place in an enumeration of mental conditions.

We cannot have the benefits of special use and ordinary use at once. Ordinarily we say that we are acquainted with certain facts when we have not yet decided what to make of them. But we are already allowing that we know these facts as such, that we have noticed them. And to notice something is always to notice *something about it*, even if only to notice that it is distinguishable from something else—and this is to make a perceptual observation. We cannot isolate 'objects of acquaintance' or 'pure sensations' within our actual experiences; the existence of such a 'stage' is simply an inference—and, I believe, a perfectly sound inference—from an examination of that experience, which *is of objects in certain relationships*. It is true that, since we perceive relationships, there must be elements which are related. But it is a further, and unjustified, step to say that we *must perceive the related elements as elements*. All we can claim is that they must, in some way, be 'presented to us'. To quote G. F. Stout:

'it thus appears that we can never have absolutely pure sensation, sensation absolutely devoid of meaning either original or acquired. We may even go further than this and lay it down as a general principle that sensations always have derivative meaning; for retentiveness and association operate from the very beginning of mental life. It may be urged that this cannot be the case in the earliest moments of experience. But even if we set aside what may perhaps be due to the results of ancestral experience transmitted by heredity, we have to recognize that the first instant of conscious life is only an ideal limit, which we cannot definitely mark off so as to consider it separately. Thus, even from this point of view, the concept of absolutely pure sensation is an artificial abstraction'.[1]

The point is that sensation, the set of distinct activities each causally dependent upon a particular sense-organ, is something we discover by normal perceptual means like any other of our bodily activities. It is not in itself a mental operation; it is below the level of consciousness. So let us say that it is a physiological activity, unique only in that it is *the* physiological activity out of which perceptions arise. Just as we can move our feet and know that they are moving forwards or backwards, so we can visually sense and know that we are sensing *in that* we are seeing trees and houses; 'see' is a cognitive term as we normally use it. In neither case are we conscious that the 'physical activity' *precedes* the 'mental activity'. At most we assume that it 'must do so'.

Sensation, then, is simply the physiological activity by virtue of which appearances are presented to us. And, like any physiological activity, it develops a capacity for its own repetition. Having once 'sensed an appearance' as the result of external stimulus i.e. had that appearance 'presented to us', we are physiologically competent to sense the same appearance again without having it 'presented to us' by an external object. We may be 're-acquainted' with that we were previously 'acquainted' with. But 'sensing an appearance' (or re-sensing it) is not, in itself, being aware of the appearance *of* anything. It is simply a prerequisite of such awareness. Just as the original acquaintance could occur only as an integral part of a perception, a 'knowledge of', so can the re-acquaintance (though here we speak not of perception but of memory). I am suggesting that *the appearance presented by an event is 'retained' because we have a physiological capacity for reproducing sensed appearances in imagery*, and that thereby we have the means, as a permanent physiological capacity; of making factual judgments about physical events after those events have occurred with the same right of assurance as we could have made them when the events were occurring.

Now, my contention throughout has been that the ability to

[1] *A Manual of Psychology*, p. 124.

image is simply the ability to retain and re-actualize sensed appearances; that is what I mean by calling imagery the memory of *how* things appeared. Thus *we have found in imagery*, if not a 'physical element' of the past physical event itself, at least *a physiological element of the past perception of that event*. And we have found in memory the element we were looking for which is prior to any interpretation of the event remembered. The objection that the imagery may not be of *actual* past events is anticipated by my argument that 'imagination images' *are* memory-images:[1] correctly identified, all images are seen to be memory-images.

But 'correctly identified' is a quite considerable qualification. I argued in Chapter VI that the proper question about imagery is not 'Whether this was' but 'When these were', and considered various factors which might lead us to accept a piece of imagery as a case of remembering, a presentation with the actual past. But still it may be felt that this is not enough, that we have a better right, and a different kind of right, to be sure about what is going on around us in the present than to be sure about what has gone on around us in the past. To decide what justification there may be for this feeling we need to consider 'the past' and its relationship to 'the present'.

THE PAST

There are two distinct, though obviously related, problems about the past: how we know the past when it is no longer here to be known, and how we know about such a thing as pastness at all—how we come to have our concept of temporal sequence. On the second question I believe that, subject to certain modifications, the naive view is the right one; our concept of the past originates with our own memories, as the 'home', so to speak, of the events we remember. But this presupposes that we are competent to distinguish actual happenings from imaginary happenings without recourse to any notion of a 'real past' as a criterion. It is imperative, therefore, for those who wish to deny that there is any unique memory-experience, and who wish to base their account of memory upon our knowledge of the past, i.e. our ability to report it correctly, to show that the concept of pastness could arise from present

[1] See Chapter VI, p. 140.

experience independently of memory. But before examining any of their suggestions as to how this could be, let us look at the first question: how can we know the past?

There are various ways of knowing what happened in the past: we can read about it, or be told about it, or work out what must have happened for things to be as they are now. Or we can remember our own past experiences. The first group are all quite simple and intelligible—once we understand clearly what we mean by 'the past'—and they are not directly connected with memory. We simply 'place' certain events in a former time.

But with our memories of our own experiences there is no question of *placing* events in a former time; in being remembered they are already so placed. We are aware of certain events, and at the same time aware that they belong to the past. Now, it would be possible to accept this and yet still to feel that to say that certain basic kinds of remembering directly acquaint us with the past is to make a strangely paradoxical claim. It may be felt that, taken literally, it is simply absurd—for the past is past—and, taken metaphorically, it reduces to the trivial assertion that the events we remember are always past events.

I do not believe, however, that this feeling would be justified. The 'reduction' cannot be sustained because there is a difference, however we may characterize it, between actually remembering an event and simply remembering propositions about it. Whatever it is that we are calling 'being actually presented with a past event' is at least a particular identifiable kind of remembering. The charge that the claim is absurd arises, I contend, from the confusion of 'being presented' with 'being present with', and a misunderstanding about *what* is presented in both memory and perception. We can *be present* when an event occurs, and we are then *presented with* an appearance of that event (or *by* that event). We are not presented with the event; we merely witness it. When we remember the event in imagery we are again presented with the same appearance, but this time by our own 'retentive mechanisms', whatever they be, not by a current happening in the world. If it be protested that the appearance presented is the same qualitatively but not numerically, then I ask what mere numerical difference between qualitatively similar appearances could mean. Appearances, as such, are neither spatial nor temporal though the things which present them are both. An appearance is simply how such things appear to observers. It instantiates or exemplifies a particular set of relationships within a particular sense field. If I ask *how* the Mona Lisa looks, the reply—enigmatic—makes no reference to where it is or when it is looked at. Of course, the 'how' cannot generally be put neatly into a word like this. But our *knowing* it —our being presented with it—though we might be quite unable to give any description of it at all, makes the difference between present awareness of a perceived past event and mere knowledge about it. I am not using the term 'appearance' to stand for an activity; any object which does not change presents the same appearance on any number of occasions to any number of observers who happen to be suitably placed. These presentations are numerically different, as are the 'perceptual acts' of the observers. But we are concerned with the appearance (how it appears), not the appearing (that it appears), and the only criterion of identity which can be applied, therefore, is qualitative sameness. If I may use an analogy: The same joke may be told many times by many different people but it remains the same joke. Numerical difference can apply only to the occasions of telling it.

Actual presentation with the past demands only that we be in effectively the same position as we were in at the past time for noting and identifying events which then occurred. It is surely misleading, then, to characterize direct presentation of the past in such ways as this: 'Just as it is asked whether the sense-datum is a mental representation of an external object or a constituent of that object, so it has been asked whether the memory image is a present symbol of what occurred in the past or the past event itself'.[1] To suggest that an *image* is itself a past event is an obvious absurdity. If there were some entity properly called 'an image' then obviously it would be a present 'event' not a past one. But there is nothing absurd in asking whether the appearance presented to me in memory-imagery on this present occasion is the same appearance as was presented to me in sense-perception on some past occasion. It is no more absurd than asking whether, in hearing a gramophone record, we are presented with a past performance of an orchestra, and the case for a positive reply seems somewhat stronger. For in that case it could be argued that what we are

---

[1] From an article by C. Landesman—'Philosophical Problems of Memory' *Journal of Philosophy* LIX. 3. February 1962, p. 57.

really presented with is the effect of vibrations set up by the record, whereas, once we have got rid of the 'entity image' notion, there is nothing we could be presented with in the memory case except the appearance of the event itself. If anyone should wish to push the analogy to what may be its logical conclusion, and say that we are really presented with the mnemic effects of certain of our own physiological retentive organisms reacting to a stimulus, then I have no objection—for these 'effects' simply are the presentation to us in imagery of a certain appearance which has been presented to us before.

Notwithstanding all this it is understandable that people may balk at saying that in memory we may be actually presented with the past. Very well: let us say only that in memory we have an access to the past which is effectively equivalent to the access we have to the present in perception. A case could be made out for either description, and this would simply be an argument about English usage. The important thing is not how we choose to describe the facts, but that we are clear as to what facts we are describing.

I have maintained that in imagery we are re-presented with the appearances originally presented to us by past events. When what we are remembering are propositions, these are already, as remembered, interpretations of, or inferences from, the appearances presented by past events. In his article 'The Empiricist Theory of Memory'[1] Holland cast doubt upon the possibility of making any sharp division within propositional memories between those arising from the perception of events and those arising from reports and inferences. He does, however, allow that 'There is, of course, one way in which I can recall the Rugby Match [which he had witnessed] that is not open to me in the case of the Boat Race [which he had not], and that is by picturing to myself parts of it as I saw them; and it seems likely that it is recollections in which visual imagery occurs that Woozley has mainly in mind when he segregates one sort of remembering from all others as being cognitive. Yet if this is the case, one wonders why he does not say so plainly'.

I agree that the only intelligible distinction of kind we can

[1] *Mind*, Vol. LXIII, 1954, p. 482. Holland is criticizing a distinction drawn by Woozley in his *Theory of Knowledge*.

make *within memory occurrences* is that between propositional memory and imagery. But, arising out of this is a distinction *in memory-claims*. It is based upon situations in which memory-imagery of the event claimed as remembered *could occur* and those in which it could not. The distinction is not based upon memories in which imagery *does* occur and memories in which it *does not*.

In fact, our memories of events we have actually witnessed generally include both propositions and imagery, and the essential difference between the memory of the Rugby Match and the memory of the Boat Race is that the former can be supported by the memory 'presentation' of the event itself, whilst the only 'presentations' which can support the latter are of *other* events—reports of the race in newspapers or from friends. The question: 'What is it you are actually remembering?' is here very pertinent.

Having once acquired a piece of knowledge, by whatever means, I may remember it. But if that knowledge was acquired as the direct result of my perceptual experience I have in general[1] thereby a far better warrant for certainty than if it had simply been imparted to me secondhand. In the latter case I may always suspect that my informant was mistaken or untruthful; in the former case, the more I ponder on the memory, the more likely it is that 'supporting evidence', both imagery and remembered propositions, will be forthcoming. Compare, for instance, my two memories: that Magna Carta was signed in 1215, and that I spent some time in Rio de Janeiro in my youth. In the first case I could be convinced that I had misremembered the date by exactly the same kind of means as I could be reassured that I had remembered it correctly—by historical records and the authority of experts. I may be surprised, but I would not be astonished; this is the kind of 'memory' we are used to getting wrong.

If, on the other hand, everybody I knew denied that I had ever visited Rio, I could only suppose that they were having some sort of joke with me. I would find it quite impossible to account for the vivid imagery I have of that city, and the supporting memories I have of the voyages to and from it, in terms of any books I may have read or films I may have seen. If people, to show

---

[1] There are, of course, exceptions which are clearly explainable. If I have a propositional memory of an occurrence in history, supported by an actual direct memory of learning the fact in question from an unimpeachable source, then this memory will carry more weight than a very vague direct memory of some trivial experience in my own past life.

that they were not joking, produced documentary proof that I *could not* have ever been in Rio, then I would have to allow that I was suffering from what I called in Chapter I a 'mnemic hallucination', and visit a psychiatrist. But, as I have observed before, it is just a fortunate fact that hallucinations of any kind are very rare indeed.

Furlong says:[1] 'The sensuous imagery supplies context to what we remember; it places our recollections; it focuses our attention'. This is certainly true, but imagery has a more fundamental role in memory than this. Additional propositional memories supply a kind of context to what we remember—as when I remember *that* once I drank a whole bottle of brandy, and also remember *that* I was subsequently very ill. *The thing which only imagery can supply is not context but content to our memories*—the past events as we perceived them. I could have been ill through drinking whiskey, or because of a stomach infection. But if I have visual and gustatory images of the bottle in my hand and the brandy in my mouth this possibility hardly matters. With imagery the relationship is of 'direct evidence' to conclusions, not—as with additional propositions—of 'circumstantial evidence' to conclusions.

This is why I reject Ryle's claim:[2] 'The question "How can I faithfully describe what I once witnessed?" is no more of a puzzle than the question, "How can I faithfully visualize what I once witnessed?". Ability to describe things learnt by personal experience is one of the knacks we expect of linguistically competent people; ability to visualize parts of it is another thing we expect in some degree of most people. . . .' In the first place, the ability to describe things has nothing to do with whether they were learnt by personal experience or not. And in the second place, the ability to digest food is also something we expect of most people, and this is not a puzzle at all—or, if it is, it is a different kind of puzzle. To remember how to describe something *so that we know that we are describing it correctly* demands the mental retention of a great many propositions, sufficient to support each other, to form an adequate[3] context for the memory. But imagery demands no *mental* retention, only physiological retention. It is enough that the body can reproduce an appearance or part of an appearance when stimulated appropriately, in just the same way as it can

---

[1] *A Study in Memory*, p. 87.   [2] *The Concept of Mind*, p. 276.
[3] For the significance of the term 'adequate' see Chapter IV. p. 81 ff.

reproduce muscular movements. In being re-presented with (or re-presenting to myself) *how* the object looked I am in a position *to decide what it was*. That I know about the past by means of memory may mean that I am remembering propositions made in the past, or that I am interpreting my present imagery, or both together; but there is a perfectly familiar distinction between knowing and knowing of or about. I know the man next door whereas I know of or about the Prime Minister but I do not know him. I can *know the past*, as distinct from knowing about it, only when I am having imagery of it.

We can turn now to the second question: how we conceive pastness at all. If we ask how we come to have a concept of space we may be told we simply perceive it directly or that it arises from our perceiving objects in certain relationships which we characterize as 'spatial'. But to claim that we conceive time only as the result of perceiving (or being aware of) events in a certain relation which we characterize as 'temporal', presupposes that our memories of events are identifiable as such, and form a temporal sequence, leading up, so to speak, to the here and now. Once I have the idea of *my* past and also the idea of existents outside and independent of myself, then it is a straightforward step to the idea of *the past*. But, without the aid of some memory-indicator to differentiate, within the thoughts I entertain, what actually has happened from what logically could happen, how could I come to conceive *my* past? It has been suggested that our idea of the past grows up, so to speak, with our use of the past tense in speech. I do not doubt that the use of past tense helps to clarify the concept of *the* past, but I fail to see how a past tense could ever *come into use* unless and until people had at least some concept of their own past lives to which to apply it. Those who deny that remembering is a unique experience, and as such identifiable, are thereby obliged to claim that we perceive temporal sequence directly, that memory is a concept derived from our acquaintance with the past, and not vice-versa, and they are led to what is, in my opinion, a very contrived and unconvincing argument.

Their claim is that the present, though we treat it as simply an ideal limit, has in fact a very short duration—just long enough for us to perceive the temporal sequence of events. So that *what*

I am now perceiving has within it one event succeeded by another. Thus I can grasp the notion of temporal sequence from present perceptual experience alone, and from this evolve the notions of past and future. Furlong, for example, speaks of 'a succession of sounds which we can apprehend in one act',[1] the rat-tat-tat of someone knocking at the door. And he says: 'Thus from this familiar mode of experience, the specious present, we can learn what it means to say that an event has occurred, and that one event is before another. And indeed this is likely to have been the way in which we first acquired this knowledge, for it is hard to see how else we could have obtained it'.[2]

Now, I do not want to deny that we apprehend rat-tat-tats 'in one act', nor to deny that this *could be* our first introduction to the idea of temporal sequence. What I do want to deny is that it is either correct or necessary to maintain that this apprehension is 'in one present', whether we call it specious or not. I find it odd that so many philosophers have cheerfully embraced the notion of a temporally extended present, notwithstanding its *prima-facie* absurdity. Consider for instance this argument by C. I. Lewis: ' "The present" is "long enough" for the genuine apprehension of the data of experience; because otherwise there would be no such thing as direct experience, of which anyone could be aware or even mention as what we do *not* have'.[3] He argues that unless there were a present *in which* we could learn what we subsequently remember about the world as presented to us, memory could never even originate. 'Either the pristine given character is there to be inspected, or there is nothing there the inspection of which would inform us of what has just escaped'.

Now, I grant that perceptual judgments may 'take time'. But I deny that the perceptual judgment which I remember must have been made within a single 'present'. If we regard the present as simply the ideal limit of the recent, then, though our sense-organs may be functioning continuously, our perceptual judgments are being made, as it were, up to the present rather than *in* the present. *An* event is whatever we *consider as an event*, and a 'present event' is simply an event, so isolated, which is not yet completed. So long as we have the faculty of retaining what is presented to the eyes, ears and so on, we can still make perceptual

---

[1] *A Study in Memory*, p. 95.   [2] *A Study in Memory*, p. 96.
[3] *An Analysis of Knowledge and Valuation*, p. 331 (his italics).

judgments; we need only allow that they are being made about the immediate past as given in memory, not about the present as given in 'sensation'.

By taking this stand we avoid the problems which must arise from such claims as this by Russell: 'The specious present includes elements at all stages on the journey from sensation to image. It is this fact which enables us to apprehend such things as movements . . . .'[1]. For here, if we take the 'fading of sensations' (Russell's description of the transition) literally, we must expect that seeing a car move down the street would involve seeing one firm shape with a series of ever fainter ghost shapes behind it, as we do in fact see shooting stars which move too fast for our eyes, or objects in photographs when the camera has been left open too long. And if we do not take it literally, can it mean anything but that we see the car where it is and also remember it where it has just been, that a single perceptual judgment embraces both the 'present sensation' and an indefinite series of memory-images of past sensations (or the appearances given in past sensations)? This seems to be the only intelligible interpretation, and, since the seeing of changes must in any case involve memory-imagery, why can we not dispense with the 'present sensation' *as a distinct kind of experience* altogether?

Only by making such a move can we avoid the difficulties we are bound to meet in explaining how and when a sensation 'becomes' an image. According to Russell 'We have seen no reason to think that the difference between sensations and images is only one of degree',[2] yet, within the specious present,[3] 'a sensation fades gradually, passing by continuous gradations to the status of an image'. It is by no means easy to see how anything can pass by continuous gradations from being one thing to being another unless the difference *is* simply one of degree. This surely is how we would normally define a difference of degree as opposed to a difference of kind.

It was, I think, this same reluctance to deny that sensations are different in kind from images that created the greatest difficulty in Hume's account of knowledge. He was faced with the problem that there seemed to be no way of distinguishing between the 'liveliness' by which he differentiated sensations from images,

[1] *The Analysis of Mind*, p' 174.   [2] *Ibid*, p. 147.   [3] *Ibid*, p. 174.

and the 'vividness' by which he differentiated memory from imagination imagery. This fact he tacitly acknowledged by interchanging the two terms quite frequently throughout his work. Why did he not simply accept that between present perception, memory-imagery and imagination-imagery there is a single difference of degree only? Why not allow that they all lie on a scale of vividness/liveliness, with present perception at one end and wild imagination at the other?

I have already argued that the difference between memory and imagination imagery can be one of degree only.[1] I have also argued that in all our perceptions we are, in fact, employing memory imagery; to deny this is to embrace the apparent absurdity of a 'present' of unspecified duration. Surely the next step is to allow that when we speak of present appearances we are simply referring to that memory-imagery which, due to the proximity in time of its 'external causes', approaches the ideal limit of memory-authority.

It may be objected here that this would leave out entirely the unique quality of 'substantial existence' which belongs to the subjects of present perception, that we would be like people who have lost the use of their sense-organs and can 'see' and 'hear' things only in imagery, having no direct contact with the world they are actually living in. But this is not so. For we have *not* lost the use of our sense-organs; on the contrary they are operating busily all the time, constantly introducing to us novel situations. I have stressed that 'sensing' is very like imaging—so like it in fact that the only effective distinguishing feature is that we 'cannot get away from' our sensations.[2] Whatever other imagery we may have, our 'present sensations' remain firmly, involuntarily and persistently with us. But, if we regard 'present appearances' as being given in memory-imagery like any 'past appearances' except in that they arise out of the most recent sense-activity, is any of this going to be different? All memory-imagery occurs as the result of some stimulus, and if that stimulus, which in this case is the effect of physical events upon our sense-organs, is being constantly reinforced (by the continuity of those physical events), then the memory-image *must keep occurring*. And it must have the maximum 'firmness', the minimum of 'controllability' and a complete, coherent context.

[1] See Chapter VI, p. 139.   [2] See Chapter VI, p.154.

CONCLUSIONS

We no longer have any problem about 'continuous gradations'. There is a single transition from imagery which reproduces the appearances presented by 'external events' in exact and perfect detail, to imagery which so distorts and rearranges those appearances that the perceptual origins of their various characteristics could hardly be traced.[1] The visual experience of a moment ago is only fractionally less 'firm' than that of this present moment, and we need not postulate a temporally extended present to explain our seeing things as they are, either still or in motion. Nor is it any objection to point out that we may have both 'sensations' and images at the same time. I have shown that there is no logical or causal reason why the presence of one image should exclude the presence of any other, and that there are excellent reasons, quite apart from this present argument, for believing that it does not.[2]

In his article, 'Philosophical Problems of Memory', C. Landesman admits that there is a natural, almost inevitable, tendency to analyse memory in terms appropriate to perception. But he points out, as the one seemingly insurmountable difficulty: 'In perceiving one usually learns something that one has not previously known; perception is an acquisition of new knowledge. However, it is essential to memory that what one remembers one does not know for the very first time'.[3] But I have established, I think, that memory-images can be reinterpreted when they occur. If we regard such reinterpretations as part of our remembering performances, then to that extent we do gain new knowledge in memory. There is a problem only if, on the one hand we exclude from remembering *all* interpretation, and on the other hand we think of remembering as a kind of perceiving. Once we allow that remembering is the major class and perceiving is simply the limiting case of that class, i.e. that perceiving is a sub-species of remembering, the problem dissolves. For then all knowledge, new or otherwise, is seen to be gained in memory.

We are able to distinguish 'present perceptions' as a unique class *because* they are the means of acquiring new knowledge of the

---

[1] For example, the monstrosities which appear in nightmares may *seem* to be wholly unlike anything we have ever seen.
[2] See Chapter VI, p. 151 ff.
[3] *The Journal of Philosophy*, LIX. 3. February 1st, 1962, p. 50.

external world. But 'present sensation' is only an ideal case, one which we can assume as the initial cause of imagery but never experience as such. For this reason arguments about such questions as whether we can properly be said to see movements raise quite unreal problems.[1] We really see things as moving just as we really see things as stationary.

I want to make it quite clear at this point that I am not proposing any startling or revolutionary new theory of knowledge. On the contrary I am simply trying to eliminate the inconsistencies in the traditional theory of knowledge, advanced by Hume, and adhered to with minor variations by every 'British Empiricist' since. I am simply accepting the conclusions to which I feel myself to be committed by that theory.

Certainly, nothing I have said need in any way weaken the force of the normal, and very necessary, distinction we make between present perception and memory. The words we use in our perception-claims—'see', 'hear', 'touch', and so on, are perception words. When I say that I see a bird on the windowsill I am asserting that there is a bird there *now*, not that there has been one there. The distinction between our perception-claims and our memory-claims is perfectly clear: both refer to objective reality, one to how it was, the other to how it is now.

But this sharp distinction lies in what is being claimed, not in our right to make the claims. Memory-claims are based upon memories we are having of our own past states at the time we make the claims. But perception-claims are not *based upon* some equivalent cognitive states called 'perceptions', for to perceive something is already to make some claim about a 'present state of affairs', to assert the existence of a particular factual relationship. As I argued in Chapter VII, even recognizing is always recognizing *that*.[2] Perception-claims are based, like memory-claims, on the memories we are having when we make them, but in the case of perception claims these memories consist very largely, though not entirely, of 'immediate memories'.

It is important to note that the basis of perception-claims does not consist entirely of 'immediate memories'. It is generally acknowledged that any perceptual judgment (any perception

---

[1] Consider e.g. H. A. Prichard, 'Seeing Movements'—*Knowledge and Perception*, Oxford University Press, 1950, p. 41 ff.

[2] See p. 163.

in the way that I use that term) must 'go beyond' the present 'given', depending at least as much upon memory and the expectancies created by memory as upon 'present sensation'. The 'pristine given character', as Lewis calls it, is always to some extent tainted by the dubious authority of memory as soon as we advance to any pronouncement about matters of fact. This is the point Stout was making in the passage I quoted earlier in this chapter. My certainty that the door is now closed may rest much more heavily upon my memory of closing it a minute ago and not opening it since than upon the cursory glance I have just cast towards it. And when I have just switched off the light in my room, my certainty that my coat is hanging on the door is likely to arise from my having seen it clearly a moment ago rather than from my present perception of the vague shape which I now take to be my coat hanging on the door.

'Common sense trusts memory, not blindly, but because it has found memory to be trustworthy', Furlong says.[1] But with memory-imagery as such the question of trusting does not arise; we simply have it. It is only when we identify that imagery, when we say 'this happened' and advance further to beliefs about when and where it happened, that the question of trusting our memories arises. And surely exactly the same could be said of our perceptions. So, to say that we have found our memories trustworthy is surely only to say that we have usually found that our own interpretations of the appearances which are presented to us, either 'in sensation' or 'in imagery', are coherent with each other and with the reports made by other people, and therefore we accept them as knowledge about the world. To say we have usually found our interpretations to be coherent is to presuppose the trust we have in memory. But we are not here doubting that trust; we are only attempting to explain it. I do not suggest that we normally think about their coherence at all, only that we are rarely in fact surprised. It is only the surprise resulting from periodic incoherences that draws our attention to the normal coherence of experience at all. When these 'interpretations' are about what is happening now we call them perceptions and when they are about what *has* happened we call them memories—without being too precise about our qualification of events as 'occurring now'.

---

[1] *A Study in Memory*, p. 18.

To return now to the question of how we come to conceive of a past at all, I suggest that 'past' is simply a classificatory term we apply to all those events which present themselves to us (present appearances to us) without that persistence by which we identify present events. It is no accident that 'present' is the contrary of both 'past' and 'absent'. The constant reinforcement of our imagery 'gives the present to us' as persistent, coherent experience which we can neither disbelieve nor ignore. Events which we are aware of *as real events*, but which are not presented with this persistent continuity—which are in fact discordant with the events so presented—are thereby negatively classified as 'not present'. That I am now thinking of my friend's appearance, i.e. how he looks, though I am not now seeing him, entails that I have seen him at another time and also that, if he still exists, he is in another place.

My claim is that the concept of the past simply arises from the distinction of 'the not-present' from 'the present' within 'the real'. And it is interesting to note that this is at least suggested in a passage by Furlong (though I do not claim that Furlong had any such idea in mind or that he would necessarily accept the view I propose, especially in the light of his claims, which I quoted above, for the specious present). 'The imaginary' he says 'is what we invent, what is largely dependent upon our will. The real is what comes to us without our asking; its main characteristic is involuntariness, spontaneity . . . . Now in memory there is also this involuntary, spontaneous character; it is understandable therefore, that we should ascribe reality to what we remember. But we can clearly observe that what we remember is not now happening, and so we place it in the past, thus assigning to it a reality of a sort'.[1]

The only amendments I would want to make to this are that the distinctions between perceiving, remembering and imagining are not the sharp distinctions of kind which it suggests, and that we do not 'place' remembered events in the past; rather we exclude them from the present.

THE ULTIMATE AUTHORITY OF MEMORY

I have argued that our current memories are the basis of both our perception-claims and our memory-claims; there are differences

[1] *A Study in Memory*, p. 98.

of degree, but not of kind, in their value as 'evidence' for the claims made. Thus the perception claim is not in any specially privileged position. As a matter of empirical fact it is less likely to be wrong, but this is only because the sense-evidence on which it is based is up-to-the-minute evidence, not because it is better evidence in some other way.

When Holland speaks of 'the distinction which we certainly draw in ordinary life between those recollections which can only be supported by further recollections and those which are supported by something better',[1] he is speaking of a distinction which simply does not apply to the authority of memory as such, but only to the comparative authority of one's own memories and the claims made by other people. He says: 'If I claim to remember putting some money into a box and certain other people saw me do it and later the box is destroyed by fire, then, supposing my recollections to be called in question, there may be no better means open to me of supporting my claim than to bring forward these other people to bear me out by saying that they also remember my putting money in the box. But suppose the box is not destroyed. Then I can if necessary fetch it and display its contents. How can it be said in this latter case that my recollection is only supported by other recollections in the way it was in the former case?'.

The important question is: What is it that causes us to make this distinction in ordinary life? The answer may be: to convince people that we did put the money in the box, or even: to convince people that there is money in the box. Surely it is not: to convince ourselves that we remember putting money in the box. I certainly do not deny that people are more readily convinced by what they see with their own eyes than by other people's memory-claims. But this fact does not, as Holland suggests, free us 'from dependence on memory in general'. My arguments above show that we *can* say that the recollection is still supported only by other recollections, even though these are the 'immediate recollections' of the people who witness the opening of the box. Their greater conviction arises, not from the fact that a memory is replaced by a present perception, but from the fact that someone else's claim is replaced by their own experience. Whether this is perceptual experience or memory experience is of minor importance. It is also true that people are more readily convinced by their own

[1] 'The Empiricist Theory of Memory', *Mind* LXIII, 1954, p. 476.

memories than by the claims of other people. These previously sceptical people would *remain* convinced five minutes after the box had been closed up again.

The important point is that all cause/effect confirmation must involve sense-perception, and once we allow that 'perceiving' is simply our name for that remembering which 'runs up to' the ideal limit we call the present, then it follows that the coherence by which we judge our memories to be true operates *wholly within memory*. And, as we have seen,[1] the most recent memory is not necessarily the strongest and most reliable.

We *judge* our memory-claims to be true by their coherence with other memory-claims, our own and other peoples. But we *feel* our memory-claims to be true because of their seeming *accord* with the mass of our own remembering. We should never lose sight of the fact that, in the overwhelming majority of cases, when we feel them to be true they *are* true. Von Leyden is perhaps right when he says that we may rule out the suggestion that the *only* characteristic of memory is 'the experience of being under the influence of some sort of an impression, and of a confidently held belief, concerning one's own past'. But I do not accept his claim that: 'It is impossible that the nature of this experience by itself should constitute the "essence" of memory, since an unjustified *or even disproved memory-claim* does not cease to be associated with, and even upheld by, precisely that same sort of experience'.[2] The feeling of belief arises out of an *initial* contextual coherence, and it is true that, on occasions, belief attaches to a memory-claim before the context of the memory has been expanded sufficiently to justify this belief. But, if the claim *has been disproved* (and I take it that Von Leyden means disproved *to the claimant*, else his claim is utterly trivial), then this can only have been by the introduction into the memory-context of some fact which is not coherent. When this happens the claimant *must* see the need to amend or modify his memory-claim, and the feeling of belief *cannot* persist. What I do, or do not, believe at any moment is simply a matter of fact which can be explained in terms of the 'evidence' I am at that moment aware of.

It is always possible, of course, to 'believe too soon'. And because of this we can never achieve 'absolute certainty' about matters

[1] See p. 205.   [2] *Remembering*, p. 105 (my italics).

of past fact. But this need not distress us, for we can never achieve 'absolute certainty' about matters of present fact either. If we suspect that we may have made a perceptual error, or even if we are just particularly anxious not to, we look again—or in some cases keep looking—until *we are satisfied* that our perceptual judgment is right. But sometimes it is by no means easy to be satisfied. We may look at a distant object for some time, seeing it sometimes as a man and sometimes as a bush blowing in the wind. Looking again is not a sure-fire way of becoming certain; at most it is a means of knowing whether we are certain or not—*or of just how much we can be certain*. And exactly the same applies when we 'look again' in imagery at the events we have witnessed in the past. But in this case it is generally necessary to 'look again' harder, more often, and more carefully, for we have to decide not only *what it is*, but *when it was* as well. This is to say, we not only have to be sure that we have identified the remembered objects or events correctly. We have also to be sure that these objects or events do belong to a particular past perceptual occasion.

The 'immediate memories' we employ in perception are felt to be immediate, and the question of their temporal location does not arise. The remembered appearances presented to me in imagery all belong in my past, but in what part or parts of my past may not be at once apparent. Some philosophers have claimed that when we have memory-images we 'see', as it were, the temporal location of the event imaged, i.e. the comparative 'distance' of the event from the present moment, almost as we see objects as more or less distant from us in space. Furlong, for instance, writes: 'We seem also to have some ability to judge what we might call "temporal distance" by means of vividness, detail and spontaneity of our imagery. To image this morning's breakfast is one thing; to image that of yesterday is another. The vividness and other such qualities of our imagery are "secondary signs" of temporal distance.'[1] Now, I believe that this is substantially true, especially in the case of our more recent memories. But, when we consider our more remote memories, it is clear that the notion of 'judging temporal distance' requires some further analysis. It is not enough to speak of 'vividness'; my memory-imagery of some very exciting happening in my youth is likely to be much more vivid than my memory-imagery of the humdrum events of this morning.

[1] *A Study in Memory*, p. 99.

First and foremost, our memories are temporally located by the other memories coherent with them. I know, for instance, that my present imagery of my children in a boat is a memory of my last holiday because it 'runs off into' other memories: of the scenery, the house we stayed in, the journey home, and so on. But this is not enough; there must also be some fixed reference point. All these events were (roughly) at the same time; but what time was that? To fix the temporal location of a remembered event seems possible only if we connect it to the present moment by an unbroken chain of coherent memories. And this is, I believe, what in fact happens.

This does not necessarily mean that to remember when anything happened to us we must also remember everything that has happened to us since. My claim seems much less odd when we realize how very indeterminate the memory of 'an event' can be. A set of coherent memories may be narrow and highly detailed, or it may be much wider and very sketchy; or it may be both at once—a nucleus, as it were, of detailed memories, fanning out into an extended context of less detailed memories, until it extends, however sketchily, over the whole of our past experience.

This extension of the context is made possible by the use of 'fixed markers'. If I wanted to colour in the eighteenth fiftieth part of a line drawn across this page I should not divide the line into fifty equal parts and then count along it. I should halve it and then halve one of the parts and so on, and the marks I made would remain on the page as a ready-made guide for any future endeavour of the same kind.

Our 'temporal markers' work in much the same way, and we all establish them for ourselves in the course of our lives. My own are mainly such things as the size and general appearance of my family, the places where I have lived and the kind of work I was engaged in. As soon as any expanding memory-context embraces any such 'marker' the memory can take a short-cut, as it were, to the present time. The noticeable inability of small children to distinguish between the recent and the comparatively distant past may well be due, in part at least, to their lack of adequate 'markers'.

I am satisfied that in this way most of our memories do 'come labelled' with the temporal location of the events remembered—with a greater or lesser degree of determinateness. On occasions I remember some event but have only the haziest notion of when it happened, but every memory of a past event in my own life has *some* degree of temporal determinateness and that temporal determinateness tends to increase with any expansion of the memory-context.

At the end of Chapter VI, I stressed that imagery, as such, is non-fallible; error can arise only in its interpretation; the imagery itself is only evidence for our memory-claims, it does not enter into those claims. There must, therefore, be a certain arbitrariness in any distinction we may make within memory-claims between what we really saw and what we took ourselves to be seeing.

We can make a distinction between seeing what is in fact a book, and seeing what we take to be a book (whether it is or not). But, in the case of memory, the very point at issue is whether or not what we took to be a book was in fact a book. We can distinguish between remembering seeing a book and *remembering the visual appearance of a book*, but this is only the distinction between remembering a particular event and remembering a particular individual. The distinction we cannot make is between remembering seeing a book and remembering seeing an appearance, for, as I argued earlier, we do not normally see appearances.[1] Appearances are presented to us by the things we see. To see is always to see something *as* something, even if only as a patch of some particular colour. The only distinction of kind we can make is between *how* we saw (our evidence) and *what* we took ourselves to be seeing (our claim). The problem is that some initial degree of interpretation must be put upon our imagery to allow it *to function as evidence*. To assert that the man was bleeding on the strength of our memory of *how* he looked we must at least identify what we saw as a red patch spreading over a white patch.

At this point I must say, quite boldly, that the ultimate justification for our memory-beliefs is not logical but psychological. In Chapter III, I made the distinction between what we (psychologically) *could not* see as anything but a certain object or event, and what we see as a certain object or event as a result of expectancies we happen to have at the time, or judgments about what it 'must be'. Having made this distinction in any given case, we have reached the terminal point of checking of our memory-claim.

[1] See Chapter VI, p. 148 ff.

But this situation is not peculiar to memory. We cannot reach logical certainty about matters of fact, whether they be of past fact or of present fact. To 'verify' a claim, whether it be a memory-claim or a perception-claim, is simply to confirm it—not to put it beyond the reach of doubt. The question 'Are you sure?' is really only an invitation to reconsider, and the reply 'Yes I am' is only a rejection of that invitation.

I have claimed that the context of most of our memories spreads, so to speak, throughout our entire past histories, very sketchily except in the 'immediate vicinity' of the event which is the subject of the memory-claim, but clearly enough to enable us to 'locate' the remembered event, and to indicate to us with what degree of determinateness we are entitled to 'locate' it. In the case of our present perceptions practical certainty is usually immediate. They are in a favoured position in that they rest, in part, upon the imagery of appearances which are still being presented, and this is sufficient to account for the greater likelihood of error in memory, a likelihood which increases as the events remembered 'fall away from' the present.

But the recentness of events is not the only factor which makes for 'firmness' in the memory of them. The extent to which we noticed them, i.e. the extent of the observed context, is ultimately of greater importance. That is why I can be more certain of my memory of travelling from England to Australia many years ago than of my memory of stubbing out a cigarette a moment ago, or even of my perception, in which I have no interest at all, of the people and cars now passing my window.

We trust our memories in the same way, and for the same reasons as we trust our eyes and ears—and with the same kind of justification. The advantage on the side of 'present perception' is that the context expands automatically with the passage of time. The compensating advantage on the side of our more distant memories is that they are concerned only with those events which did interest us, did command our attention, whether we realized this at the time or not. Because of this the supporting memory-context is not only always available to us, it is in fact already 'present' as the setting to the memory. It is only the presence of this context that gives us our beliefs about the past and enables us to claim to be remembering.

INDEX

Acquaintance, 172, 191
After-images, 137
Alexander, S., 24
Appearances, 53 ff., 58, 61, 149 ff., 158, 169–75, 190–3, 195, 211
Association of ideas, 98
Austin, J. L., 183
Ayer, A. J., 105, 134, 168, 176

Bartlett, Sir R., 142, 147
Belief about the past 43, 208
Benjamin, B. S., 132, 173
Broad, C. D., 51, 73, 107, 180

Causal connection in memory, 80 ff. 107, 121, 197
Certainty about the past, 101
Chisholm, R. M., 149, 172
Claims about the past, Ch. IV, 131, 189, 207
Complete and adequate memories, 81
Complexity—its relation to accuracy, 84
Concepts, 66–70
and images, 148, 169, 183
Confirmation of memories, 25, 98–104, 207 ff., 212
Conflicting memories, 21
Contexts of memories and images, 142, 197
Controllability, 141

Deja vu, 20
Determinateness—and accuracy, 85–88, 97
Dispositions and occurrences, 24, 46, 102, 108, 119, 127–9, 166
Dreams, 143

Eidetic imagery, 137, 176
Errors of memory, 16 ff.

Events—
memory of, 30, 51, 54, 98–101
reconstruction of from memory, 55–63, 189
what is one event? 130, 200

Facts—memory of, 59
Fallibility of imagery, 155–6, 211
Familiarity—feeling of, 20, 42, 96
Forgetting, 17, 114
Furlong, E. J., 82, 92, 133, 145, 159, 161, 198, 200, 205, 206, 209

Galton's questionnaire, 176
Generic imagery, 183–5

Habit, 71–74
Hallucination, 153–5
Harrod, Sir R., 35
Holland, R. F., 42, 144, 196, 207
How to—memory of, Ch. V, 37–8, 44, 71, 188
Hume, D., 42, 58, 67, 141, 153, 201, 204
Hunter, I. M. L., 138, 148, 157

Imageability, 92, 148–56, 197
Images, Ch. VI., Ch. VII
checking and interpreting, 189, 205
comparison of, 57, 174
and concepts, 67–9, 148, 169, 183
as entities, 144, 157–62, 169, 196
identification of, 34
of imagination, 64, 140 ff.
of images, 144, 152
as inspectables, 56, 93, 95–7, 152, 159–62, 169
kinaesthetic, 111, 132, 146, 177
as memory, 44, 101
metaphorical, 168
as pictures, 159
privacy of, 172
and recognition, 162 ff.

214　MEMORY

Images—*cont.*
　and sensations, 153–5, 201–3
　simultaneous, 151 ff., 175
　spatial location of, 178–80
　as symbols, 158, 168, 195
　verbal, 66, 147
Imagination confused with memory 19, 23
Immediate memory, 47, 204
Independent evidence of the past, 26 ff., 41, 99, 186, 207
Individuals—memory of, 51–54, 58, 187
Initial authority of memory, 14–16, 28, 36, 41–2, 186
Intelligence, 116, 121–7, 188
Intentional behaviour, 75, 118–20

James, W., 32, 36, 42, 171

Knowing—remembering as, 33, 121
Knowing the past, 35 ff., 194 ff.

Landesman, C., 195, 203
Learning and not forgetting, 37–39, 111.
Lewis, C. I., 200, 205
Locke, J., 174

Misleading memories, 30, 103
Mnemic hallucination, 19, 22, 43, 198
Motor-response, 75, 107, 113–15, 119, 128–30, 134, 156, 164
Negative remembering, 94–8, 113, 152

Objects of memory, 43 ff.

Pastness, 32, 36, 193–206, 209
Perceiving, 60, 85, 89, 138, 156, 172, 190, 199 ff.
　and sensing, 203–5, 211
Persistence of sense-experience,154
Physical element in memory, 91, 103
Potential memories, 35

Price, H. H., 29, 41, 85, 122, 124, 133, 155, 158–9, 164 ff.
Prichard, H. A., 204
Projecting images, 179
Propositions—memory of, 30, 52, 60 ff., 65, 187

Reality of events, 206
Recognition, 62, 69, 74–8
　as classification, 75
　of imagery, 162–3
　by imagery, 164–6, 171
　of individuals, kinds, qualities, 74–7
Repetition—its effect on memory, 73, 123
Retentiveness, 47, 166
Russell, B., 32, 59, 83, 96, 134, 143, 150, 152, 153, 156, 160, 174, 182, 201
Ryle, G., 33, 110 ff., 198

Sceptics, 13, 28
Seeming to remember, 36
Sensing, 146, 151, 153–6, 190–3, 202
Sentences—memory of, 63 ff.
Skills and sub-skills, 115 ff., 133
Specious present, 199–201
Stout, G. F., 85, 147, 154, 192

Temporal location of the remembered, 209 ff.
Total momentary experience, 150

Vagueness, 82–84, 182
Verbal description, 173 ff.
Visual memory—predominance of, 146
Von Leyden, W., 22, 42, 89, 173, 208

Waismann, F., 39
Ward, J., 154
Wittgenstein, L., 39, 79, 171
Wollheim, E., 149
Woozley, A. D., 151, 196